The Marquis and the Chevalier

THE MARQUIS
and
THE CHEVALIER

A STUDY IN THE PSYCHOLOGY OF SEX
AS ILLUSTRATED BY THE LIVES AND
PERSONALITIES OF THE
MARQUIS DE SADE (1740–1814)
AND THE
CHEVALIER VON SACHER-MASOCH
(1836–1905)

by

James Cleugh

GREENWOOD PRESS, PUBLISHERS
WESTPORT, CONNECTICUT

The Library of Congress has catalogued this publication as follows:

Library of Congress Cataloging in Publication Data

Cleugh, James.
  The Marquis and the Chevalier.

  Bibliography: p.
  1. Sade, Donatien Alphonse François, Comte, called
Marquis de, 1740-1814. 2. Sacher-Masoch, Leopold,
Ritter von, 1835-1895. I. Title.
HQ79.C55 1972   157'.7'35   70-142317
ISBN 0-8371-5920-2

First American Edition published in 1952 by Duell Sloan & Pearce,
New York

Reprinted with the permission of Hawthorn Books, Inc., New York

Reprinted in 1972 by Greenwood Press, Inc., 51 Riverside Avenue,
Westport, Conn. 06880

Library of Congress catalog card number 70-142317
ISBN 0-8371-5920-2

Printed in the United States of America

10 9 8 7 6 5 4 3 2

DEDICATED TO
JAMES WHITTAKER
FRGS FRHS MIEx

in Friendship

Contents

CONTENTS

Illustrations

The Marquis and the Chevalier

Prologue

THE Marquis de Sade (1740–1814) and the Chevalier von Sacher-Masoch (1836–1905) happen to illustrate with singular clarity, both in their private characters and in their published works, the only two possible corner-stones for a soundly monumental psychology of sex.

The present work does not pretend even to indicate the plan of any such piece of architecture. It is wholly non-technical. It only hopes to serve as a temporary pointer for those who feel that they would like to know a little more than they do about Sade and Masoch. It is only concerned to indicate aspects both of the men themselves and of the roots and workings of that sex instinct, the tyranny of which they each accepted, greatly to the potential advantage of posterity, far more frankly than the vast majority of us do, even today.

Contrary to general belief, both the Frenchman and the Austrian attracted outstanding minds, in their own as well as in succeeding generations, not only as thinkers and as literary artists, but also as kindly and tolerant, often industriously benevolent, rarely less than fascinating human beings. The Marquis de Sade, even in his embittered old age, to say nothing of more agreeable periods in his life, devoted a great deal of his time to pleasing people from whom he could expect little or nothing in return. The Chevalier von Sacher-Masoch exhibited positively heroic patience, almost to the end of his days, in bearing with those who steadily repaid his disinterested generosity with deliberate malevolence.

In each case early sexual experiences were extremely disappointing. The marquis's most satisfactory love affairs came too late in his life, after too much moral damage had been done to him, to be comprehensive in their compensations. The Chevalier never had any quasi-permanent connections which he could enjoy whole-heartedly.

It is true that these two remarkable men were both in revolt against the social system of their day and that they would find even more to criticize in our own. But in the first place they share this trait even with their superiors in intellect, culture and character. And, secondly, they were each far too sensible to allow their opinions to drive them into open and violent rebellion.

Finally, the state of psychological understanding at the present time owes much of its confidence to the thought and to the actions of de Sade and von Sacher-Masoch. Without their closely argued and uncompromising declarations, without the documented proof which we possess that the feelings which led them to behave as they did were perfectly genuine, the researches of Freud and his successors would not have been so securely based, nor would our reading of the past and present history of human nature have been so relatively free from bewilderment.

Such seem to be the several justifications for writing again, however briefly and therefore inadequately, about Donatien de Sade, who has continued into our own day to draw serious attention from persons not in the habit of wasting their own time or other peoples', and about Leopold von Sacher-Masoch, who has, on the contrary, been so contemptuously ignored, in general, by reputable authors, except as a labelled dummy in the works of professed psychologists, during the fifty years which have elapsed since he disappeared into an oblivion few as yet have troubled to disturb.

The subject of this book, in the abstract, is sado-masochism, or, as the phenomenon was first called by Schrenck-Nötzing in the late nineteenth century, algolagnia, from the Greek words *algos,* pain, and *lagneia,* salaciousness or the act of coition. The best definition of this commonest of all psycho-neuroses is still that of the psychopathologist Eugen Duehren, composed about 1899.

It is the relation, either deliberately contrived or coming about by accident, between pleasurable sexual excitation and the occurrence, either actual or imagined, of terrifying events, appalling acts and destructive exploits, threatening or extinguishing human or any animate life, health or property and imperilling or annihilating the continued existence of inanimate objects; in all such events the human being who obtains sexual pleasure from them may be actually their direct originator or may cause their inauguration by others, or again he may be simply a spectator of them, or else, finally, the voluntary or compelled object of attack by any such agents. (*The Marquis de Sade and his Time*, 1901, pp. 414–5.)

It will be observed from this quotation that algolagnia is as old as human nature and as widespread, at all times, including our own, as the sex instinct itself, of which it is, indeed, the most primitive and simplest expression. Neither Sade nor Masoch were responsible for it. Prehistoric witch-doctors, pagan tyrants, the Christian fanatics of the Middle Ages, the renegade sensation hunters of the Renaissance, the extravagant mystics of the seventeenth century and the cold, doctrinaire sensualists of the early eighteenth all preceded, as conspicuous instances of the neurosis in its extreme forms, the two men whose names were selected by the sexologists of the nineteenth century to designate the phenomenon of 'sado-masochism.'

These two men were both highly articulate, highly educated and socially privileged members of a society which was just beginning, as Sade reached maturity, to substitute free scientific enquiry for superstitious, priest-ridden fancy. Many fields and especially those of biology and psychology were then being explored in this spirit. Accordingly, first Sade and then Masoch made full use of the new opportunity to define and explain in detail, without serious fear of the consequences, the more or less open secret of the material and mental mechanism provided by nature for the propagation of life.

Since their day the subject has been heavily overlaid with intricate theory, not all the parts of which have been strictly scientific, since some of them have been inspired from quarters primarily interested in ethics, theology, administration or even aesthetics. The study of mysterious topics is best begun with the thinkers who were the first in time to deal with them clear of the shadow of such pre-conceptions. The budding metaphysician starts with the ancient Greeks. The man or woman who, without intending to become a professional sexologist, wishes to gain a better comprehension of one of the most powerful instincts in human nature, is not entitled to lay down the law in this matter before at least getting some idea of what sort of people Sade and Masoch really were, what they actually did in their lives and what present-day society has since come to owe to them.

This book is a brief and simple attempt to convey some elements of this, as I think, desirable information.

It should be added that the sources, both known to exist and conjectured, for the lives of these two men have not even now been exhaustively studied in the one case or completely identified in the other. The compilation of a definitive biography of either figure would occupy many years and demand special linguistic, scientific and moral qualifications in the writer. The present work is based only upon such data as have hitherto been made available.

Book I

The Marquis

~~~~~~

*Au comble de la solitude
un accent inconnu de grâce et de fureur.*

GILBERT LÉLY, *Morceaux Choisis.* 1948.

~~~~~~

CHAPTER ONE

Stars and Eagles

In 1740 the Paris of Louis Quinze resembled the camp of a luxurious army, living on its wits in the midst of a sullen but impotent population. France was still the richest country in Europe, as well as the most highly civilized. The prestige won during the long reign of Louis XIV the present king's immediate predecessor, had not yet diminished. The English, the Prussians, the Austrians, the Spaniards, the Italians and even the Russians were all uneasily conscious of their inferiority beside the brilliant intelligence, the charm and the polish which the Great Century, as it was generally called, of Molière and of Racine, of Turenne and of Colbert, had imparted to French culture.

But this wit and grandeur were concentrated at the centre. The Court glittered. The lawyers and the business men, beyond this magic pale, struggled in an apprehensive twilight. The shopkeepers and the peasantry, the great majority of the people of France, still largely illiterate, superstitious and excluded, in principle, from all hope of economic advancement, seethed helplessly in an outer darkness. They still called their handsome young king Louis the Well Beloved. They still enjoyed the reflected glory of his palace, the Tuileries. But France, socially, was Paris; and Paris, socially, was the throne and the nobility.

To be born into that inner circle meant to have the best of the contemporary world at one's feet, to be familiar, if one chose, with its arts and sciences, to be an honoured guest among its material splendours, to dispose freely of its power and wealth. Such inordinate privileges led inevitably, for the majority of those who exploited them, to an arrogant and cynical extravagance of self-indulgence and in particular to a frank sensuality, ungoverned by any but fashionable considerations, which would today be impossible for any but a few astute master-criminals.

This half savage, half exquisite world of *fêtes galantes* and ferocious public executions, of graceful refinement and systematized debauchery, has been given the name of *rococo* by art historians, derived from the French word *rocailles,* which was used to designate the artificial grottoes and fantastic arrangements of rocks in the gardens of Versailles. Freedom and irregularity were its keynotes. It was the final phase of intellectual pride which had rationalized all deep feeling out of existence and substituted titillation.

Such was the setting for a birth which took place that year at the Paris residence of the great Condé family, near the Luxembourg Gardens, on the site now occupied by the Odéon Theatre. The Condés were a branch of the royal house of Bourbon. It was a Prince de Condé who, in 1643, at the age of no more than twenty-two, broke for ever, at the great battle of Rocroi, the Spanish military hegemony in Europe and so cleared the way for French political ascendancy.

The great-grandson of this formidable personage preferred to be known simply as the duke of Bourbon. He was one of the chief ministers of Louis XV and died in the very year, 1740, in which a son was born to one of his wife's ladies-in-waiting, actually a cousin of hers, Marie-Eléonore, comtesse de Sade, married to a soldier-diplomatist who had recently been very successful in certain secret negotiations of the French Government with the British Prime Minister, Sir Robert Walpole.

The curtains, coverlets and cushions of the boy's cradle were embroidered with stars and eagles. For the arms of the de Sade family were an eight-pointed golden star on a red field, surmounted by a spread eagle, sable, with open beak and talons, and a red diadem upon its head. The child was christened Donatien Alphonse François and became a marquis at birth, since the de Sades' eldest sons always bore that title immediately they appeared, becoming counts only on the father's death. In most other families of this rank the rule was the exact opposite.

The duchesse de Bourbon or princesse de Condé — she had a right to either title — considered little Donatien quite exceptionally pretty and robust, though slightly undersized.

"Where does he get that girlish look?" she asked the mother one day. "White skin, golden hair, big blue eyes! He's got all the attributes the poets always give their ideal mistresses. And such grace of movement, such a sweet little voice! Neither you nor Jean-Baptiste, my dear, if you will forgive me for saying so, resemble him in the slightest."

The dark, rather severe-looking countess returned her lively principal's thrust with impassive courtesy.

"I think he must be referred to Laura de Noves, *madame*. You know that our fourteenth-century ancestor, Hugues de Sade, had been her husband for two years before Petrarch ever saw her. They say that Fabrice, the son of Hugues by Laura, was a bad lot. But he had decent brothers. And since then the de Sades have been, I believe, all brave and faithful servants of God and of their country. I expect no less from Donatien."

The princess pursed her full lips ironically, though without interrupting the gay sparkle in her eyes. She was a good deal older than her lady-in-waiting and also a very thorough woman of the world.

"I'm sure I hope so, my dear friend! But . . ." She rose majestically, sweeping her enormous skirts together with one hand and menacing her attendant with the fan held in the other. "*Gare les femmes!* Look out for the women, sweetheart!"

The countess lifted her stately shoulders slightly, without answering, as she moved to follow her mistress. Her calm face did not change. As if one did not know that women, certain women, were always a danger to men, handsome or otherwise. But neither her own family nor her husband's had ever been fools in that respect, so far as she was aware, always excepting the incorrigible Fabrice of the fourteenth century, a comparatively barbarous age in any case.

Fabrice, it seemed, used to help himself pretty regularly, on his rides abroad, there and then, to the more prepossessing of his female serfs, whether they or anyone else liked it or not. Provençal blood! Those who objected were quite certain to have less than five minutes of life left in which to regret their boldness. Still, Fabrice was only a collateral ancestor of Jean-Baptiste, her husband. Marie-Eléonore had a mind and a will of her own. She did not, just then, expect to have more than the usual puberty and adolescent worries over the seductive little marquis. If she could have seen twenty years into the future her smooth features would have turned yellow with fear, horror and disgust under the rouge and powder. But she would have stood her ground, not fainted. She was not a niece of the late duc de Richelieu, nor a cousin of the magnificent Condés, for nothing.

All the ladies, great and small, who surrounded that princely household, naturally enough spoilt Donatien. The higher they were in rank or reputation and the more dazzling their personal attractions were considered, the more they kissed, tickled and played with the fascinating de Sade baby.

He soon began to order them about, even to abuse them, stamping his small feet and sulking when they teased him. A rather shocking temper made its appearance in his character. But sly, self-willed, obstreperous and vindictive as the child certainly was, Donatien de Sade did not differ in the least, at this kindergarten age, from any other infant pampered by rich parents. He did show, however, as time went on, an extraordinary delicacy and brilliance, not only of that hair, eyes and skin which his mother believed resembled those of Laura de Noves, but also of intelligence.

The strangely subtle remarks and behaviour of children under five are amusing because so unexpected from human creatures at this early stage. Few of the experienced adults who notice them, generation after generation, suppose that these pearls from the mouths of babes, these daringly eccentric performances in public, are more than accidental. But actually they are nearly always due to the successive impacts of a fresh, unprepossessed mind, not necessarily deep or even vigorous, upon the endless complexities of a new environment. The imitative instinct, however, soon outgrows, unfortunately, apprehension and reflection. Children often seem geniuses from two years old to six and at least abnormally gifted from seven to twelve. But the vast majority then relapse into sedulous copies of other people. They may become estimable or detestable, but certainly not as illustrious as it once seemed they might grow to be.

Accordingly, what is reported or may reasonably be conjectured about the little marquis de Sade before he reached the age of ten or eleven, when he was undoubtedly the mental equal of the average child of twelve or thirteen, cannot have decisive weight in any final judgment of his nature. Similar anecdotes could be told about almost anyone's babyhood. He used to cry, it seems, like other over-indulged brats, whenever he couldn't get just what he wanted.

Once, when his blue eyes, which had an odd habit of turning greenish in anger, were full of these sullen tears, the young comtesse de Brécourt, a conspicuous beauty, knelt and put her arms around his neck, murmuring consolatory endearments. He gave her an inscrutable look, suddenly dry-eyed. Then he stiffened. Swift as a cat's, both his little claws shot out, scoring her cheeks.

There is no need, even for a professional psychologist, to see anything particularly significant either in this outburst or in those so lucidly recorded by the marquis himself in the course of a partly autobiographical romance, *Aline et Valcour,* which he wrote in middle life and which unquestionably had, among other objects, that of explaining his personality to posterity, an exercise rarely so readably performed by those whose personalities are undistinguished.

"I was born in Paris," he makes his hero say, "and nurtured in luxury and profusion. As soon as I could think at all, I came to believe that nature and fortune had combined to heap their gifts upon me. I believed it because people were foolish enough to tell me so. This absurd assumption made me conceited, domineering and touchy. I thought that everyone ought to give way to me, that the whole universe ought to obey my capricious orders and that it was nobody's business but my own to conceive them and get them carried out."

This masterly and serenely objective piece of self-analysis was executed by a man who, at this date, already had a reputation, along the boulevards, which can be compared only with those of Heliogabalus, Cesare Borgia or a modern concentration-camp commandant.

Louis Josèphe de Bourbon, son of the duke of that name, or prince de Condé, as the father had the right to call himself, had been born four years before Donatien de Sade. The latter, in *Aline et Valcour,* continues:

> "Since I was being brought up in the palace of the illustrious prince to whom my mother was related and who was nearly the same age as myself" — a pardonable exaggeration in what was, after all, supposed to be a work of fiction — "I was encouraged to seek his company, so that I might eventually, as having been known to him ever since my childhood, be able to count on his support for the rest of my life. But my vanity at this time, when I still knew nothing of such calculations, caused me, one day when we were playing together, to take offence because he refused to let me have something I wanted. My exasperation was aggravated because, no doubt with perfect justification, he seemed to think that his rank warranted his refusal. I punished his contumacy with a rain of blows nothing could induce me to stop. It was only by the exercise of brute force that I was at last dragged away from him."

There are few little boys of spirit who have not been guilty of some such 'sadistic' attack on conceited children somewhat older than themselves. The marquis, at the time when he was writing *Aline et Valcour,* was concerned with pleading a special case for himself and magnanimously 'confessing' to sins common to most of the rest of humanity.

In August 1744 the Condé household moved to Chantilly, a resort 25 miles north of Paris, where they had a country house. Donatien was by then beginning, in the princesse's opinion, to be rather in the way. He was sent to stay with his paternal grandmother, the dowager comtesse de Sade, at Avignon. She seems to have been a rather sentimental old lady and to have therefore continued the 'spoiling' process. His temper had by no means improved when, three years later, it was judged that the time had come to give him a little education.

He was taken, for this purpose, in 1747, to live with his uncle, the Abbé François de Sade. This gentleman, the younger brother of Count Jean-Baptiste de Sade, had taken Orders in accordance with the custom in noble French families at that time, when the eldest son normally went into the Army and the second son into the Church. François was forty-two years old and a typical worldly priest of his time and country. He had led a gay life in Paris in earlier years and was said to have been the last lover of Madame de la Popelinière, the famous mistress of the duc de Richelieu. But the elegant and blue-blooded Abbé was by no means, like so many of his colleagues, a mere playboy. He was not only a naturalist, with cabinets full of beetles and butterflies, but also a man of high general culture, with a serious interest in history and literature. He was engaged at this time on research into the life and works of no less a person than Petrarch, the great Italian poet and humanist, who had lived at Avignon and loved Laura de Noves, the wife of old Hugues de Sade, four hundred years before. The book which François de Sade wrote on the 'sweet singer of Vaucluse'—the department of France of which Avignon is the capital—was published in 1764 and is still one of the principal authorities for the study of the poet.

François, comfortably off in his practical sinecure of the Abbey of Ebreuil and in his life-tenancy of the lordship of the adjoining village of Saumane, divided his time between insects, the fourteenth century and certain less arduous recreations. His bachelor's household included an attractive as well as businesslike manageress and at least two charming maids. Young Donatien was already used to having good-looking girls about him. He was as sharp as needles and no doubt saw more than he was meant to in the way of natural history, in which subject, properly so called, the debonair Abbé was, however, glad to see him also take an intelligent interest.

But it is unnecessary to argue precocious sexual development from this cause alone. He was barely six when he arrived, barely ten when he left. At such ages, however highly sexed one may potentially be, the pursuits of country life, with a background of chapel, library and private museum, will take up quite as much of one's attention as the sexual indiscretions of one's uncle, whatever gossip there might be in the neighbourhood about him.

Donatien was taught Latin and Provençal by this gay and learned preceptor. He was also, of course, familiarized with the ancestral tale of Petrarch and Laura. It is improbable that he learned much theology. The Abbé François, though his scholarly tastes made him conscientious in the fulfilment of the few formalities demanded by his office, took little or no interest in them. He was not pious. But neither was he, in spite of the housekeeper and the maids, a libertine in any way comparable with some of his Parisian friends of a dozen years before.

There were plenty of frivolous priests, at that date, who would not have troubled their heads about the possible effects on a nephew of nine of their domestic revels. Some of them, such was the malicious scepticism of the period, might even have enjoyed initiating a child into the mysteries of questionable entertainments for adults. But François de Sade was, after all, fundamentally a serious person, a historian with a strong sense of personal integrity, a scientist with a strong sense of categories in conduct as well as in coleoptera, an aristocrat with a strong sense of the code of manners required by his social position. His morals were not those of the Geneva Calvinists or of his contemporary John Wesley. But they precluded what we should now call bohemianism.

It is fairly safe to infer that, by the time the comte de Sade summoned his son to Paris, in 1750, to begin a more conventional education, the boy's acquaintance with the intricacies of sexual behaviour, which were to preoccupy so much of his future life, did not yet equal that of a typical street-arab of his own age, whether in 1750 or 1950.

Molière and Voltaire had preceded him at the smart Jesuit college for boys named Louis le Grand, after Louis XIV, at which he was now enrolled. Robespierre and Victor Hugo, among many other distinguished pupils, were to follow. The type of schooling here imparted, based almost exclusively upon Christianity and the Greek and Latin classics, conformed to the generally accepted pattern of the day. It reached a high standard. For there was little that the Society of Jesus, then as now, did not know about the art of instruction.

Thoroughly up to date, the staff bestowed a great deal of attention on acting, for the stage was already believed to be an even more powerful social instrument than the pulpit. The Fathers kept up the Renaissance practice of turning schools into theatres for the performance of plays both in Latin and in the vernacular. The marquis's life-long devotion to the drama dates from this period.

Another peculiarity of the system at the college of Louis le Grand was that each class was officially divided into two competitive sections, with a 'consul' at the head of each and a decreasing hierarchy of 'censors,' 'tribunes,' 'senators,' and other ranks of the ancient Roman social order. Each officer was put in charge of a sub-section, the ambition of which was, again officially, to defeat the other groups in the school examinations.

This arrangement had been carefully thought out and certainly had its points. It at least gave the boys a vivid appreciation of the civilization which produced Latin grammar, a discipline still in those days, after so many centuries, the only conceivable foundation of European secular education. But it is doubtful whether the young marquis ever displayed any particular enthusiasm for it. His mind was already restlessly inquisitive and rebellious, intolerant of all conventional control.

However, his Latin and Greek were found excellent, though his mathematics were considered poor. His lack of a cool head for figures was to be a disadvantage to him in later life and to lead him, at various times, into all sorts of absurd calculations. Throughout his school career he obtained no particular distinctions and underwent no particular punishments. As little could be said of the boyhood of many another man of exceptional mark at that time or this.

As for his moral behaviour, there is no real evidence that it was any worse than that of his companions. No doubt many of these softly nurtured and over-indulged scions of wealthy families soon grew vicious. But the Jesuit despots were strict, understood perfectly well what was bound to go on in this line and had their own tested methods of dealing with it.

The marquis himself drops a hint, in *Aline et Valcour,* of a certain corruption in his conduct at this period. But, as has already been suggested, the tone throughout this work is somewhat unctuous, approaching the strained and high-flown style, not untainted with hypocrisy, of the contemporary English novelist Samuel Richardson, whose vogue in France was enormous at the time *Aline et Valcour* was composed. The hero is here in fact making a pompous appeal to the charity of possible critics. We may take the passage with more than a grain of salt.

"I returned to Paris," says 'Valcour,' "to continue my studies under the supervision of a strict and highly intelligent man, without question an ideal guide for my youthful education." This seems to be a reference to an *abbé* of a rather different sort from François de Sade, one Amblet, from Geneva, who attended young Donatien after school hours. "But, unfortunately for myself," continues the dignified penitent, "he was not with me long enough."

As soon as the marquis had reached the age of fourteen, his father, himself a Lieutenant-General, decided, as was normal in those days, that he was ripe for regimental life. The boy had not grown very tall. He was never to be, according to the police records of a later date, more than five feet two inches all his life. But his constitution was extremely robust, his physique excellent. The girlish good looks, as remarkable as ever, were confined to his countenance. He wore his clothes with distinction, bore himself as a young noble should and, though reserved in the presence of his elders, possessed a ready tongue. He had shown aptitude, the Fathers reported, for dancing, fencing and riding, as well as a considerable talent for acting, an ability not without its advantages in a raw subaltern. The comte was very satisfied with him.

Jean-Baptiste, like so many of the fathers of men who subsequently make an equivocal noise in the world and come to be as much detested as admired, appears to have been a dry stick of a man, pedantic, conventional, absorbed in his diplomatic and military work and rather inhuman in his relationships with his fellow-beings. The marquis, who still hardly knew him, was only to be closely associated with him for a very few months in his life. But that period was to have a decisive effect on the son's subsequent career.

The boy had now passed the age of puberty. It is not necessary to believe, with the nineteenth-century journalist Jules Janin, who wished to make out a special and sensational case, that by this time "the lad was already spreading around him an obscure kind of poisonous atmosphere, which made everybody hate him." We need not doubt, however, though no contemporary concerned with him at this stage has left any record of it, that the marquis, at fourteen, was sexually precocious, a practitioner of all the schoolboy's vices in this connection and determined, the moment he was free from the expert supervision of the Jesuit Fathers, to explore to the full all the sexual gratifications open to wealth, leisure, an ardent imagination, a coolly daring intelligence and a reliable physique.

His later life, in the light of the general history of mankind, does not permit the supposition that the impressionable years from twelve or thirteen to twenty-three, when trustworthy evidence as to his career becomes much fuller, could have been sexually sluggish or even normal.

As a military cadet, then, he was probably already quite capable of astonishing his companions with his erudition, recollections and powers of improvisation in the erotic field. The stage of regular experience with the other sex now began. It could hardly have been initiated at the Louis le Grand college under the rigid control of the Jesuit Fathers and the supplemetary attentions of the worthy Abbé Amblet. But the cadet schools and garrisons of France, and of every other country in Europe at that time, were a very highly remunerative source of income to the brothels lucky enough to be established in their neighbourhood. The boys visited them in droves, week by week.

It remains noteworthy that absolutely no evidence of any specifically 'sadistic' conduct on the part of young Donatien on these occasions, which were of course peculiarly open to such abuses, has come to light. At the end of his military service as at the beginning of it, the marquis was not distinguished from his brother cadets or officers by remarkable feats of any kind, either on or off duty. There are plenty of young men between seventeen and twenty-two today, in all social classes, who regularly lead far more 'monstrous' lives, sexually, than can be proved against Donatien de Sade between 1754 and 1763.

The marquis served for two years as a cadet in the Royal Light Horse Guards, an extremely aristocratic regiment. It had been issued with the carbine as well as the sword in 1745 and wore a white tunic and breeches under a uniform cloak of scarlet and gold, with a white cockade in the busby. France was for the moment at peace. But she was surrounded by enemies, of whom England was the chief. Military training was taken as seriously as was practicable in a regiment officered by young noblemen who could not be coerced on account of their important relatives and few of whom intended to become professional soldiers or in fact do anything but enjoy themselves and their gorgeous accoutrements.

In 1755 England suddenly attacked France at sea — India and Canada were at stake — and King Frederick II of Prussia, the 'Great,' who had been allied with France in the war, ending in 1748, of the Austrian Succession, threw in his lot with the English. Louis XV turned to Austria for help and the French armies began to move into the Austrian-governed part of the Netherlands. Commissions began to be distributed to the cadets. The marquis de Sade was made a sub-lieutenant in an infantry regiment. On his promotion to ensign in January 1757 he was transferred to another crack corps of dragoons.

By this time the Seven Years' War was in full swing. Prussia, whose British ally was weak in land forces, faced not only France and Austria but Russia, Sweden and Saxony. Frederick's military genius, however, was equal to the occasion. He beat the Saxons soundly at Pirna in 1756 and the Austrians and their allies again and again in the following year. The French had been more successful, and were in Hanover and Brunswick. But they could make little headway while the Austrians retreated, the Swedes seemed to be asleep and the Russians had not yet come fully into action. When they did, in 1758, Frederick drove them back at Zorndorf, though he found them a tougher proposition than his other enemies.

Ensign de Sade may or may not have been eager to play his part in these thrilling events. He was eighteen years old, physically energetic and adventurous by temperament. But his intelligence was not of the kind that turns naturally to war. The very reverse of a coward or a pacifist, he nevertheless cared nothing for the real business of a soldier's life, though he enjoyed the uniforms and the parades, the respect and envy of civilian males and the capitulation of their wives and daughters to the handsome young cavalry officer.

In April 1759 he was made a captain, for promotion, especially for the blue-blooded, came fast in those days. He was appointed to yet another famous regiment, the Burgundian Cavalry, whose uniforms were blue and scarlet. But here the fact that his father, though a Count, a General and of ancient lineage, was a comparatively poor man began to interfere with the marquis's natural extravagance, a *sine qua non* in the Burgundian Cavalry. He discovered that the world, after all, was not yet quite at his feet. His temper, never very equable, deteriorated. He grew to be, as young men will on these occasions, rather morose and vindictive.

That year Frederick at last beat the French soundly at the great battle of Minden, near Hanover, in August. The allies started to pull themselves together. But even this reverse did not rouse Captain de Sade from his apathetic ill-humour. He continued to bombard his father with requests for money. The comte began to consider the question of a rich marriage, to solve the problem of this inconvenient drain upon his limited resources.

"My father," continues the semi-autobiographical *Aline et Valcour*, "summoned me to Paris in the winter of 1759 and I hastened to obey him. He wished to discuss the question of my marriage. His health was declining and he was anxious to see me set up a home of my own before he closed his eyes."

If we are to take *Aline et Valcour* seriously as autobiography, the last sentence of this passage can only be a rhetorical flourish. The General was barely fifty-seven. But the echo of Richardson is again evident in this sentimentally flavoured paragraph, which reads remarkably like a fragment from a speech for the defence. In 1788, the period of its composition, the marquis certainly desired to appear 'normal' to the general public. The artificially smooth style, quite unlike his usual vigorous language, was part of the disguise.

The matrimonial project eventually fell through owing, no doubt, to lack of co-operation on the other side. The marquis was sick of Army life and would have been glad enough, in accordance with the custom of the day, to submit to his father's judgment. A wife of any reasonably tolerable sort would be a change from the Burgundian Cavalry mess and would not interfere in the slightest with his private pleasures, which there is no reason to suppose differed at all, just then, from those of any other headstrong and self-indulgent young aristocrat. It is probable that the failure of the negotiations to mature was simply due to the inadequacy, in the comte's view, of the settlement proposed by the girl's parents.

It was, therefore, as still a bachelor that the marquis accompanied his regiment, in 1760, to the front in Hanover.

"We went on active service," observes the respectable 'Valcour,' "and I think I may say that I did quite well . . . our regiment, after getting a hammering in the last campaign but one, was retired to garrison duty in Normandy. I was then just twenty-three years old."

This reference, in its casual brevity, is unmistakably contemptuous. The marquis was not interested in the Seven Years' War, or in any other war. For the rest, the official records of the French War

Office compliment the young Captain, among many other officers on service at the time, for 'heroic conduct.' One need not take this formal phrase too seriously. The fact is that the marquis distinguished himself no more as a soldier than he had as a schoolboy. He was not the man to have omitted a more trenchant boast than that contained in *Aline et Valcour* if there had been any real justification for it. It is obvious, however, that he did his duty, if no more.

'Valcour,' in the romance just mentioned, describes a love affair in 1762 with a young woman named Adélaide. It does not differ, in any substantial detail, from a hundred other such associations between a young cavalry officer on garrison duty and a girl of respectable family resident in the town. Donatien's affections do not appear to have been very seriously engaged. One may conjecture that he was bored with regimental life and that it was the fashion to have a socially presentable mistress. The exchange of vows of eternal fidelity went on for about six months. Then the regiment was transferred, the lovers parted in eloquent distress and Adélaide does not ever seem to have seen her Captain again. She appears, however, to have been harder hit than he was. For two years later, says 'Valcour,' she announced her intention of retiring to a convent and begged her former lover to use his social influence in recommending her to a suitable institution. This transparent device for renewing their interrupted relations failed. The marquis in 1764, as we shall see, was a very different sort of person from the sulky but, from a normal girl's point of view, tolerably romantic and dashing young soldier of 1762. He declined to entertain the suggestion and probably told her not to be a fool. In any case she duly married three years later and played no further part in his life.

The Treaty of Paris, which put an end to the Seven Years' War, was signed at Hubertusburg on the 15th of February, 1763. Both sides were exhausted and terms were adjusted on a *status quo ante* basis. Captain de Sade was at rest billets in Normandy. In March the regiment was returned to a peace footing. Meanwhile the comte de Sade had been renewing his attempts to improve the family's financial position by marrying his son into money. Early in the year preliminaries were satisfactorily settled with an old acquaintance, Claude René Cordier de Montreuil, President of the Third Chamber of the High Court of Paris, who had an eligible daughter. M. de Montreuil, apart from his comparatively humble origins, was a man after the comte's own heart. A sound lawyer and business man, he was quiet and unassuming in manner, utterly devoted to his profession, in which he had made plenty of money and looked like making plenty more. He was delighted with the dignified attentions of a contemporary so far above him in social position and yet as businesslike and free from ostentation as he was himself. He agreed to all the comte's proposals, referring him only, for their due ratification, to Madame de Montreuil, who wore the breeches.

The tactful and anxious nobleman found Madame charming. He saw at once that she was a woman of considerable force of character, who always had got and always would get, in the end, exactly what she wanted. But she knew how to do it without ruffling people up the wrong way. A noble son-in-law, the comte discovered, was just what she wanted for her daughter Renée-Pélagie. She set out deliberately to make a conquest of her husband's reserved and formal, but unquestionably respectable as well as blue-blooded, business acquaintance. She succeeded perfectly.

The comte, for form's sake, took a look at Renée, a tall, dark girl with a somewhat blunt but extremely modest cast of countenance. He found her a little clumsy in her movements but obviously well brought up. Jean-Baptiste was no connoisseur of women. If they behaved themselves and didn't put on airs he was always perfectly satisfied with them. Renée, he decided, would do excellently for Donatien.

In March he sent for the marquis and informed him of these preliminary manœuvres.

"The girl whom I intend for you," said the comte, "belongs to a highly respected family and is extremely well dowered. What do you say?"

The marquis remained silent for a moment, eyeing his father's prim and unfamiliar features with a certain anxiety. The young man understood well enough that, with this sort of parent, a rich marriage was the only road to freedom from the maddening restrictions of life as a poor aristocrat. But it was to be hoped that the instrument of this salvation would not be too awful. Some of the tradesmen's daughters he had been obliged to meet in garrison towns and on service in Hanover had sent cold shivers down his spine.

"Is she pretty, Sir?" he asked quietly, at last.

"What the devil does that matter, Sir? I have told you how she is situated in the world and that is enough. If you do not consider it enough I shall have to take steps to persuade you to change your mind."

Father and son again crossed glances. The eyes of both were hard. But the younger man knew what the older meant. Any nobleman of the period could obtain a *lettre de cachet,* an arbitrary warrant for imprisonment, from the King, which would enable the applicant to lock up any social inferior he pleased for any length of time he chose.

Captain de Sade, like Edward Gibbon at a slightly earlier period, recognized the obligations of filial duty. He bent his head.

"Very well, Sir," he said. "No doubt everything has been arranged for the best. What do you wish me to do about it?"

"Why, that's talking sense, man!" The comte rose and clapped his son on the shoulder. Then, taking Donatien's arm, he began to walk him up and down the room.

"You may or may not know M. de Montreuil, the High Court Judge. I am under considerable obligations to him financially. He is a very decent fellow for a *bourgeois.* He has a very clever and agreeable wife. And I want you to marry his daughter. I have prepared all the ground for you on his side. You have only to go and make the acquaintance of the family, pay your court to the girl and report what progress you make to me. I hope it will be rapid. For I don't mind telling you, in strict confidence, now that you are no longer a boy, that our whole family is extremely hard up."

Jean-Baptiste added, for his son's private information, certain details as to the income, estates and appointments which might be expected to follow the marriage. They sounded highly satisfactory. The young man's spirits began to rise. He gathered from his father that Renée was neither hideous nor affected, a perfectly normal, respectable girl about his own age who would give him no trouble whatever. Money, after all, in these days, the comte observed, rather bitterly, gave on the whole better results, socially, than a long pedigree. In any case, money was really essential if the family were not to fall, like so many others of equal rank, into misery and obscurity. Donatien owed it to his ancestors to keep up the state which they had bequeathed to him.

Both men knew well enough, though the comte's dry character forbade him to say so, that marriage, with or without affection, would not be expected by society at large to prevent a discreet, wealthy and aristocratic husband from having as many mistresses as he pleased. That was commonly the case and no one, least of all a well-brought-up wife, could possibly object to it.

Meanwhile, time pressed. The marquis, in April 1763, went off to pay his first visit to the Montreuil family in a mood of only very slightly chastened anticipation. He had already learned, in the Army, that the world was not completely at his private disposal. But it would not be his fault if Renée de Montreuil did not hand him a good slice of it.

CHAPTER TWO

Frustration

THE reception room at the house of the Montreuil family in Paris was enormous. It was furnished with a sober magnificence precluding any idea of the *rococo* frivolity so much in vogue in the palaces of the nobility. The marquis did not feel particularly at home in it. But he could not help being considerably impressed. His father had evidently been quite right about the financial standing of these people. Donatien immediately determined to exploit it to the full. The devil take it! It was not every day that a damned stuffy old notary's brat — the young officer's conception of the function of High Court Judges was a good deal hazier, just then, than it was to become later — managed to land a marquis whose ancestors had practically ruled Provence in the fourteenth century.

While waiting for Madame de Montreuil he strolled about the room, shrugging his shoulders, swinging his cane and glancing into the mirrors. He saw a perfection of delicate elegance, the faintly insolent blue eyes and complacently curling lips set in features of a refined regularity, rather small in scale, as befitted his neat, agile figure, and roseate as a girl's. The cobalt, white and scarlet of his closely cut cavalry officer's uniform, the faultless peruke, coquettishly waved, the shapely hands and feet, the grace of each separate movement, the composed assurance of his bearing in every attitude, gave an unmistakable impression of breeding and imperturbable courtesy. Not so often, he thought again, with gratified condescension, could this great, pretentious barrack of a place receive so truly distinguished a visitor.

He crossed over to the vast windows. Beyond them lay formal gardens, terraces, statues, fountains, flower-beds and geometrically cut hedges, groups of trees placed at cunningly contrived intervals, all flecked with the spring sunlight, the new leaves stirring in a gentle breeze, the green turf glowing. The marquis, however, was not lyrically given. He was turning away from this peaceful prospect, with a slight yawn, when his half-closed eyes distinguished a female figure bending over a bed of daffodils near one of the boxwood hedges.

This apparition was much more in the Captain's line than vegetation, however ornamental. He stiffened at once, throwing back his aristocratic head. Good God! What a lovely creature!

He could not see the face. But the hair, wig or not, gleamed richly golden, falling in apparent carelessness about the slender shoulders in a fashion which indicated that the head was that of a very young girl. The figure, too, he could see, was prettily curved and instinct with adolescent charm. The expensive gown could not be that of a servant. Could this child-goddess be the 'modest and respectable' Renée de Montreuil, his future bride?

She stood up and turned towards the house, her arms full of the pale yellow blooms. The marquis gasped, one knee on the window-ledge, his nervous fingers twisting in the heavy curtains, his eyes intent. This was no goddess, but a vision of enchanting beauty, mischief and intelligence, a witch, a fairy, a romp destined to turn the heads of kings. Just as she tossed her fair head and began to run up a path leading to the house, he heard a footstep in the room behind him.

Good manners obliged him to turn. But his heart was beating with such violence that he could hardly bring himself to adopt a conventional attitude. Madame de Montreuil was, fortunately, still some distance away from him as she sailed, smiling gravely, up the great room. In an instant he had recovered himself and was bowing with all the accomplished grace of which he had long been a master.

While he kissed her hand and, after they were both seated, exchanged compliments with her, the mistress of the house looked him over very carefully. Madame de Montreuil was a very experienced and very astute observer of men. On this occasion she liked what she saw and heard. This was a true aristocrat, she thought exultantly, self-possessed, handsome, suave and by no means stupid. He had real charm, too, a ready smile, an agreeable wit, an excellent leg. And how he wore his clothes! It was easy to see he had never done a stroke of work for his living. So far as the Montreuil family was concerned this was a chance not to be missed.

She laid herself out to be gracious and gay, even a little coquettish. This was one of the very rare moments when Madame de Montreuil wished she had been twenty years younger. Normally, for her, middle age, the middle age of a wealthy, shrewd and energetic woman, seemed vastly preferable to youth, with its ignorance, leading strings and disastrous impulses of reckless generosity. It was a very long time indeed since Madame de Montreuil had felt generously inclined. Now she experienced all the emotions of a large-scale philanthropist. That stick Renée would be luckier, if all went well, than her looks and personality entitled her to be. As for the young marquis, his bread too, would be buttered for him if he played the cards expected of him.

He seemed to intend to do so. Madame de Montreuil noted, within his perfect manners and easy charm, a real enthusiasm, even an anxiety, to make a good impression upon her. Was his financial position even rockier than Claude had given her to understand? She had been snubbed often enough before by aristocrats, including those few whom she had interviewed on Renée's behalf. But this de Sade was treating her like a queen. Well, so much the better. Everyone would, in the end, be satisfied. Whatever he might privately think of Renée, he would not be such a fool as to let private inclination interfere with public prospects. So much was obvious from his present attitude.

This first interview, then, went off splendidly. The marquis took his leave with actual rapture. In less than a week, the mother had promised, he would meet her daughter. That brilliant little face, under its golden hair, that audacious, almost athletic shape, that exciting, enchanting suggestion of adventurous gaiety he had identified, beyond any shadow of doubt, in the garden! What a wife for a man! Hang it all, what a mistress . . .

He was with his father the same night, announcing himself absoultely delighted with the whole affair, especially the 'inexpressibly delicious' bride-to-be.

The comte stared, a little grimly. That awkward booby of a girl 'inexpressibly delicious?'

"Eh? You didn't run into her at the house, did you?"

"No. I saw her through the window."

"Hum. Delicious, hey? Well, well. I'm not much of a judge of women, I dare say. If you are satisfied with her person, so much the better. I'm glad all is going so well."

A formal reception was held a few days later at the house of the Montreuil family. Captain de Sade, as he crossed the threshold of the *salon,* at once perceived his garden-goddess, very modestly and soberly dressed, and evidently on her best behaviour, seated with her mother and father and some other ladies and gentlemen at the end of the long room. He had never felt so clumsy and stupid in his life before and actually felt himself blushing. His heart thumped painfully as he bent low over the mother's hand.

Straightening, he hardly glanced at the dumpy judge, who was greeting him with shy effusiveness. The girl looked up at him. He could have sworn, though his agitation was so great that he could scarcely see her, that her blue, mischievous eyes sparkled into his. Then, still staring at her, he heard the murmur of the introduction. "My daughter Renée, *Monsieur le marquis —* "

Someone, a man, chuckled softly and maliciously. Then there was a general burst of feminine laughter. His father was dragging violently at his elbow. He heard the comte whisper savagely:

"Are you mad, Sir? Look in front of you. . . ."

He turned, saw a strange young woman looking at him with a nervously ingratiating expression, mixed with fear and awe. The features were swarthy and heavy, shapeless after that other's. The eyes were quite fine, tender and dark. But there was something, to his taste, nauseatingly sentimental and banal about the whole figure, tall and even majestic, but crudely poised and absurdly apologetic in effect.

"*Mademoiselle* . . ." he stammered, bowing and frowning at his own awkwardness. Everyone was watching him, the mother with indulgent censure, the father with his mouth open, the rest with more or less frank amusement. He recovered himself almost immediately, his features smoothing into a fine mask of punctilious courtesy that veiled an inferno. He talked to Mademoiselle Renée-Pélagie de Montreuil with practised gallantry, hitting the precise note of dignified deference that suited the occasion. The comte drew back, satisfied. Madame de Montreuil turned to her other guests. The incident, socially, was over. But under the conventional flow of small talk that he uttered the marquis was battling with a tide of fury that carried everything but his outward demeanour before it.

He had been trapped. The daughter was as wretchedly negligible a type of shallow-minded, vulgar and servile fool of a *bourgeoise* as he had ever met. He could see her whining, nagging, boring him with endless details of household management and trivial gossip, disgracing him before his friends with her asinine chatter, betraying him to the servants, interfering disastrously in his business affairs. The whole thing was impossible. He would never go on with it. The comte must see reason. The devil take it! He had made nearly as big an idiot of himself as that silly girl, with her pitiful manners and obtuse misunderstanding of everything he said, was making at this moment.

He excused himself as soon as he decently could and devoted the rest of the evening to attempting to make contact with the golden-headed fairy of his vision in the garden. He discovered that she was Renée's younger sister Anne-Prospère, commonly called Louise, sixteen years old and only present at this gathering of adults in view of its family importance. It was relatively easy for him, in his new and detested capacity of a suitor for the elder sister's hand, to get a few words with the adorable infant. He found her, as he had expected, exceptionally self-possessed and intelligent. She let him see that he pleased her and that she would be delighted to flirt with him if he were not already practically engaged to her sister. He was entranced with her alternate pertness and mock-modesty. But etiquette, the presence of others and the formality of the occasion obliged him to maintain, for the moment, merely the attitude of an elder brother, a pretence which deceived neither of them. By the time Louise was called upon by her mother to exhibit her social accomplishments, playing and singing very prettily to the harp, the cavalry captain and the judge's youngest daughter were very heartily in love with each other.

Donatien tackled his father as soon as they were alone in the carriage together, on the way home.

"This is impossible, Sir. You told me that there was only one daughter. I find that there are two, the eldest, for whom you destine me, a fool, and the younger, a child still in a convent school, an angel."

Jean-Baptiste regarded him sternly.

"I said no such thing, Sir. Only one of the daughters is marriageable. The other, a mere child, as you say, was not even mentioned to me in this connection. The match with Renée is perfectly suitable in every respect. I must ask you, for the reasons I have already given you, to raise no frivolous objections to it."

The marquis hissed between his teeth:

"I shall call upon Madame de Montreuil tomorrow and inform her that I am not prepared to proceed, that I do not wish —"

"You do not wish, Sir? What are you thinking of? To whom are you talking? What have your wishes got to do with the matter? You have entered formally into an engagement. Do you now propose to break it? There is a word, Sir, which has never yet been applied to members of my family. It is dishonour. I shall be obliged if you will take care, Sir, like your ancestors, to keep that word out of our history."

"But if I consent to marry the other —"

"You consent, Sir? And will the parents consent? A child at a convent? The younger before the elder? You would be condemning your betrothed to an insufferable humiliation, and making enemies of a set of people with whom, I tell you frankly, I cannot afford to quarrel. Enough of this! Behave yourself, Sir! Fulfil your obligations like a man of honour. Or I shall know what steps to take."

The young man, pale to the lips, held his tongue. The trap had been closed by this unnatural father, whom he now began to hate to the depths of a being with a singular capacity for hate. He said no more, either then or at any other time, on any but the most indifferent subjects, to the comte de Sade. But after a night of rage and despair, ending in a bitter and cold resolution which made the dashing, if occasionally sullen young captain of dragoons a person who now seemed to belong to a wholly alien and utterly irrecoverable existence, he went to see, in secret, Madame de Montreuil.

He exerted every resource of his formidable social charm upon that equally formidable lady. He told her, acting, with brilliant virtuosity, the part of youthful diffidence, that he had an uneasy presentiment that a mistake might possibly have been made. He hinted at his admiration of Louise, appealing to what he hoped might be a mother's partiality.

But Madame de Montreuil was not this kind of a mother. Less sentimental even than the marquis, she made it clear to him that this shift of the contractual ground was out of the question. Louise was far too young to think of marriage, she pointed out. There had been no thought, at any time, of her being the daughter whose disposal was open to discussion. The redoubtable matron remained courteous and sympathetic, but inflexible. She made a joke, from the height of her twenty years' seniority, of the young suitor's qualms. Then, blandly, she changed the subject to the matter of Renée's dowry.

The figures, added to those of the prospective bridegroom's own expectations, as promised by his father, meant that the future marquis and marquise de Sade would be extremely wealthy people, even by Louis Quinze standards. Madame de Montreuil drew a dazzling picture, cunningly adorned with the sensual overtones likely to attract extravagant young aristocrats, of the life of leisure and enjoyment which marriage with Renée would bring to her fortunate husband. She added a few conventional praises of her elder daughter's meekness and sobriety. The marquis need have no fear, she strongly implied, that Renée would prove any hindrance to his doing precisely as he pleased. She promised her own support in any possible matrimonial debates. Then she returned to the glittering material prospects, basing them upon the hardest possible facts, which she was prepared to support, if necessary, by documentary evidence.

Donatien kept his temper, expressed his gratitude for so much tactful consideration of his feelings and complimented the lady, quite sincerely, on her grasp of practical affairs. He gave her to understand, however, that he still required a few days to think the deal over.

But there was no way out, for an eighteenth-century nobleman, of this dilemma. One horn or the other of it had to be accepted. To go into hiding from the inevitable *lettre de cachet,* to carry Louise off by trickery or by force and take her abroad, were expedients that did occur to the marquis. But his innate breeding rejected them absolutely. One would become a penniless outlaw and criminal, sooner or later exposed to disgraceful punishment. Such acts could be and had been committed by common citizens and even by men of rank who were their own masters. But they were out of the question for a bachelor marquis still utterly dependent upon his father.

He would have to go through with the marriage, then. It was a vile business and he would never forgive his father for it, or that bitch of a lawyer's wife either. The ephemeral fits of sulkiness which the young captain had experienced while he was on service hardened and solidified into a black mood of resentment against the whole world. This attitude was rarely to leave him again. Even his feeling for Louise underwent a change. He was going to have her, that was certain. But the affair could now be, at best, only of short duration, a brief, doomed ecstasy. What was that beside the lifetime of happiness he had dreamed of at the window overlooking the garden?

On the 17th of May, 1763, the fatal marriage took place, with extraordinary pomp, at the church of St. Roch in Paris. Louise was not present. Her mother had packed her off to her convent with extreme promptitude, immediately after the interview with Donatien which had shown her which way the wind blew. The almost regal solemnity with which the wedding was celebrated enabled the bridegroom, without offence to etiquette, to preserve an expression of gloomy arrogance, which, for once, exactly corresponded with this born actor's thoughts. Renée, sedulously coached, and exalted by the honour of becoming a real marquise, behaved with much less of her usual clumsiness. Tall, dark, grave and statuesque, she went through her part with only an occasional over-long stride to mar for a moment the serenity of her mother's watchful eye.

The bride's dowry, the guests at the church whispered, amounted to an enormous sum, the equivalent in British purchasing power today of something like £250,000.

Nothing could be more inviting, from any point of view, except that of a highly-sexed young husband who had just 'fallen in love' for the first time with a girl not his wife, than the outlook for the newly-married couple. The less than prepossessing Renée herself was of course delighted at her unexpected good fortune. She had landed a partner who seemed to have every attribute of a fairy prince, except wealth equal to her own and an explicitly fervent adoration of his young bride. But the girl was too modest to have anticipated such transports. It was enough for her that she was the authorized consort of an exceptionally handsome and courtly young aristocrat of ancient line and unimpeachable social eminence. She did not realize that he was also exceptionally intelligent. If she had guessed the fact, she was not herself intelligent enough to have felt uneasy about the discovery.

Her innocence and enthusiasm led her, that day in the church of St. Roch, to make a private as well as a public vow to love, honour and obey her magnificent husband for as long as they both should live. She was a girl, like so many of her type, of genuinely deep and loyal, positively blind, affections. Fortunately for herself, her lack of imagination saved her, in the sequel, from suffering the agonies of disillusion that would have tortured a more sensitive nature. She believed and hoped almost to the end, then suddenly gave up. But it took a marquis de Sade to bring Renée de Montreuil to that point of pious resignation. A mere rake would have retained her unquestioning devotion to the very brink of the grave.

The marquis, for his part, for the first time in his hitherto, on the whole, very enjoyable life, had now quite despaired of ever attaining that serene and confident level of steady participation in the more enduring pleasures of existence which he had been brought up to suppose would easily become his by right of birth, education and experience. He was by no means a born intellectual. But he had already begun to savour the fine arts. He knew something about painting and sculpture, had even tried his hand at them. He had learned from the Abbé François and the Jesuit Fathers to take an interest in history and classical literature. He had put himself to the trouble, unlike most of his brother officers, to learn German while he was campaigning in Hanover, if only the more easily to make love to the female population under forty. He was intensely devoted to the theatre, fond of music, dancing, all the entertaining amenities of cultivated society. Now he had lost the chance of acquiring a clever and charming wife, was married to a rich dunderhead and had nothing to look forward to but boredom in her society and, when he left her in this temper, what he could buy with her money to relieve it.

He felt furious with his bloodless father, his dangerous mother-in-law and the entire contemporary apparatus of social convention that could compel a man with brains, looks, birth and at least some money to saddle himself with a lifelong companion inferior in all these respects except the last. He had no feelings whatever, one way or the other, about Renée. She was a nonentity. He did not, perhaps, just then, intend to make a noise in the world, though he was already conscious of the impact of new ideas, transcending what he saw about him, the environment which, within a generation, was to vanish in the shadow of the guillotine, never to revive again.

But Donatien de Sade certainly intended to go on enjoying himself, if not in step with a society which, he considered, had victimized him, then at its expense. And how the devil was one to do that with a creature like Renée for ever hanging on to one's skirts?

Even at twenty-three, with a fairly riotous life as an Army officer behind him and a mind singularly susceptible to the revolutionary ideas in politics, sociology and metaphysics which Voltaire, Jean Jacques Rousseau and the encyclopedists were then disseminating, the marquis had still not yet developed that formidable arrogance of his to the point of absolutely defying his family and the conservatives of Louis Quinze society. As already suggested, such rebellion would have been an almost unthinkable step for a man in his position to have taken in 1763. It was not quite unthinkable, however. And there is little doubt that he did think of it, in connection with Louise at any rate. That in fact he took no such action is the measure of his immaturity at this time and of the mental gulf between the bridegroom who, impassive without, enraged within, entered the church of St. Roch on the 17th of May and the deliberate debauchee who hired a house called L'Aumônerie, at Arcueil, some two hours' drive from Paris, a month later, for purposes which, at that time, he would scarcely have dreamed of if it had been Anne-Prospère-Louise de Montreuil he was marrying.

The sexual climate of the doomed aristocratic circles of Paris in the 1760's was already feverish. It still retained something of the burlesque ferocity of earlier days, when a king like Henri Quatre could shock mistress and wife alike by his boisterousness. But the eighteenth century had added what the Middle Ages, the Renaissance and even the Great Century of Louis XIV had hesitated to embrace, to wit, a thoroughgoing scepticism. The effect of the withdrawal of the fear of hell from the cultivated strata of society was cataclysmic. It became fashionable to have new vices, the more appalling the better.

The raw materials for the analysis which the marquis de Sade subsequently inaugurated already existed, under Louis XV, in abundance. The scenes at the public torture and execution of Damiens, the would-be assassin of the king, in 1757, when women were openly violated in the tightly-packed crowds of wildly excited sightseers in the streets and at the windows, are alone sufficient, without adding innumerable other instances from the police records of the time, to prove a general recklessness in sexual morality which had not been seen in Christian Europe for many hundreds of years.

Every great and wealthy city of which historical notes survive has had its open and its secret face, the one splendid with palaces, gardens, rich costumes and dignified manners, the other lurid with lust, violence, fraud and misery. Formal history is mostly concerned with the power and the glory of human achievement. But it is salutary to remember also the decadence and the shame, which have been at least as operative in moulding the general character of humanity. Men of sufficient ability to write history at all have usually been more attracted by the events which may be interpreted as showing an ascent of earth to heaven than by the reverse process, by the nobility of Greek art and literature rather than by the sordid greed and frivolous irresponsibility of the Athenian *demos,* by the charms of Horace and Cicero rather than by the orgies of Nero. So it has been throughout history, so that, when the average man thinks of Louis Quinze, he thinks primarily of *rococo* furniture, of Fragonard and Boucher, of the exquisite flower of a culture more elegant than any of Italy's, more ingenious than any of its own previous manifestations, as full of revered names as any in Europe has ever been.

But the mid-eighteenth century in France did not mean only the genius of its dramatists, novelists, historians, philosophers, statesmen and scientists. It meant also the monstrous corruption of financial and political life, an almost universal cynicism in public morals, paralleled by a degradation, in particular, of relations between the sexes which thickened and poisoned the air of every meeting between a man and any woman under fifty.

Women ruled France. And yet Denis Diderot, the most energetic mind, apart from Voltaire's, of the century, could declare that women are essentially merely harlots. Montesquieu, the greatest philosophic historian of the age, considered them no better than amusing children, J. J. Rousseau called them playthings and Voltaire ciphers. All these highly civilized men, nevertheless, spent far more time with attractive women than their 'opposite numbers' would today, when the social emancipation of feminine Europe, which the marquis de

Sade foretold, is far more advanced. Hardly a Frenchman of note, in those days, including the clergy, could do without an almost continual resort to the female society which, as *savants,* they affected so heartily to despise.

It seems a strange situation to those who look back over two hundred years from communities in which, on the whole, women are as much feared as rivals or appreciated as companions, as desired physically or for mental relaxation. The atmosphere through which the du Barry swept or one of Restif de la Bretonne's 'little working girls' tripped had been prepared by centuries of bitter subjection and exploitation. A female child learned at a very early age that she could expect to get little or no pleasure out of life and no respect at all from the other sex unless she set out to play, coolly and with unrelenting vigilance, upon the universal, inordinate and unscrupulous concupiscence, with which she was, at every step through life to the climacteric, surrounded.

There could be no question, for her, of the 'fun' which a boy could legitimately expect. For a girl sex was the whole business, a deadly serious one, of existence, her only chance of reasonable prosperity and happiness. And the penalties of failure at the game amounted to the loss, practically, of recognition as a human being at all.

The best men of the age could not see, on their intellectual premises, the horrible injustice of this situation. Here and there an exceptionally generous mind, like that of the Abbé Prévost, author of *Manon Lescaut,* pitied those of this vast population of 'white slaves' who happened to be pretty and good-natured. The Abbé made poetry out of the pity. Others followed him. But the enthronement and glorification of the prostitute which became general under Louis XV (the king setting the fashion with his enormous brothel of the Parc Aux Cerfs, run by an ex-whore who had won his favour) owed less to the romantic reflections of the good Abbé than to the characteristically materialist recognition by Frenchmen who had ceased to be frightened by hell-fire that pleasure was the highest good in life, sexual pleasure was the most intense of pleasures and the harlot the most readily accessible source of it.

The marquis, therefore, when he turned, in acrimonious frustration, from his hopes of life with Louise to see how he could best drown his sorrows, found an extremely comprehensive banqueting-table set out before him. It was a very crowded scene. Most of his contemporaries and elders were already tirelessly jostling for the best places. He had only to present his title, his wealth, his forceful personality and his determination to drain all cups to the dregs, in order to get well to the front of this gigantic trough of Epicurus.

He found that the general attitude of his competitors was pretty well uniform. One could not enjoy the various forms of sexual gratification with proper concentration if there were any nonsense about romantic love in the affair. The object of lust, despite the intensity of its magnetism, was scarcely thought of as human. It rather resembled an ingenious piece of mechanism or furniture, at best an idol. You could do what you pleased with it if it didn't behave properly, as certain savages thrash their gods when the rain or the harvest is not forthcoming in the desired abundance. This view was heavily reinforced by the fact that you were paying in hard cash for the usufruct. The marquis, who had been struck at an early age by the importance of money and never ceased to worry about it all his life, was particularly impressed by this aspect of the matter. From the point of view of that logic which was his birthright as a Frenchman it seemed omnipotent.

As an aristocrat, however, the marquis disliked crowds and publicity. He soon deserted the swarming streets, theatres and brothels, even the fashionable night-clubs, where a gentleman's amusements were likely to be interrupted at any moment by a murderous brawl or a visit from the police. Instead of these vulgar localities he chose, like other young and old noblemen of the day, a discreet country cottage, a *petite maison,* as these inconspicuous establishments were currently called, to which he could invite the participants, male and female, of his pleasures.

L'Aumônerie, a former farmhouse lying well off the main road from Paris in a relatively isolated position and snugly embowered in its orchard, with a low wall running round its grounds and more than one concealed entrance, was a typical *petite maison*. Its exterior did not attract attention. It looked just like any other moderately well-off peasant's cottage. But indoors it was furnished with taste and even a certain degree of luxury. All the latest improvements were installed. There was a permanent small staff of servants. The walls were exceptionally thick and all the doors had locks. The marquis and his friends visited it two or three times a week, always bringing with them a number of human subjects for erotic experiment. Sometimes, however, the tenant appeared with only a single companion. The kitchen staff were then usually expected to keep out of the way.

Most of the villagers knew that L'Aumônerie was being used by some great lord for immoral purposes. But there were other such places in the district. The practice was common and it was none of their business. The local police and the more important residents had no objection so long as there was no open violence or scandal. Until nearly the end of the summer of 1763 they had nothing to complain of.

In fact, there is no evidence that the parties with expensive prostitutes or ladies of less openly professional status, which took place this year at L'Aumônerie, differed at all from familiar examples of such jollifications throughout the ages, except that they were, perhaps, a little more imaginative. Donatien's boon companions are known to have included the prince de Lamballe, four years later to be married to a celebrated beauty, who became the favourite of Marie Antoinette in later years and was hacked to death by the Paris mob in 1792. Another friend was the duc de Fronsac, a young scapegrace with a decided talent for engineering, who had invented a special armchair for obstinate females. The latter had only to sit in it to be instantly thrown backwards, legs in air, a hopeless position, in the eighteenth century, if an active and resolute seducer were present.

The bawdy tales of the day, and the engravings which often accompanied them, describe many such rough tricks played by the gilded youth of the eighteenth century upon girls, some of whom were professionals and well paid for their humiliations, while others were respectable enough by the easy standards of the time but generally inferior socially to their rascally hosts. Most of the stories and nearly all the illustrations are quite good-humoured, though the humour is distinctly 'broad.' They are mere reactions, of course, against the insistent courtly convention that the elaborately dressed and stiffly posed 'lady' of the period could not be conceived in any but a condescending attitude.

Pornography, it has often been suggested, is one thing, obscenity another. The police of Louis XV drew a clear distinction between printed matter designed to make a 'broad'-minded man laugh and paragraphs deliberately concocted with the object of putting ideas into people's heads which might subvert public order. Accounts of a seducer's stratagems might pass, for they would at any rate fore-warn a possible victim. But details of performances which, if they were imitated, might lead to rowdyism, were barred.

This last consideration was the reason why the police did some-times interfere when prostitutes, as happened fairly frequently, got hurt less by accident than by design. Then as now the guardians of the law were very closely and intricately concerned, as they had to be, with paid traffic between the sexes. Abuses were rife on both sides. A rich and well-known debauchee was never safe, unless he was very near the king's person, from fraudulent prosecutions by whores who saw a chance of lucrative blackmail or by policemen who either had been or expected to be bribed, or who felt the time and the opportunity ripe for their promotion.

The marquis and his new wife had gone to live, after their mar-riage, with Madame de Montreuil, at Echauffour in Normandy, for a reason which is still obscure. Perhaps the comte's estates in Prov-ence were not yet ready for their occupation. But it is possible that Donatien, during the first few days of his married life, had given Renée some reason to suspect, if not his 'fury' and intention to 'submerge the ruin of his life' in a flood of ceaseless dissipation, at least his frigid indifference towards her. Or he may have, in his bore-dom, tried to play one or two mildly 'sadistic' tricks upon her. In any case, circumstances were such that the girl's mother seems to have wished to keep an eye on her eldest and not over self-reliant

daughter. The marquis had no objection whatever to these arrangements, since he spent as little time as possible, at this period, in any
house where his wife might happen to live.

Madame de Montreuil, if she made any discoveries about her
'charming' son-in-law at this date, was not the woman, as we shall
see in due course, to keep them to herself. A quiet word from the
wife of a prominent judge, dropped into the ear of a high police official, would be enough to cause the authorities to watch with at least
a fatherly interest the marquis's private proceedings at L'Aumônerie.

However that might be, the first brush between Donatien de Sade
and the representatives of the law occurred at the *petite maison* itself
a few months after the much-talked-of ceremony at the church of
St. Roch.

Early on a September morning a police inspector, with two
subordinates, drove up to the house in a closed carriage. The officer,
leaving his constables to watch the door, announced himself to the
lackey who answered it. While the inspector waited in the hall the
servant ran upstairs and knocked at the door of a room on the first
floor.

As there was no sound from within and the man found the door
unlocked, he entered. Sunlight shone, through the carelessly-drawn
curtains, across the bed. In it, fast asleep, lay the marquis de Sade and
two young women. All three were snoring. The lackey had to give
his master's shoulder quite a shaking before Donatien opened his
eyes.

He stared at the servant with an amazement that almost instantly
changed to fury.

"What the devil are you doing here at this hour, you impudent
scoundrel? Get out! Do you hear me? Get out! Leave my service!
Leave my — ah, pest . . ." He clicked his tongue against his dry lips.
"Get me a glass of water, you vagabond!"

He sat up, with protruding tongue. The valet hastened to obey
him. Then, as the marquis, after a convulsive grimace, opened his
mouth again, the man muttered hurriedly.

"Someone to see you, my lord marquis. He's waiting downstairs."

"Tell him to go to hell!"

The young aristocrat settled down to resume his slumbers. But the servant insisted.

"*Monsieur le marquis!* It's the police!"

De Sade opened one eye, then two. The girls woke up and began twittering and exclaiming. Their patron turned savagely upon them.

"Silence, animals!" He nodded to the valet. "All right. I'm coming."

The man fled. De Sade got out of bed, put on his night-gown and went downstairs. The inspector greeted him with apologies and respect.

"You are the marquis de Sade?"

"I am."

"Inspector of police Marais, at your lordship's service. I am sorry to have to tell you that I bring the king's warrant for your arrest."

De Sade frowned. He had not expected this.

"On what charge?" he demanded sternly.

"I have not been informed of the charge, my lord marquis. Here is the warrant."

He held out a sealed parchment. The other waved it aside impatiently.

"There has been some mistake," he said, with haughty condescension. "Wait here. I shall be with you again in a few minutes."

He returned to the bedroom. A quarter of an hour later, after ordering his valet to pay the women and see them off the premises, he left the house with the inspector. They entered the carriage, the two constables mounted behind it and the driver took the road to Paris.

"What is our destination, fellow?" the marquis enquired negligently, after they had been bowling along at a smart pace for some minutes.

"The prison of Vincennes, my lord," was the quiet answer.

It is still not known for certain why de Sade was arrested on this occasion. But, from the letter quoted below, it seems indubitable that the charge involved certain written matter for which the marquis was in some way held responsible and probable that this book, pamphlet or manuscript described technically criminal debaucheries in a certain house in or near Paris, but not L'Aumônerie. A nobleman of de Sade's standing could hardly be clapped in gaol for anything less. Relevant extracts from this extremely curious document, which throws, for the first time, a flood of light on the marquis's character, are subjoined.

"TO
    M. de Sartine,
        Lieutenant of Police.

                                    Vincennes Prison,
                                    2 November, 1763
SIR,

In the unfortunate situation to which I am reduced the only consolation I can afford myself is to beg you to inform my wife of my unhappy condition . . . please also write to my mother-in-law, Madame de Montreuil, at Echauffour in Normandy. . . . I feel that I have deserved God's vengeance; all I can do is to weep for my sins and abhor my wicked behaviour. . . . I should be obliged if you would allow me to see a priest . . . also my valet, a thoroughly decent fellow, I assure you, he had nothing to do with what I am here for. . . . I rely upon you not to inform my family of the true reason for my detention . . . the date of that wretched book is only June, I was married on the 17th of May and I can assure you that I have not set foot in the house in question since June. Moreover, I have been in the country for the last three months. I was arrested only a week after my return. . . ."

The tone of this communication is utterly unexpected. The supercilious young marquis and seasoned ex-Guards officer writes like a hysterical schoolgirl who has been caught reading a forbidden novel in the lavatory. It is quite certain that the marquis had never, in all his born days, been this sort of nincompoop. But we know that he was already a first-rate actor and we now find that he could express himself pretty well on paper. Therefore, he was playing a part, the part which he knew officialdom would expect of him. He had enough experience of the conventional world that posed before the less agreeable aspects of society to be almost sure that M. de Sartine, like most heads of disciplinary institutions, at any rate in the eighteenth century, would only be accessible to a supplication accompanied by appeals to heaven and protestations of abject repentance. The remarkable thing is that the obstinate and embittered youth could bring himself to perform these antics with such a convincing air. One can only put it down to his passion for the theatre, motivated by a shrewdness in the diagnosis of his elders' hypocrisy and conceit which is quite startling in so young a man, with so profound an innate contempt for age and authority.

After this exordium the marquis resumes for a moment the character of a dignified and misused gentleman, who is at the same time a genial man of the world. He begs, in somewhat colloquial terms, for the services of his valet, but again shows his guilty conscience in the hasty assurance that the fellow is only wanted for his professional, not for improper, attendance.

There is some slight indication here that the 'book' referred to dealt with unnatural vice, to which the writer was later to show himself earnestly addicted, less by native tendency than by intellectual conviction. Sodomy was punishable by law at this time, as mere fornication was not. There would be definite grounds for the arrest even of a nobleman if printed or written matter bearing his name provided evidence that he had committed this crime, or some kindred offence, or condoned it. A mere account of reprehensible dealings with women, even if alleged to have been accompanied by some degree of violence or outrage, would not in itself be sufficient.

However that may be, the rest of the letter carefully sustains the tearful, penitent note. "Don't tell my people, it was all before my marriage —"(assuming the 'book' to have been printed after a certain lapse of time) "I never do that sort of thing nowadays, I don't even live in Paris now," etc.

The circumstances of the marquis's actual arrest, which must have been communicated to Sartine by Marais, would invalidate this plea if de Sade had in fact only been arrested for scandalous fornication. The prisoner, it seems practically certain, must be here telling his gaoler, not that he has given up frequenting whores, a sacrifice which would not interest the policeman, but that marriage has cured him of certain abnormal inclinations.

It is true that de Sade had been officially domiciled in Normandy since his marriage. But it is also highly probable that he was more often in or near Paris than in the banal surroundings of Echauffour. The country always bored him except as a hiding-place.

From this letter the conclusions are almost inescapable that de Sade, at twenty-three, was already deliberately bi-sexual, could resort with perfect confidence to any amount of barefaced bluff when it suited his purpose and had no more moral sense than a jaguar. There are plenty of clever and popular young men, everywhere in the world, at this moment, who combine all these characteristics and yet not only manage to keep out of gaol but even out of notoriety.

This letter succeeded in procuring the prisoner's freedom within a few days. The order of release was signed by Louis XV on the 13th of November. But Sartine warned the marquis that he was to stay away from Paris, that hotbed of temptations, for an indefinite period. The facts fit a theory that the crime was homosexual practice but that the criminal was too important a member of society to be heavily punished. Sartine was really only concerned to keep down the rising tide of erotic dissipation in the capital, Louis to save the face of one of those old families he relied on to protect him against his reforming, decentralizing ministers, ultimately against revolution.

Madame de Montreuil, who can hardly have been kept in ignorance of the real reason for the arrest, also had the object in view of preventing serious scandal from depreciating the prestige of the clan she had married her daughter into. Perhaps, at this stage, she still hoped to be able to teach her son-in-law a lesson, not too severe a one. She may or may not have been privy to Sartine's decision to lock the young man up for a time. There is little doubt that she was instrumental in procuring his release at an early date, probably feeling that the shock of the arrest had already proved a salutary one, though it is unlikely that she was deceived by the prisoner's lachrymose appeal from his cell, if Sartine ever showed it to her. From this time on, at any rate, she watched this incalculable addition to her family, not only with the unsleeping eye and poised talons of a mother eagle defending her young, but also with the inflexible purpose of a social climber and an upholder of the established framework of society.

The marquis returned to Echauffour towards the end of the year 1763. His wife received him with open arms. He took little trouble, but had no difficulty, in persuading her that the whole episode of his brief incarceration had been an absurd blunder by M. de Sartine. Madame de Montreuil, in her less effusive way, appeared quite ready to share her daughter's indignant view of the matter. She played house-detective on her son-in-law for a few more days. Then, satisfied with his behaviour — no doubt he was acting again — and with Renée's reports of her own more intimate observations, she left the house, as the winter deepened, for a prolonged visit to Paris.

CHAPTER THREE

The Eddying Stream

THE marquise de Sade, delighted with her consort's new docility, was imprudent enough to invite her younger sister, whose education had now terminated, to visit the house at Echauffour. Louise, still not yet twenty, duly arrived and found her brother-in-law even more fascinating than she had thought him at the reception given to celebrate his betrothal to her sister. She was intrigued, perhaps, as much by the dark rumours of his outrageous, but to her obscure, debaucheries, as by his intelligence, good looks and perfect manners. Both she and Donatien were fairly accomplished musicians. He accompanied, on the harpsichord, her singing of ballads by Lully and played Rameau to her. They took walks together when the weather improved.

The marquis's first, idealistic infatuation for the girl, differing little from any other young man's, had undergone a change. The months which had passed since he had first seen her in the spring of '63 had hardened and darkened his character. He allowed her, at times, to see the sensual passion beneath the compliments and gaieties which enlivened the hours they spent in each other's company. These were pretty frequent, for Renée took her household duties very seriously and in any case bored them both to extinction with her incomprehensible babble, proclamations of the obvious at inordinate length and tedious sentimentalities.

It could have been no surprise to Louise when there was a discreet, but unmistakably masculine, rap at her bedroom door one night. She had admitted him, however, before she quite realized who it was. He was tender at first, then became pressing. A certain amount of struggling ensued, towards the end of which the terrified girl, repenting of her originally indulgent attitude, struck her importunate brother-in-law a violent blow in the face. He at once released her, bent his head and then, without a word, left the room. Either some remnant of respect for this first inspirer of a romantic sentiment still lingered in him, or he considered that he could not afford to permit the scandal of a rape committed on his own wife's sister to get abroad.

In the morning he apologized to her in suitable terms, declaring that he had been unable to resist an impulse rooted in a profound obsession with her personality. He was duly forgiven, for it seems that Louise still remained, in secret, deeply attached to him. But shortly afterwards, whether by previous arrangement or fearing her own weakness, she went off to join her mother in Paris.

In April 1764 M. de Montreuil, good-natured as only those can be who are entirely wrapped up in their professions, obtained permission from the king, after due consultation with Madame de Montreuil concerning the earnest solicitations he was receiving from his son-in-law, for the marquis to return to the capital for a period not exceeding three months. In Paris Donatien, for Louise was now kept sedulously out of his way by her mother, who may or may not have been apprised of the recent acceleration of the marquis's interest in her second daughter, gradually began to look up his old associates in sexual experiment.

He renewed his attentions to an old mistress, Mademoiselle de Beauvoisin, a courtesan of the highest rank, who owed her position less to her appearance, which was far from agreeable, than to her erotic erudition. She was a short, bunchy little creature, some thirty-five years of age, utterly unscrupulous, extremely lascivious, quite impervious to any kind of decent feeling and alarmingly intelligent. Since she was also well off and knew everybody worth knowing from the sexual point of view, she was an ideal companion, the marquis considered, or perhaps accomplice would be the better word to express her association with a noble patron, for his designs to extend and complicate the field of personal lubricity.

This early specimen of night-club queen maintained, as a rule, the most cordial relations with the police, whom she kept indulgent by bribes and an imperturbable discretion. But at this date M. de Sartine was being rather troublesome. Things were getting altogether too hot in Paris, both from his standpoint and hers. Too many undesirable people were getting hold of too much money, owing to the general craze for sexual orgy, and the finances of the whole country were being disorganized, with consequent discontent in the provinces. Louis was forced to drop a strong hint to his home administrators. Police regulations in the capital were drastically tightened.

Mademoiselle de Beauvoisin, therefore, was glad to accept her friend the marquis's invitation to spend a few weeks with him at his *château* of La Coste in Provence, which had now been placed at his disposal by the comte.

The two highly imaginative experts in the service of Venus fitted up the place as a super-brothel, with paintings by degenerate Bouchers and Fragonards, furniture of erotic design by disciples of the duc de Fronsac and one room at least decorated with libidinous frescoes on every wall, depicting the various unorthodox uses to which the clyster, a fashionable surgical instrument of the period, could be put.

Lavish entertainments began at La Coste. Comedies were acted in which both guests and hosts took part. Revels were organized at which aphrodisiacs, both solid and liquid, were freely dispensed. The marquis, during the latter scenes, was in the habit of concealing himself in a specially constructed observatory and taking notes, which he carefully preserved. He was already beginning to find himself better pleased by contemplation of the transports of others than by contriving his own.

In September the busy owner of La Coste received, through his mother-in-law, the king's unconditional withdrawal of the sentence of exile from Paris. "The King revokes, without qualifications," ran this document, "His order to M. de Sade to remain in retirement at Echauffour" — (where he was officially supposed to be). Louis, as usual, disliked having to keep any of his valuable aristocrats under even a formal shadow of official displeasure.

The marquis at once returned to Paris, which he always regarded as preferable to even the most luxurious country seat. Here he seems to have left Mademoiselle de Beauvoisin very much to her own devices for the time being. The new, or possibly resuscitated, favourite was a bawd of the name of La Brissaut, upon whom he relied for introductions to new pleasures.

Marais now again began to watch the ex-prisoner closely. On the 30th of November, 1764, the inspector warned La Brissaut to stop her association with this awkward customer, whose activities might well bring him a second time into conflict with the State authorities. Marais reports to his chief on the 7th of December:

> "The Marquis de Sade, whom I escorted to Vincennes at the King's order a year ago, obtained permission, this summer, to come to Paris, where he still is. . . . I have advised La Brissaut in the strongest terms, without going further into the matter, to refrain from supplying him with prostitutes for his visits to country cottages."

The age was, indeed, an exceptionally licentious one. Those who had money to burn were not expected to maintain high standards of sexual morality. Behaviour which would today lead to prosecution or at least exclude a man from decent society, such as the forcible abduction and rape of girls of good reputation but modest social position, or the brutal ill-treatment of professional courtesans, who, in general, could not look to the police for protection, passed almost unnoticed. In this corrupt atmosphere a man had to do something rather drastic before he achieved the sinister notoriety which now began, as Marais' report makes clear, to gather round de Sade.

It becomes necessary, therefore, at this stage, to ask what solid foundation there really was, in 1764, for the brazen glare, as from a torture-chamber or the mouth of hell, the red and black of a demoniac vision, that some people appeared to see flickering dangerously behind and around the dapper little marquis.

As usual, a good many of these rumours must be discounted as simply malicious or exaggerated. Plenty of talkative persons envied the marquis de Sade. Plenty found his name a good peg on which to hang inventions which they hoped would bring themselves fame as thrilling story-tellers or righteous moralists. As de Sade himself subsequently wrote in a letter to his lawyer, if you are once seen to kick the cat, the neighbours are sure to say, sooner or later, that you daily torture it. Journalists and novelists like Restif de la Bretonne cashed in heavily on their imaginative ideas of what went on at L'Aumônerie or elsewhere.

But even after we have made these allowances the probability still stands high that the marquis had, by 1764, already gone some considerable distance along the road of 'sadism.' We must not forget that he had seen active service in war, with its inevitable accompaniments of sexual violence and cruelty. He may have seen ocular evidence of such events. He must have heard sensational tales of them, and at a highly impressionable age. The effects of these experiences on a youth of innately excitable and aggressive temperament, with an ingrained contempt for people of inferior social standing, must have been exceptionally powerful.

The Paris debaucheries which followed, with their colder, more deliberate and artificial heightening of sexual feeling, ranging from the horseplay of de Fronsac and other aristocratic young ruffians to the vulgar brutalities of the public brothels and the heartless cynicism of the scientific amorists who discussed theories of sexual exploitation with Mademoiselle de Beauvoisin, strongly reinforced the now thoroughly aroused urgency of de Sade's appetite for new sensations. He had undoubtedly, with the Beauvoisin, enjoyed the humiliation, very likely also the fear and the pain, of the less sophisticated guests at La Coste.

It must also be remembered, as a contributing cause to the nature of the marquis's sexual peculiarities, that he had, in '63, received a crushing rebuff to an adolescent passion which, if it had been conventionally assuaged, would probably have resulted in his being known to posterity as a political and social reformer rather than as an erotomaniac. A naturally proud and impulsive character reacts far more restively to such checks than more reflective, inhibited or diffident persons. He had tried to stifle the memory of the loss of Louise in the salacious revels which were open to noblemen of great wealth and considerable physical attractions in the most shamelessly prurient of European cities.

But the marquis, though not much given to meditation, was endowed with a restlessly probing intelligence which, so far from being confounded by oddities or even horrors, positively delighted in them. He would have made an excellent field anthropologist, though his reports would, perhaps, have been a little one-sided in their emphasis upon the sexual factor. Accordingly, he became extremely attentive to the byways of physiology and psychology, so far, at any rate, as they bore upon the erotic sphere; these were just then beginning to form the subject of not always wholly disinterested study among the many contemporary Frenchmen who were scientifically inclined. De Sade listened eagerly to their pronouncements and speculations on the connection of the nervous system with the philoprogenitive instinct, on aphrodisiacs, on the interaction of mental and physical pains and pleasures, on the artificiality of ethical dogmatism and the power of primitive emotions.

He was beginning to grow weary of the multiplicity of parts to play in the welter of exorbitant voluptuousness, to turn more and more to the role of spectator, of investigator and tester, materially passive, intellectually active; to savour, at last, the half appalled raptures, not only of a laboratory specialist, but of an observer at a pagan amphitheatre or a Christian public execution, like that of Damiens or of the two pederasts burnt alive at Paris in 1750.

It is likely, therefore, that some, as yet relatively slight, foundation for the horrific narratives of Restig and his competitors was already being laid in the 'little house' at Arcueil and other more or less private resorts of the marquis; that it had come to the notice of the police and also, very possibly, to the attention of Madame de Montreuil.

All these 'experiments' cost a great deal of money. Donatien gambled and borrowed, to meet his debts. But they steadily rose as the ensuing year went on. In August 1765, he applied to Mademoiselle de Beauvoisin for a loan. That astute little lady agreed to a gift of, it is said, the substantial sum of 10,000 livres (purchasing power today about £7000), but demanded in exchange a permanent secured income of 500 or something like what £350 p.a. would be worth at present. The money was raised by La Beauvoisin through the sale of certain jewellery. It is significant that shortly afterwards the marquis quarrelled definitely with his former associate. There is no evidence that any part of the 'income' was ever paid to her.

De Sade, in these financial manœuvres, was concerned far less, however, with solvency than with immunity. The ideal was to have enough money to put himself beyond the interference of the law with his amusements and experimental operations. Of course, this ideal was unattainable. But it could be and was approached.

Another expedient, less direct but likely in the end to be as efficacious, was put in hand towards the end of 1764, shortly after Marais' net of inquisitions and prohibitions began seriously to incommode the marquis.

In those last years of aristocratic privilege in France a nobleman might, by hunting up a sufficiently impressive pedigree, and getting it acknowledged by the king, live under royal protection to an extent which would enable him to do pretty well as he liked, short of committing high treason. In such circumstances a charge of murder, rape or unnatural vice could be fairly easily disposed of by the defendant, against whom no one would care to press the accusation, for fear of the king's displeasure, especially as a thumping bride could usually be collected long before the matter became anything like public.

Donatien, with these considerations in mind, asked his uncle François, the literary Abbé of Ebreuil, to conduct the necessary researches and also co-opted the social influence of Madame de Montreuil. The letters are phrased in the friendliest and most courteous manner imaginable. Both the addressees hastened to agree to the writer's proposals, for they both foresaw the kind of career their young relative was going to have and how useful the duly authenticated genealogy was therefore likely to be. They worked fast. By the middle of 1765 the papers had reached the king and received his formal approbation.

Two further letters in de Sade's hand, one to his aunt, the Abbé's and his father's sister, and one to the Abbé himself, by this time sixty-one years of age and now promoted to the rank of Vicar-General, are about the only documents at present available which can be relied on for information as to Donatien's experiences between the end of 1765 and the autumn of 1766.

The more interesting sentences from these letters are quoted below.

"La Coste,
1765.

Your reproaches, my dear aunt, are couched in somewhat strong language. To tell you the truth, I hardly expected to find such violent expression proceeding from the mouth of a holy nun. I neither permit nor endure nor authorize the person with whom I live here" — this was Mademoiselle de Beauvoisin, who must therefore have returned to La Coste some time this year, perhaps just prior to the negotiations for the loan in August — "to be considered as my wife. I have told everyone the exact opposite. A certain priest advised me as follows: Never give people to understand that she is your wife, but let people say she is if they want to, in spite of your unequivocal declaration that it is not the case.

I took his advice. When one of your sisters, married like myself, was living here in public with her lover, did you then consider La Coste 'an accursed spot'? I am doing no more harm than she did and it is not going to worry either of us in the least. As for him to whom you owe the information you now pass on to me, he may be a priest. But he always has a couple of trollops — pardon the expression, it is one of your own — living with him. Is his house, therefore, a seraglio? Personally, I should call it a brothel.

Excuse the oddness of my phrasing. I am catching the family style of wit. If I have one reproach to tax myself with, it is that of having had the misfortune to be born into such a collection of fools and scoundrels. God preserve me from the swarming antheap of their absurdities and vices. I shall think myself positively virtuous (almost) if God is merciful enough to save me from adopting more than a few of them. I send you, my dear aunt, my best respects."

It appears from this smart rap over the knuckles administered to an interfering spinster relative that the gay Abbé Francois had been gossiping with his sister about their errant nephew. Whether the stones thrown from the Abbé's glasshouse were bigger than those with which the marquis retaliated from his does not matter much. What is interesting here is the profoundly embittered tone of the sarcasm. The sentences, it seems to me, express neither the impudence of a flippant rogue nor the bluster of an uneasy villain. I should say that they were written, in their rather laboured style (for the correspondent was still only twenty-five and had not yet acquired the fluency of his later years) by a lonely, frustrated and therefore vindictive young gentleman, with an intolerable and irremovable load of grievance crushing heart and brain. He bites and scratches like a cornered rat. This is not the attitude either of a cynic or a monster.

The second letter, that to the Abbé, is dated nearly a year later and reads very differently.

"18th October, 1766

I have only one more favour to ask of you, my dear uncle. It is that you will forget faults committed in the blindness of a passion which I was unable to control. Please believe that the proofs so maliciously and indiscreetly laid before you were only written down at the dictation of the siren who was depriving me of common sense at the time. In my normal state I should have been incapable of such base conduct and now that my illusion has been entirely dissipated I blush for it and find it inconceivable.

I beg and adjure you to pardon all this and believe that, in all the remorse I feel for the errors into which I have been led by that wretched creature, the worst is my shame at having dared to attempt to crush in my soul, by such horrible means, the affectionate and grateful sentiments towards yourself with which I shall always be imbued; but I shall never, so long as I live, pardon her who caused you to read such stuff."

These passages are difficult to interpret in the absence of other data. But it seems clear that there is a real connection between the letters of 1765 and the following year. One may, perhaps, legitimately conjecture that the Abbé, having offended the young man by informing the latter's aunt (the former's sister) that their nephew was telling people at La Coste that a courtesan with whom he was living there was the marquise de Sade — there is a certain humour in putting poor Renée's label on the Beauvoisin — the affronted mistress in question persuaded Donatien to revenge himself on his uncle by overwhelming that gentleman with a flood of outrageous 'proofs' of the Abbé's own delinquencies.

The 'proofs' referred to in the letter may, of course, relate to the marquis's, not the Vicar-General's, aberrations, with which Donatien may have been induced by his 'siren' to taunt or shock the priest. But on the whole this seems less likely. It is certain, in any case, that the marquis, in a fit of temper, had insulted the Abbé and now thought it as well to apologize to a relative who had already done a lot for him and from whom, moreover, he may have expected a legacy.

The apology is a shrewd one. It is clothed in precisely the dress most likely to soften the resentment felt by an elderly tutor and man of letters at the conduct of a 'young rascal,' to whom he really stood in the relation of both father and mother, for neither of the marquis's parents seem to have wished to have anything more to do with him after the first imprisonment.

The anger with the unnamed mistress rings fairly sincere, if the pleading does not. It is evident enough that the fierce little fellow had been at last convinced, for once, that he had made a fool of himself with this woman; that with characteristic frankness and resolution he set himself to try to put the matter right, even if he had to tell a few conventional lies in the process.

The period to the end of 1767 is an obscure one. The marquis was in money difficulties. He was under constant police supervision. He felt, no doubt, that he was making mistakes and irritating influential people against him. It is highly probable that for the time being he took fewer risks, meditated more and kept out of the lurid limelight as much as possible.

The death of the comte Jean-Baptiste de Sade, on the 24th of January, 1767, removed most of the worry about money. Donatien now became the head of the family and could safely defy financial misfortune. On the 27th of August the marquise, to her intense delight, bore him a son, whom they called Louis-Marie. The terrible monster of the columnists of Paris seemed in a fair way to becoming a domesticated, provincial paterfamilias.

Yet, on the 16th of October in this year, Inspector Marais could write:

> "We shall soon be hearing further news of the *horrors*" —
> the word is underlined in the original — "of M. de Sade. He
> is doing all in his power to get La Rivière, of the Opera, to
> live with him. He has offered her twenty-five louis a month,
> provided that on the days when she is not dancing she will
> visit him at his place in Arcueil. The young lady has declined
> this offer."

M. Marais probably used the word 'horrors' ironically. It was the usual term bandied about whenever the 'monstrous' marquis was mentioned in society gossip. What the inspector had to report was in fact a triviality. No doubt Mademoiselle Rivière received a dozen such offers a week. No one thought the worse of any wealthy young man for running after well-known actresses. Such pursuits were, on the contrary, considered proof positive of pluck, fashionable eminence and sound financial standing. Marais could not have had much to do on the 16th of October if he thought this item worth noting. It could only have interested those who could not get the marquis out of their heads. Perhaps the experienced detective was being badgered by his anxious superiors, spurred on, possibly, by Madame de Montreuil. Perhaps he felt a proprietary attachment to the important figure he had once already taken in a closed carriage to the prison at Vincennes. Certainly he smelt promotion if he could repeat the exploit. And no doubt he was of the opinion that a cat watching a mouse cannot afford to ignore any of its movements, however apparently unalarming.

A study of the surviving documents in any way relevant to the marquis's life at this time really does not reveal him as anything more than a tireless, impatient and occasionally irritable young skirt-chaser, whose money and social position made his feats in this line, when they could be discovered or invented, more provocative of talk among Parisians than those of less prosperous or exalted noblemen. The only actually odd thing about his arrangements was the unusually large number of houses, apartments and 'country cottages' that he seemed to dispose of. It is useful, of course, for a man fighting a war of manœuvre with the police to have more than two or three addresses.

The representatives of the law, however, were soon to come to know M. de Sade as a rather more bizarre character than the merely highhanded young libertine they were reporting on in 1767.

On an April morning in the following year the nobleman in question happened to have business in the Place des Victoires. After alighting from his carriage he was ascending the steps of the house he proposed to enter when he heard a female voice at his elbow murmur something about charity and the love of God. The intonation and language were respectable and respectful. The early hour, for it was only nine o'clock, made common prostitution unlikely. The marquis glanced, with careless curiosity, over his shoulder.

The woman who had spoken was poorly but decently dressed. She seemed about thirty. He observed automatically, with the practised eye of the rake, that her face and figure would pass muster if set off to advantage. Her present pose, the slightly hunched shoulders, uptilted head and expression of humble supplication suited her, he thought, raising a delicate eyebrow.

"You surprise me, *madame!*" The lazy tone, the half-veiled glance, bantered her with ironic gallantry. "What brings you to this pass?"

She explained, in a diffident whisper, that the death of her husband, a confectioner, the week before, in a public hospital, had obliged her to resort to beggary, since he had died in debt and she had no friends or relatives to turn to.

Donatien, listening to her submissive stammer, appraising her rounded features and graceful gestures, felt the blood in his temples begin to beat a little. This is just the type, he thought. If one could only get her to oneself! Well, probably she'll do anything for money. Let's try. So long as I take care not to frighten the bird away before I've caged it . . .

Aloud, he advised her, in his kindliest manner, rather to look for some sort of honest employment than to go about begging in the streets. She answered, half tearfully, that she only wished she could find such work. But, unfortunately —

The cool, handsomely garbed young aristocrat seemed to come to a sudden decision. He cut short her faltering phrases.

"Your name, *madame?*"

"Rose Keller, *monsieur.*"

"Well, Rose Keller, how would you like to act as housekeeper in one of my own establishments?"

She almost threw herself at his feet in her gratitude, would have kissed his hand if he had not kept it out of her reach.

Maintaining an impassive dignity, the better to hold down his own rising excitement, the marquis intimated that he would be ready, at three o'clock that very afternoon, and on the spot where they were now standing, to convey her in his carriage to Arcueil. There, if she pleased, she could enter upon her duties immediately. Rose rapturously agreed to the plan.

She was punctual at the rendezvous. Her patron drove up, a few minutes later, in a hired vehicle. He complimented her, quite sincerely, on her improved appearance since the morning and wished to know whether she was still of the same mind. She assured him that it was so. He assisted her into the carriage and got in beside her.

The drive to Arcueil lasted two hours, during which Rose's new master behaved with perfect decorum. He asked her only such questions as any employer in similar circumstances would ask. He told her merely that the house at Arcueil was a small one and that the servants she would have to supervise would all be men and boys.

On the outskirts of the village the marquis stopped the carriage. He informed Rose that they might as well walk the rest of the way, a matter of a few minutes only. He pointed to a green-painted gate in the wall of a small estate a few hundred yards from the roadside.

"That leads to my garden."

They alighted. De Sade paid and dismissed the driver. He then conducted the girl across the grass to the garden gate, through the garden and into the house, which was, of course, L'Aumônerie. All this time they saw no one.

"My servants are all out for the day," observed the young man negligently. "They will be back this evening. I will show you over the place myself."

The house comprised, on the ground floor, two rooms only in addition to the kitchen. On the first floor there were two bedrooms.

"Your own room will be on the top floor, my dear Rose. This way." After mounting a second flight of stairs they found themselves in a passage, with a door at the end of it. De Sade ushered Rose Keller into the room beyond, which was rather dark. She could make out only that it seemed somewhat sketchily furnished, with a bed, a wardrobe, a chest of drawers and two or three chairs.

The girl, turning back to her host from this cursory examination of her future quarters and about to make some light remark, perceived that the marquis was in the act of locking the door.

With a sudden gasp of misgiving she called out involuntarily: "Why, what are you doing, *monsieur?*"

De Sade put the key in his pocket.

"Take those clothes off, my little angel. And be quick about it."

Rose had been expecting some such development for some time, though one never quite knew with these serene young gentlemen. For form's sake she fell on her knees with a wail of anguish, clasped her hands and begged for mercy.

"I am an honest woman, *monsieur*," she sobbed. "Spare me!"

He answered coolly, with an impatient gesture:

"Do as I tell you. Or it will be the worse for you. Hurry up!"

She thought fast. There might be money in this, if one stuck to it that one had been lured here under false pretences. She gazed at him stupidly, blinking in assumed terror.

The marquis, losing his temper, stamped furiously and drew his sword. The rasp and glitter of the blade made the girl shriek. He shook the point under her nose.

"Now, then! You want me to spit you like a pullet? Undress, or you'll get it through you! It hurts, you know."

She became really a little frightened, now, at the flash in his blue eyes. But she kept to the part she had decided to play, jumping up and backing away, her arms crossed over her breast.

"No! No! I'd rather die."

"Pshaw!"

The marquis pitched his rapier into a corner of the room and flung himself at the woman. He picked her up, easily mastering her struggles, and threw her across the bed. Then, holding his left arm rigid over her throat, he stripped off her outer garments.

Rose, her mind solely on the report she was going to make to the police, put up a considerable fight. But eventually her assailant managed, with strips torn from her chemise, to tie her wrists behind her back, then her ankles firmly together. Finally, he gagged her with a piece of firewood.

Leaving her bound, naked and helpless on the bed, de Sade next crossed the room to the chest of drawers, opened it and took out a handful of knotted cords, a candle, a small pocket-knife and a stick of what appeared to be sealing-wax.

He placed these articles on a chair beside the bed and lit the candle. Then he turned the body of the girl face downwards, seated himself on her shoulders and gripped her waist between his knees.

He began to flog, with the cords, Rose's twitching body about the loins, arms and thighs till the skin reddened and a little blood began to trickle from the weals.

Next, he reached over to the chair, took the pocket-knife and proceeded to make, with surgical precision, a number of small, circular cuts in the swollen marks made by the flogging. He then heated the stick of wax or whatever it was at the candle and anointed the cuts with it.

After a brief inspection of his work, he got off the girl's shoulders, untied her limbs and withdrew the gag. Then, standing beside the bed, he ordered her in a cool tone to rise and dress.

Moaning, shuddering and weeping, Rose managed to get to her feet. She began pulling on her clothes. The marquis seated himself and took snuff.

After a moment or two he rose abruptly, kicking away the chair.

"Perhaps you will come to your senses later," he remarked contemptuously. "I am going to leave you now. I shall be back in three hours to finish what I intend to do with you. Till then!"

He picked up his sword, slammed it back into the scabbard and left the room, locking the door from the outside.

Rose now considered she had enough evidence. She did not intend to wait for more if she could help it. She found that she was able to open the window, which gave on to the garden at the rear of the house. After searching the room she discovered a further supply of cord in a corner. With this and her own torn garments she made a sort of rope down which she climbed into the garden, where night was already coming on.

She made her way among the trees and bushes until she came to a low wall, with a ladder, most conveniently, lying beside it. She scaled the wall, dropped down on the other side and ran towards the public highway.

She heard shouts behind her and running feet. Glancing round, she perceived a man, not the marquis, rapidly overhauling her. He was calling loudly:

"Wait, *mademoiselle!*"

She stopped for an instant, watching him warily. The man came up puffing and blowing, holding out a purse.

"From *M. le Marquis, mademoiselle*. He orders me to pay you." But Rose was out for something more substantial than a few livres. She shook her head, frowning, and made off again, taking the road towards the village. The man grinned, moving his shoulders a little and swinging the purse. But he did not attempt to pursue her.

A week later, on the 10th of April, the marquis was arrested and taken to the fortress of Saumur on the River Loire. Here he was confined for nearly three weeks. On the 30th Marais transferred him to the Pierre-Encise gaol at Lyons. Here his imprisonment was much more rigorous. On the 15th of May he was liberated on parole and requested to come up for judgment in Paris on the 10th of June.

We may now turn to the evidence given at this hearing. Madame Lambert, wife of the local notary at Arcueil, deposed that Rose Keller was brought to her by a village woman on the night of the 3rd of April, suffering from bruises and cuts. Madame Lambert put Rose to bed and sent for the surgeon of the place and the police.

Dr. Paul Lecomte, the surgeon in question, stated that he found the complainant's loins excoriated, slightly cut and reddened. There were some dozen small cuts, about the size and shape of a six-sou piece. They had not penetrated the epidermis. He found no trace of sealing-wax or burns, merely some drops of what appeared to be a solidified ointment of some kind, which could not have had a caustic effect.

The Abbé Amblet stated that he had been at one time the defendant's tutor. On the 7th of April he was called to the residence of Madame de Montreuil, where he met Maître Sohier, a Court lawyer, and was told that the defendant had been reported to the police by a prostitute. The Abbé accompanied Maître Sohier, at the request of Madame de Montreuil, to Arcueil, where he saw the complainant, who was in bed, and on a second visit, again at the request of Madame de Montreuil, paid her the sum of 2400 livres, an amount which both the lawyer and he himself considered excessive in the circumstances. The Abbé added that he had since examined the *petite maison,* the scene of the matter in dispute, and found nothing unusual there. He was at a loss to understand the accusations of brutality that had been brought against the defendant, who was a good-natured young man, though certainly of an 'ardent' temperament.

Rose Keller said that the outrages had occurred, not in the house, but in a hut in the garden. She stated that the marquis had poured boiling red and white sealing-wax into her wounds, threatened her with death and told her to make her last confession to him. The rest of the complainant's evidence, with the exception of a few trifling details and some statements about comings and goings between the hut and the house and also concerning some ointment, towels, water, food and wine which she said the defendant had given her, corresponds with the account given above.

The marquis's story was that he invited Rose to accompany him to Arcueil 'for a wild party.' He denied that he had used threats or force, admitted the flogging, said he had not used a knife but had put small touches of an ointment of his own invention on the weals in order to test its curative properties. He added that the girl did not appear to be distressed by these proceedings.

The only completely satisfactory witnesses were the doctor and the priest. It is perfectly obvious that Rose Keller, who could not read or write, was in the business for what she could make out of it and that her volubilities were unscrupulously directed to this end alone. The marquis, who spoke with airy and vague composure, was for his part only concerned to give the whole affair the look of a semi-scientific frolic. In the end, after showing his *lettres d'abolition,* documents bearing the King's signature, which rendered the holder immune from all but the most serious prosecutions, he was simply fined two hundred livres and warned to keep away from Paris until further notice.

Between the arrest and the trial, however, there was plenty of sensational gossip. Madame du Deffand, on the 12th and 13th of April, wrote the current version of what had happened to Horace

Walpole. This was more or less what Rose had told Madame Lambert, a tale of violent assaults by a cynical degenerate upon a terrified and helpless victim. There were other even more lurid accounts of the matter. Papers at the Châtelet, the seat in Paris of the jurisdiction of the Lieutenant General of Police, contain statements that the actual scene of Rose's 'torture' was the garden, where she was said to have been stripped and tied to a tree.

The medical evidence of the highly respectable Dr. Lecomte is, however, decisive. There was no 'torture.' At worst there were threats, a rough-and-tumble, a deliberate attempt to frighten and some very peculiar incidents. The moral and legal codes of the day could not regard the bruises and scratches inflicted upon an extremely well-paid prostitute as a serious crime.

An amusing footnote may be added before this much-publicized event is dismissed. The defendant swore, with characteristic impudence, that he had been merely carrying out an experiment with a certain unguent which he had devised for the immediate cure of open wounds. He told the lieutenant of police that society owed him a debt of gratitude, not a prosecution, for what he had done.

The marquis cannot yet be considered, in spite of Rose Keller, a case for the professional psycho-pathologist. He is still no more than a disappointed young man with a ferocious sexual appetite and an insatiable curiosity about the means which might be employed to satisfy it. At this very time he engaged in a proceeding which, if highhanded, is far more readily comprehensible.

The moment he was released from the prison at Lyons, on bail, on the 15th of May, before the final hearing of the Rose Keller case, he paid a visit to the convent to which Madame de Montreuil had despatched her youngest daughter on the marquis's return to Paris in the previous year.

He coolly announced to the Mother Superior that Madame de Montreuil had sent him, as Anne-Prospère's brother-in-law, to fetch the girl for a holiday at La Coste. He was allowed by the unsuspecting nuns to carry her off. No doubt she was delighted to accompany him. For there does not appear to have been any idea in his mind, at this time, of seduction. At La Coste he was on his best behaviour, while he awaited the commons from Paris.

But the local residents gossiped. Probably at Louise's own request he sent, on the 19th of May, for Renée to join him. The letter informs her that he intends her sister to remain at La Coste at least until the following November. It seems, however, that the marquise, for some reason, never received this communication.

May passed into June. The trial was held and resulted in what was virtually an acquittal. The marquis returned to La Coste in triumph. Louise was waiting for him. The degree of intimacy in which they were then living still remains obscure. But no doubt the reunion was hilarious for the time being.

Then doubts began to occur to Donatien. He cared nothing for the chatter of the neighbours. He was indifferent to what his wife might think, do or say. But his mother-in-law was bound to know of Louise's abduction by this time. She could not have him arrested for it. He was the head of the combined families of de Sade and Montreuil. But she could concoct another charge against him and bring about a separation in that way. Even now she was probably laying such plans. He resolved, by a bold and unexpected stroke, to bring them immediately to ruin.

CHAPTER FOUR

M. de Sade and the Detectives

~~~~~~

"My angel," he told Louise with great seriousness, a few days after his return to La Coste. "We must get away from here at once. Or M. Marais will be coming up the drive."

She pouted.

"Oh, bother him! I like it here. But where shall we go, then, you abominable monster?"

He smiled gaily.

"To Italy! To Florence, Rome, Naples! See them and die! And, yes, I had almost forgotten, Venice, the world-famous paradise of all lovers! To Italy, my child! Prepare yourself! It is a command! We start today!"

The night when Louise had slapped his face in her bedroom at Echauffour was long past. She seems now to have been as infatuated as he. At any rate, whether or not it was the first time she had yielded to him, she made no resistance on this occasion.

They were away together in all probability for a whole year, during which de Sade appears to have remained consistently devoted to his sprightly 'angel.' It is certain that the girl was initiated into a good many strange byways of eroticism, as well as of Italy, which in any case, at that period, rivalled Paris in its obsession with sexual enjoyment, with the difference, due to the national temperament, of a more exuberant playfulness, a less intellectual approach to the eternal preoccupation of the eighteenth century.

Yet there is no evidence that Anne-Prospère de Montreuil's formidable mentor ever caused her a moment's distress at this time. The period was, in short, the first and last time the marquis experienced the mutual joys of domesticity. His verdict has not been recorded. But there is no reason to suppose it to have been unmixed approval.

After L'Aumônerie, after la Beauvoisin, la Brissaut and a considerable number, no doubt, of Rose Kellers, after prisons, magistrates and policemen, after family and matrimonial jars and the poisoned air of icy interviews with Madame de Montreuil, the consummation of this perfectly genuine romance had come too late in Donatien's life. It could not now last.

In the late spring or early summer of 1769 the lovers parted for ever, whether intentionally or not cannot now, apparently, be known. It is probable that there were vows of constancy and promises of renewal of the affair on both sides. And one or other or both may have been sincere. But it is equally likely that the flame had burnt itself out in both the lady and the gentleman and that each was glad to see the last of the other.

It is only certain that Louise rejoined her mother and eventually disappeared into another convent in Paris, while Madame de Montreuil moved heaven and earth to get her married. Almost exactly twelve years later the 'angel' died, the only woman, perhaps, who can be said to have possessed all the secrets of her strange, alternately dashing and sullen, lover's heart.

Evidence asserted by early biographers that the Italian excursion with Louise took place, not in 1769, but in 1772, is not, on the whole, despite the otherwise careful chronology of Maurice Heine (d. 1940), decisive against the opinion of later writers (Amiaux, 1936, Desbordes, 1939) that 1769 was the year in question.

Renée returned to La Coste soon after the parting of the lovers. There had now been three major scandals in her husband's life, quite apart from his jollifications in Paris and at La Coste itself with Mademoiselle de Beauvoisin. But neither the arrest at Arcueil in the very year of the marriage, the Rose Keller business nor the latest humiliation of the elopement with the marquise's own sister had for a moment disturbed the devotion of this — on the purely domestic side — model wife. Renée was almost English in her obstinate myopia, her barely conscious determination to look on the bright side of things. She was incapable of theory. It was at bottom simply the instinct of self-preservation that caused her so far unshakable imperturbability in the face of events peculiarly calculated, one would have supposed, to appal a girl whose conventionality was bred into the very bone.

Intelligence is an embarrassment to steady living. Life does not bear a too unshaded scrutiny. The brilliant, as distinguished from the merely shrewd, are generally tragic figures. The unruffled, stately and silly marquise de Sade is not a character of high tragedy. She only wanted to be respectable, to keep clear of unpleasantness. This is a far stronger sentiment among civilized people than is often realized. It is practically universal below a certain level of mental alertness. It is a primary source of happiness for the majority of Western citizens. They will not often die for it, but only because they seldom have to, since they simply ignore, like the London cockney drinking tea among the ruins of his bombed possessions, all encroachment upon this impregnable obsession.

Renée, then, ignored everything about her husband except that he was a marquis and had married her. Those were the only important facts. Donatien was not the man to condescend to discuss his behaviour with so trivial a personage, even if she were his wife. Renée, in any case, would not have wished to listen to explanations which would have been quite beyond her comprehension. When the police arrested her husband, she gave no sign of being interested in his guilt or innocence. She was only concerned to get him out of the clutches of the law as soon as possible, so that he could take his place in society again, her state of mind on these occasions rather resembling that of a Civil Servant who has temporarily mislead his umbrella than that of a virtuous woman whose adored consort has been found to be vicious.

She did undoubtedly adore Donatien, much as a dog adores almost any kind of a master who does not daily plague it, and all the more on account of his obvious indifference to her. When he abducted Louise, disappearing with her into Italy for months and months,

Renée could hardly have failed to feel at least astonished and perhaps disconcerted. But here again the dominant feeling would be the desire to retrieve the vanished legal owner of her person. She must have opposed a maddeningly tranquil front to her mother's vengeful fury.

And the truant did return, cool as ever, as if nothing in particular had happened. It is not to be supposed that his wife, who had borne him a second son, Armand, in his absence, even reproached him. She set to work at once to rebuild the social life of the marquis and marquise de Sade in the only way she knew, by maintaining her usual preoccupation with the daily round of the wife of a great landowner who was now happily in residence again after a trip abroad.

Even in the eighteenth century, when legal feminine partners, especially of socially prominent individuals, did not expect for a moment that their husbands would be physically faithful to them, Renée's prosaic attitude was found remarkable. Today it would be unthinkable. Wives in our day have been known to stick by even convicted murderers, who had once married them, to the very gallows. But they have without exception been women whose ruling passions have not been respectability but the persons of their delinquent spouses. Renée was utterly unqualified, both emotionally and intellectually, for such high erotic passion.

For about a year Monsieur and Madame de Sade appear to have lived together at La Coste, that rather overwhelmingly furnished bower of carnal pleasures, without any particular friction. The gentleman was probably largely engaged in the pleasures of memory, the lady in the enjoyment of her new-found return to normal routine. At any rate, by April 1771 a third and last child, a daughter, who was named Laure, after the famous de Sade ancestress, had been born to this oddly assorted pair.

Madame de Montreuil, however, had not forgiven her son-in-law. She was not the kind of woman who ever, under any circumstances, forgives. Profoundly astute, patient and subtle as an international financier, a born intriguer on the grand scale and an absolutely relentless enemy, the mother-in-law of the marquis was by far the strongest character he ever had to deal with in all his endless negotiations with all sorts of dangerous or malicious people. She was quite definitely determined to ruin him. But she was far from impulsive and she knew it could not be done openly. She laid her plans in the dark, with every conceivable precaution.

They began in a correspondence with Maître Gaufridy, the lawyer whom the marquis most trusted of all his agents, whom this declared foe of lawyers in general really liked and who knew how to respond congenially to his employer's friendliness. Donatien believed, almost to the end, that Gaufridy was on his side. But almost from the first Gaufridy was quietly promoting the schemes of Madame de Montreuil, who very soon recognized his value as a spy who understood the marquis as well as he understood the lady. She paid him accordingly.

Gaufridy, however, was by no means the only strategically placed outpost of this female field-marshal. She had powerful friends in the Army, of which the marquis de Sade was still, after all, a member. At the end of July 1770 Major de Sade, as he now was, unexpectedly received notice to rejoin his regiment. France was still at peace, though precariously, and Donatien could not understand the reason for his recall to military service. He went off, cursing, to Compiègne on the River Aisne, a northern part of the country which he disliked as a Provençal, and a garrison town which at once reminded him of all the boredom of earlier years in this heartily detested occupation.

It was no wonder that he made himself disagreeable on his arrival and was coldly received by his brother officers, who knew all about his adventures with the police. Renée's mother at once paid her a visit, ostensibly of consolation. But the real object was so to arrange matters, if possible, in the absence of the head of the family, as, if not to disillusion Renée finally with her husband, at least to render her more her own mistress and give her a freer hand in the management and exploitation of the marquis's estates, for which latter purpose consultations with Gaufridy, who was in the neighborhood, would come in useful. The principal point, for the moment, was to keep Donatien out of the way until all these matters were satisfactorily settled. There might be war with Sweden or Poland or

England. If so, so much the better. In any case, the longer he could be pinned down in the north, the sooner might Renée come to see reason.

But this last calculation was one of Madame de Montreuil's very few mistakes. The marquise had nothing to do with reason. In vain did her mother tactfully hint at the absent officer's improprieties, not to say enormities, of conduct. Renée remained adamantly inconsolable. The elder lady was obliged to concentrate upon Gaufridy, whom she found much more amenable. After coming to a definite understanding with him, she left again for Paris, promising her tearful daughter that the marquis's renewed devotion to his country should not, at least, go unrewarded.

She was as good as her word. In March Major de Sade was promoted to a rank equivalent to that of a colonel of cavalry. But in June the unpopular and uninterested officer sold his commission to the comte d'Osmont for ten thousand livres and returned once more to Renée's ready but unexciting bosom. Madame de Montreuil knew how to wait. With the adroitness of a born commander she had already changed her tactics.

The marquis, it turned out, now wished to give free rein, at last, to his passion for the theatre. He made La Coste a sort of Bayreuth for the staging of the plays he preferred — they were no more indelicate, if perhaps rather more sophisticated, than Paris was seeing every night in those days — and in which he acted the principal parts himself, as well as attending to the details of production. These expensive entertainments, comedies for the most part, with music and dancing, brought a number of greedy guests to the castle and cost a lot of money. When the marquis was not rehearsing, he was badgering his legal agents for loans and discussing ways and means with Gaufridy.

That gentleman, assiduously hunting with both hare and hounds, steered a dexterously tortuous course between accommodating his public principal in such a way as not to lose his confidence by landing him hopelessly in debt — in September the marquis was actually imprisoned, at the request of his creditors, for a few days — and attending to the interests of his private one, which were to encourage de Sade to ruin himself without involving his wife's dowry and other financial investments in her husband's affairs.

The disputes were endless, complicated and very fatiguing. The marquis grew even more irritable than most actor-managers have a right to be. Renée, of course, remained perfectly tranquil and quite unconscious of what was going on. She had the more reason to be complacent in that she had now borne her legitimate partner three children. It is amusing to think of her passing, in a kind of vegetative twilight of well-being, utterly innocent of either apprehension, reflection or imagination, through the hectic dazzle of life at La Coste during this period, the aristocratic receptions, the private theatricals, the outrageously voluptuous settings, with the marquis bawling at his lawyers in the library half the day and at authors, actors and stage carpenters the other half.

It is not to be thought that she ever batted an eyelid throughout these uproarious scenes, though it is certain that she considered it her duty to be present. The drawing which survives of her not unpleasing but perfectly wooden features reveals her character with remarkable precision. She must have been as indifferent to the noblest as to the basest performances of the human spirit. It was, perhaps, for this reason that she escaped more brutal treatment by her dangerous consort. The mere sight of her, eternally calm and bland, would reduce him to a condition, almost, though evidently not quite, of impotence.

However that may have been, the marquis, either because he really felt he needed a holiday or, as there is more reason to suppose, to negotiate a loan or because some rather special consignment of theatrical properties or other furniture awaited his personal inspection at Marseilles, paid that gay city a visit in June 1772.

He was accompanied by his valet, a good-looking and impudent young rascal named La Tour, who was allowed considerable freedom of intercourse with his master and may even have stood in a more equivocal relationship to him. At any rate it was the marquis's fantasy, or perhaps a prudential measure, that during this escapade, for such it really turned out, in the end, to be, the tall, pock-marked La Tour should pose as the gentleman and his much shorter but elegantly built, blue-eyed and fair-complexioned companion as the servant.

At ten o'clock in the morning of the 27th the two young men visited together a prostitute's apartments in Marseilles. Their hostess, apparently in compliance with a request made by the marquis the day before, had three other girls with her.

It is clear that orgies took place, accompanied by some flagellation and the distribution of sweets which made some of the girls ill. But, as is usual when the depositions of ladies of easy virtue have to be considered, the several accounts, given later, of what actually occurred, vary in almost every detail.

There was also a visit, paid by the marquis alone, at nine o'clock in the evening of the same day, to another whore in a different part of the town. This girl told the police, three days later, that her client of the 27th had tried to poison her. On the 1st of July all four of the women visited by La Tour and de Sade on the morning of the 27th made the same complaint in the same quarter.

Enough gossip was caused in Marseilles by these performances to enable Madame de Montreuil to take action. A warrant was issued for the arrest of both master and man on charges of attempted murder and they both felt it advisable to slip over the frontier into Italy.

From the welter of contradictory testimony given by the harlots concerned, and also, it seems, by some who were not concerned, in this affair, it is possible to extract the following fairly plausible story.

The tall and short man arrived together at the first house visited. He who appeared to be the master, but was obviously nothing of the kind, the tall, pock-marked man, threw down a fat purse and ordered the best liquor obtainable to be fetched and the entire strength of the establishment, four girls in all, to be placed at his disposal. After the wine had been brought in, he locked the door of the apartment.

During some preliminary cuddling and drinking, the short man, who was addressed as Lafleur — the usual stage name for a valet — by his companion, passed round a box of chocolates. All the women except one, who declared, with regret, that chocolates made her sick, partook greedily of these delicacies. Two of them, Marguerite and Mariette, helped themselves very liberally.

It was not long before the aphrodisiacs, aniseed and cantharides, with which the sweets had been filled, began to take effect. The girls, beside themselves with excitement, embraced first the marquis, the better-looking of the two men, then, when he repulsed them and signed to La Tour to do the same, threw themselves upon one another.

In the midst of the confused scene which followed de Sade finally allowed the valet to give free rein to his passions with one of the prostitutes. But he himself remained an outwardly calm, though no doubt inwardly agitated, spectator.

At this point Marguerite and Mariette staggered out of the *mêlée*, screaming and bent double, their hands to their stomachs. They almost immediately began to vomit with great violence. One of them shrieked out that she had been poisoned, was dying. It was clear that the dose, in these two cases, had been excessive.

The other two girls and La Tour, terrified, picked themselves up and cowered against the locked door, staring in consternation at the writhing bodies on the floor. Then they all started screaming at once.

De Sade possessed himself of the valet's sword and threatened them with it. There was no doubt who was the master now.

"Stop that row! Or I'll bleed you — "

This behaviour, and the dreadfully ferocious and determined expression which accompanied the glittering flourish of the steel, reduced the women to a condition of helpless, but silent, fright.

The terrible little marquis, followed by La Tour, left the room and the house, with his weapon still drawn.

The prostitute visited in the evening, a girl named Rose Coste, averred that she had also been given 'poisoned sweets' by the marquis, but had felt no ill effects for some hours.

Three days later Rose Coste's maid, a girl named Catherine, told the Marseilles police that her mistress had been taken seriously ill after receiving a gentleman who was now believed to have been the notorious marquis de Sade, convicted four years before of an extraordinary assault upon one Rose Keller.

The police investigation led them to the house visited by the marquis and his servant the previous week. Here the girl Marguerite, though she had now completely recovered her health, lodged a charge against the 'short man' of attempting poisoning. Others talked vaguely of sodomy. Some chocolates were found at this address. The contents were analysed. Although no deadly poison was discovered, it was decided to proceed with the charge, for it was understood that socially influential persons were interested. The chancellor of State, Maupéou, himself ordered a complete judicial enquiry. An inspector called at La Coste on the 11th of July. But the birds had flown. M. *le marquis* Renée informed the policeman, was 'abroad.'

Meanwhile Marguerite, on being told of the official chemists' report as to the innocuousness of the sweets, withdrew her accusation. That of unnatural vice could not be proceeded with, as no precise deposition to that effect had been made. It appeared, for the moment, as if nothing more would be heard of the matter.

But Madame de Montreuil declined to miss this great chance of dealing a perhaps mortal blow at her enemy. If these whores would not speak, others would, if they were properly handled. She gave M. Maupéou no rest on the subject. Luckily for her, he was a moral bigot, and, like most of the lawyers of the day, loathed the old nobility. The judicial enquiry was opened at Marseilles, in the continued absence of the presumed culprits, in August.

Marianne Laverne deposed that the defendants had called at the brothel where she was employed, bringing with them a whip (furnished with bent pins.) With this instrument she was obliged to give the marquis no less than 859 lashes, in four series — Marianne, apparently, was not much good at arithmetic — while he kept the score by making marks on the mantelpiece. After this drastic preliminary, intercourse took place with herself and also between the marquis and his servant.

Three other prostitutes testified that they called upon the marquis, by arrangement with his valet, 'one after the other, in a quiet part of the town.' They were lightly flagellated by him with a 'parchment' whip, studded with big and little nails and covered with bloodstains. He then asked them to use this implement upon himself. They refused. He thereupon handed them a 'twig broom,' with which they gave him 800 lashes. The servant kept the score on the wall. The marquis subsequently used the girls 'in the Italian manner' and was similarly abused by the valet. Finally, the sweets were passed round. Only one girl accepted them. She was sick later on.

All this rigamarole is obviously manufactured evidence. It bristles with inconsistencies, improbabilities and plagiarism. Any prostitute is willing, with or without payment, to retail such stuff, half invention, half confused recollection of isolated incidents occurring at different times, for hours on end. The marquis was not perhaps at this date incapable of such behaviour. He had made an exhaustive study of Parisian dissipation and had learned much, more recently, in Italy. But the substance of the stories is so grotesque that they cannot be literally true. The inference is almost inescapable that the women had heard garbled versions of the scene with the first four whores and of the visit to Rose Coste, and had been hired by the prosecution, since the original participants would not testify, to tell similar tales.

No honest Court would have convicted on this evidence. But the Court at Marseilles was not honest. It was packed with Madame de Montreuil's friends and agents.

On the 3rd of September, 1772, the chief criminal magistrate of Marseilles, without further ado, condemned the marquis de Sade and his servant La Tour to

"do penance before the main door of the cathedral of La Major on their knees, bareheaded and barefooted, in their shirts, with ropes around their necks and having burning candles of yellow wax, weight one pound apiece, in their hands, and there ask pardon of God, the King and the Law. After which they are to be conducted to the Place St. Louis and there, upon a scaffold erected for the purpose, the said Lord de Sade is to be beheaded and on a gallows there also erected the said La Tour is to be hanged and strangled to death. The corpse of the said Lord de Sade and that of the said La Tour are to be burned and their ashes scattered to the winds. Furthermore, the said Lord de Sade is to be fined, for the King's compensation, thirty livres and the said La Tour ten livres."

This ludicrously inept document, which says as little for the common sense of its perpetrators as it does for their sense of humour, is still to be read in the departmental archives. For all its folly, it does show the feelings of horror which the marquis, at this time, could always arouse in the minds of the simple or the bigoted. The sentence might almost have been written three or four hundred years before. It could not have been written twenty years later.

The verdict was confirmed, with suspicious alacrity, a week later, by the Parliament of Provence, sitting at Aix. The ceremony was carried out next day, in Marseilles, but on dummies, for everyone now knew that the two men who had actually been condemned were in Italy.

The whole of this queer business, of which all France was talking, could not be ignored by Renée de Sade. A false accusation and a few days' unjust imprisonment were one thing. Even an elopement with a wife's sister, though very naughty, was something which could be pardoned. But to have one's husband beheaded in effigy, on an appalling charge, by the order of the Parliament of Provence was altogether too much, temporarily, for the respectable marquise. She left La Coste and entered a convent in Paris, whence she bombarded the authorities with a rain of incoherent correspondence on the rights and wrongs of the matter.

Meanwhile, her peccant consort had arrived at Genoa, travelling as the comte de Mazan, a title he already possessed. Thence he went on to Turin. By October he was living in Chambéry, a town in Savoy, within the area which then formed part of the kingdom of Sardinia. Here he made the mistake of appealing to Madame de Montreuil. That lady was not really anxious to have him beheaded. After all, he was still Renée's husband. She had not been able to resist the pleasure of the solemn nonsense at Marseilles, the rite of execution performed on the effigy of her son-in-law. But her object was now, since she was not prepared to allow him to live at his ease, even abroad, the commutation of the sentence to perpetual detention in France.

On receipt of the marquis's imprudent letter she at once informed the French authorities where he was. On the 8th of December he was arrested, with La Tour, by the Sardinian police and lodged in the State Prison at Miolans in Savoy.

The de Sade and Montreuil families notified the governor of the gaol, M. de Launay, that they would wish the prisoner to be treated with consideration but also with sufficient rigour to prevent his escape. De Launay obtained the marquis's word of honour not to attempt any such thing. He was allowed reasonable freedom of movement and comfortable quarters. But he remained under constant supervision.

Nevertheless, he complained both to his family, to the governor and to the Prefect of Chambéry. He told the latter that M. de Launay, who seems in fact to have been a very harmless and innocent sort of fellow, as prison governors go, was 'deafer, blinder and dumber than any ancient Israelite,' i.e., would not listen to his arrogant captive's demands for this and that privilege, would not see the shortcomings of the confinement that were pointed out to him and declined to answer 'frivolous' questions.

Renée sent a haughty, threatening letter to poor de Launay, who, in his turn, lamented to the Commandant of the Duchy of Savoy that the marquis was disgustingly rude and talked openly, dispite his sworn parole, about his intention to escape.

The fact was that de Sade, whether on account of his detention or because of his previous debaucheries, had begun to suffer in health and from 'nerves.' He redoubled his fault-finding. Renée wrathfully backed him. Finally, de Launay, in a last attempt to keep him quiet, introduced him to a fellow-prisoner of two years' standing, the Baron de l'Allée. Card-parties were arranged, La Tour and the deputy governor making up the necessary four. There were quarrels, however. The marquis accused the baron of cheating and threw the cards in his face. On other occasions he smashed bottles and glasses. Once, the baron had to be forcibly removed to prevent a fight. But reconciliations always eventually took place.

The French authorities now began to snub the marquise in her persistent endeavours to secure her husband's release. But the indefatigable Renée, who had now quite recovered from her original shock and was determined, in accordance with her deepest principles, to restore the *status quo,* merely transferred her entreaties to the King of Sardinia himself. Snubbed again, she suddenly appeared in Chambéry at the head of fifteen armed men, intent on liberating the prisoner by force.

She succeeded, by a ruse, in obtaining an interview, outside the gaol, with one of the warders. She told him that her husband had been illegally accused, was being illegally detained and deserved instant reunion with his loving spouse.

When the man, whose name was Moret, jibbed at the idea of helping to stage an escape, the marquise, who must certainly have been consulting someone a good deal cleverer than herself, threatened to report him for having suggested it.

In the end a plot was duly laid. Moret tied himself hand and foot to Renée by signing a receipt for a large sum of money which she gave him. On a moonless night, the 30th of April, 1773, the marquis had word that all was ready.

He wrote a sarcastic note to de Launay, thanking him for his attentions and exonerating him from all connivance in the forthcoming escape. Next, followed by La Tour, he walked out of the unlocked door, passed first one, then another apparently slumbering sentry, met the baron, who had been apprised of the plot, since he was an old hand at this sort of thing and might come in useful, than found Moret and another bribed officer, the chief turnkey, Josèphe Violon.

The five men left the prison by a small side-door, crossed the dry moat that surrounded the building, met Renée's men, who had brought horses for them, and rode off, without a hitch, to Geneva and the Italian border.

The unlucky M. de Launay, in spite of the marquis's letter, was officially disgraced. The baron was caught a year later, Violon two years afterwards. Moret was never heard of again.

De Sade joined his intrepid rescuer in Italy. He returned with her, eventually, to La Coste, as early as the autumn of the same year. Travel in Italy with Renée was not quite the same thing as travelling with her sister had been. The reunited pair lived a very quiet life until after midnight on the 6th of Januarry, 1774, when a police agent from Paris, escorted by four archers of the Guard and a troop of yeomanry, broke into the castle by force.

But again the bird had flown. Gaufridy had warned the marquis of the imminent raid — he played Madame de Montreuil false on this occasion, not for the first or last time — and the ex-prisoner of Miolans was hiding in the neighbourhood. The police seem to have behaved badly in their disappointment. They turned the whole castle upside down, shouting, "Sade, dead or alive!" and did a lot of damage under Renée's indignant nose, treating her with 'much discourtesy.'

After their departure the marquis, as soon as he returned, preferred a charge of breaking and entering against his mother-in-law. But he took the precaution of resorting to a wandering life, staying for short periods in such places as Bordeaux, Grenoble and Lyons, where no doubt he knew how to treat himself to suitable, if inconspicuous, consolation for his grievances against the Government.

In November the marquise, who had meanwhile come to terms with her mother, found her husband living in Lyons with one of her own ex-maids, a young woman called Nanon, who had completely fallen under his influence and was supplying him with victims for treatment à la Rose Keller. Renée took back with her to La Coste the marquis, Nanon and two female children suffering, though not very seriously, from this type of assault at the hands of de Sade. They were both in their mid-'teens. The marquise packed them off to convalescence, one in the house of the Abbé François, the other in a local convent.

She now seems to have become quite resigned to her husband's peculiarities and only concerned to keep him out of prison, a project with which her partner was heartily in agreement, however much he may have regretted, on other grounds, her interference with his amusements.

But that winter the parents of the Lyons children, whether instigated or not by influences other than their own indignation, started proceedings for abduction and assault against the marquis. It was actually Madame de Montreuil, perhaps at Renée's entreaty, who eventually got the prosecution stopped. Next, however, Nanon, who was pregnant by her late protector, began to use menacing language. The humbler residents of Provence were now fully aware that money might be made out of this particular landowner's eccentricities. Renée, for the moment, soon silenced Nanon by having her arrested for theft and imprisoned at Arles. The marquise's character was hardening under all these worries. She had no mercy on anyone who looked like depriving her of her lawful husband, whatever *his* particular character might be considered to be.

The incorrigible source of all these misfortunes now took himself off, once more, as the comte de Mazan, to Florence, Rome and Naples, on the track, perhaps, in these irritating days, of memories of Louise, whose marriage to a M. de Beaumont, Madame de Montreuil had recently told Renée, awaited merely the final apprehension of her dangerous lover. The Beaumont family declined, it appears, to risk the scandal of another abduction. It is not clear whether the marquis was aware of all this. If so, the knowledge must have added a piquant bitterness to his rovings. It is improbable, all the same, that he had any idea of renewing that unforgettable liaison.

He kept up, all this time, a friendly correspondence with his superlatively devoted wife, who, for her part, saw to it that he was never short of money.

He returned to La Coste in November 1776, loaded with 'antiques,' accompanied by a charming male 'secretary' with very few literary qualifications indeed, and rather tired, at last, of the fascinating land of 'the Italian manner.'

He found, to his annoyance, that the Lyons case against him had been revived, the two girls having escaped from the custody of Abbé and convent respectively to their native cities of Lyons and Vienne. Moreover, trouble awaited him with a certain Treillet, father of one of the marquise's cooks, a girl called Catherine, who had only recently entered her service. Treillet, a rather eccentric character, tried to get his daughter away by force, since she did not seem willing to come of her own accord, from the 'corrupt' atmosphere of the castle. He not only found an opportunity to discharge a pistol at M. de Sade but also lodged charges against him with the Public Prosecutor. This affair cannot be regarded as serious. Its only interest is its indication of the growing attitude of mingled resentment and cupidity with which the owners of La Coste — for Renée now found herself coupled with her husband as his 'accomplice' — were confronted in the neighbourhood.

The marquis, somewhat wearily now, again set out on a tour of southern France, beyond the borders of Provence. Again the police arrived in force at the castle. Again they retired in discomfiture. Renée now agreed with Donatien that the place was becoming impossible. By February 1777 Monsieur and Madame de Sade were re-installed in Paris. But almost immediately the marquis, just after hearing of his mother's death, was arrested for the fourth time.

This time no charge was preferred. The custody was in the nature of what would now be called 'protective.' The official view and indeed that of the family — always excluding the marquise — was that this rebellious but distinguished personage would be better under lock and key before he came to disgrace himself beyond hope of redemption.

The Abbé François wrote at this time: "The man has been arrested and locked up in a château very near Paris. Now I can breathe again; and I believe that everyone else will be glad, too."

Madame de Montreuil adds: "Everything is in excellent and safe trim now: about time, too . . . there is no gossip about the matter here and . . . the authorities intend to prevent any further fuss either here or in Provence . . . neither I nor his wife know where he is, but he is perfectly all right."

In point of fact, as perhaps Madame very well knew, the marquis was incarcerated at his first place of detention, the State Prison of Vincennes in the Paris suburb of that name. He found his cell cold and damp, and had to make his own bed. His food was passed to him through a hatch. An hour's exercise a day was allowed, but no books, pens or paper. The captive, concluding that the place was not a patch on Miolans, raged impotently.

Renée's immediate efforts to get him out were regularly checkmated by her mother and the Abbé. The former, in pursuance of her main object of avoiding scandal, was engaged in destroying, with Gaufridy's help, as much as possible of the evidence for the marquis's peculiar occupations at La Coste. Furniture, decorations, papers and 'machines' were removed and burnt or buried. There is some reason to believe that notes dealing with sexual psycho-pathology, which had been made by the marquis in Italy, perished in this righteous holocaust.

Meanwhile, the prisoner, in the absence of any possible means of passing the time except by brooding, was working himself up into such a state of permanent fury that everyone, except the marquise, began to think he was really mad. Renée tried to calm him down. He answered in a raving spasm of rancour:

"This letter, whatever people may tell you, is to give you my final instructions, whether you are prepared to carry them out or not. Good-bye to you! If, as I suppose, your whore of a mother will be the first to read this, let her read, in full, my dying curse upon her for all her odious machinations to drive me to despair and plunge her dagger deeper, day after day, into my heart. Good-bye for ever."

She replied affectionately but stupidly. He spat back. And so the hopeless exchange of misunderstandings went on, not by any means the first or the last in which the boundless, indestructible tenderness of the mental age of eight beats in vain upon the exasperated frustrations of a mind far beyond its comprehension.

Once he asked after Louise. Renée suddenly seems to grow up in her retort.

"My silence on the subject of my sister was soundly based, my friend. This is the last time I shall speak to you of her . . . she has left home for perfectly good reasons which have nothing to do with you. She is not your enemy. I am unable to give you her address. Whatever it may be, no ill will come to you of it."

This is not very intelligible. Perhaps Louise, by this time, was married. The matter, in any case, was not mentioned again between the correspondents. Instead, de Sade threw his wife back into a paroxysm of infantile confusion by trying to teach her a complicated cipher, by means of which they could elude the prying of the prison censor. He was obliged to give up this idea in a very short time.

The next move on his part was the plaguing of police headquarters with a disingenuous parade of virtue and undeserved misfortune, even, with the coolest effrontery, calling the attention of the Lieutenant General of Police to the death of his mother and the existence of his 'beloved' wife and children.

On the 3rd of January, 1778, the Abbé François expired peacefully, aged seventy-three. The marquis, however, who owed the dead priest both a good deal of indulgence on some occasions and a good deal of backbiting and lack of sympathy on others — François had, for instance, more than once seconded the machinations of Madame de Montreuil to get her son-in-law locked up — was in no mood to mourn his uncle.

Meanwhile the family lawyers had been in conference with their official colleagues of the State. It was eventually agreed between them that there had been certain illegalities in the condemnation of the marquis de Sade to death at Marseilles in 1772. The official side conceded that the case could reasonably be reopened, with the object of a revision of the sentence. On the 27th of May, 1778, when the 'lunatic' had been continuously confined at Vincennes for well over a year, the new King, Louis XVI — his predecessor had died in 1774 — signed an order for the transfer of the marquis de Sade from Vincennes to Aix to attend the new hearing of the Marseilles charges.

Inspector Marais, his brother and four mounted constables, well armed, accompanied the carriage which conveyed the captive from Paris to Aix. All had been warned that there might be an attempt at rescue on the road, for the marquise's activities were pretty well known at police headquarters. But the journey, which took a week, passed off, after all, without incident. By the 21st of June the chafing prisoner was safe in goal again, at Aix.

The hearing lasted from the 2nd to the 14th of July. It was clearly established that the substances found in the chocolates at Marseilles contained no lethal elements whatever and that the three girls who had been ill were now in perfect health. The charge of sodomy was dropped on a technicality, nothing having been said about it until the first hearing at Marseilles was half over.

The judges ruled that the defendant be admonished, forbidden to visit Marseilles for three years, fined fifty livres and released after payment of the fine. But the Montreuils and de Sades, though they obtained this satisfactory conclusion to the illegal capital verdict of 1772, by no means intended to set their black sheep at liberty.

On the 15th of July the return journey to Vincennes began, with the same escort as before. The party reached Valence in the evening of the 16th. Marais decided to remain there for the night. During that night M. de Sade disappeared.

There are two versions of what happened, one by the inspector and one by his prisoner. Probably neither is wholly accurate. Marais had to defend himself against the charge of negligence and the marquis wished to secure the policeman's official ruin. Marais was one of his oldest enemies. The truth is almost certainly that there was more negligence than Marais admits and that de Sade was bolder in seizing his opportunity than, with his aim of blackening Marais' character, it suits him to acknowledge.

Both versions are, however, interesting, the inspector's because it is dramatic and picturesque, the marquis's because it is an excellent specimen of his intimate prose style.

Marais, at the official enquiry, deposed:

"After the carriage had been driven into the courtyard of the said inn, the witness and his brother conducted the marquis to his room, not losing sight of him for an instant. After entering he went to the window looking out on to the high road and remained there until supper-time. About half an hour after the marquis had entered the room the witness approached him and suggested that he might now take a meal. He answered that he had no appetite and would not eat that evening. The rest of us ate. Meanwhile the marquis walked to and fro. He shortly afterwards informed the witness's brother that he desired to relieve a pressing bodily need and the said trusted officer took him to the latrine.

The marquis remained in the latrine for some five or six minutes, then returned to the table. At that moment he pretended to stumble; the witness and his brother, in attempting to prevent him from falling, almost fell with him; the marquis picked himself up with the greatest agility, slipped through the hands of the witness and his brother and ran to the stone stairs near the passage leading to the latrine. These stairs, ten steps in the first section, eight in the second, lead to the courtyard of the inn and the main gateway. The latter being open, it is presumed that the said marquis left that way.

The witness and two trusted officers rushed after him up the stairs, searched the whole house, garden, stables, etc., but could not catch sight of him . . . the witness's brother and one of these officers mounted and searched the Montélimar road, the other officer that leading north from Valence . . . they returned without any trace of him . . . at daybreak the town mounted constabulary patrolled the Rhône fords. The witness employed twelve other trusted persons to search the town and the entire countryside . . . but without success."

De Sade writes to Gaufridy:

"Next day we supped at Valence and I noticed that the further we got from Aix the less supervision I had. We had scarcely arrived, on the second day out, when the escorting inspector gave me to understand, in remarkably vigorous language, that my return to Vincennes was a mere formality and that if I wished to get rid of it by giving my flight the look of an unplanned escape, I was at liberty to do so; they, he said, for their part, would ensure that the steps then taken would have the aspect of a strict and relentless pursuit and that when it was all over, provided I behaved at home in the manner which would be natural after all the misfortunes I had suffered, I should have nothing more to fear. . . .

Accordingly, I left the inn secretly that same night and walked along the banks of the river, unarmed and alone, for about six leagues . . . at daybreak I found a little fishing-boat and managed to get myself rowed, by a single individual, down to Avignon, where I arrived at six in the evening. I went to a friend's house, where I had supper while a carriage was being got ready for me. The following evening I reached home in this vehicle! . . ."

The marquis ends his letter with a sarcastic compliment to Madame de Montreuil and an equally sardonic promise to "remove the apprehensions of this worthy parent." It is evident that he is in the highest spirits again.

Renée only learned of these adventures some days later, in Paris. She at once announced her intention, as usual, of joining her husband at La Coste. But her infuriated mother threatened her with detention in a convent if she attempted to do so. The poor marquise had to be content, once more, with a somewhat one-sided correspondence. Meanwhile Madame de Montreuil set vigorously to work to counter this unhappy accident.

On the 25th of August the marquis received an unexpected guest at La Coste, no other than Louis Marais. The inspector entered by the window, followed by two archers of the Guard. The three men covered de Sade, who was in bed, with pistols. Marais, who seems to have been a little drunk on this occasion, perhaps through endeavouring to forget the official censure to which he had been subjected for his failure to hold his prisoner, threatened his host with a life sentence and said he knew all about the 'black room' upstairs, where 'dead bodies' had been found.

Meanwhile the house was searched and plundered by his men. At dawn the marquis was conveyed in a closed carriage to Lyons, where he managed to get a hurried note delivered to Gaufridy, recommending him to take a certain Mademoiselle de Rousset, with whom de Sade had left the keys of his private cabinet, into his confidence.

This lady, a resident in the neighbourhood and now aged about thirty-four, had been for some years a friend of both husband and wife. She had been a frequent visitor to La Coste. But it seems clear that her relations with the marquis were purely 'platonic.' Perhaps she was not very good-looking. She was certainly an orphan, only moderately well off, very intelligent, highly educated and a remarkably cool customer, one of those women, not so rare as one might suppose, who are often respected and admired, without physical intimacy, by 'scoundrels' in whom they 'bring out the best' and who remain permanently loyal to them, if to no one else, while the sympathetic object of this devotion much prefers it, for one reason or another, to any coming from a less 'corrupt' source.

After a halt of two days at Lyons the carriage rolled on northwards to Paris and eventually crossed the drawbridge of Vincennes on the 5th of September. De Sade was allotted a thirteen-foot square cell, again very damp and cold, on the second floor of the dungeon. Again he had to make his own bed and received his food through a hatch.

The Mind Alone

~~~~~~

THE conditions of the renewed captivity at Vincennes gradually improved during the ensuing months. The marquis was eventually provided with writing materials, of which he made abundant use, not only for correspondence, but for what he called his 'Journal,' mostly in cipher. There were also poems in Provençal, German and Italian, addressed to Mademoiselle de Rousset. The Governor of the gaol, de Rougemont, had to censor all the prisoner's letters. But it is doubtful whether he could make much of those in foreign tongues.

As for the lady, now that she was safely beyond de Sade's physical reach, her replies grew more and more coquettish. After April 1779, she felt obliged, in view of the Governor's duties, to write them in Provençal. Her letters now used the most passionate language. One would suppose, reading them, that the writer had conceived a wild, sensual infatuation for her 'dear one,' who answered her in sedulously gallant but much cooler terms. This odd exchange of views, where the 'cruel seducer' speaks like an indulgent man of the world and the spectacled blue-stocking like a reckless courtesan, can only be explained by assuming that neurosis, in the latter, which causes otherwise respectable people to chalk up obscenities in public places, and that desire, in the former, for the last pleasure of the exhausted rake, the rôle of a bashful lover.

But in less than a year the marquis wearied even of this final resort in the endless struggle to banish the tedium of his existence. It is bad enough for a quiet-living man to be thrown into prison for years on end. But for the marquis, with his fierce physical appetites and restless intellectual curiosity, to find himself, in his late thirties, relegated to gaol for an indefinite period, was to enter a hell of torment.

There came a time when he could not stand the arch endearments of the self-styled temptress of Provence any longer. His letters grew shorter, colder, rarer. Mademoiselle de Rousset retained her dignity. She, too, abbreviated and formalized her communications.

In any case, by November 1779, she was obliged to undergo medical treatment for tuberculosis. Her letters now ceased altogether. They were not renewed for another eighteen months.

By that time the prisoner had almost forgotten this correspondent in the very different preoccupations which now took up his time. And when, in May 1781, he received a further note from Mademoiselle de Rousset, its contents were the very reverse of encouraging for a resumption of friendship on the former terms.

She informed the marquis, among other matters, in which he took little or no interest, of the death from small-pox of his old flame, Louise. This news was not, perhaps, imparted by Mademoiselle without a certain amount of malice. His comments, if any, on the information have not survived. In 1781, at Vincennes, the angel of garden in Paris, of La Coste and of Italy must have seemed very far away. It was twelve years since he had last seen her. Donatien de Sade had never been a sentimentalist. He had a good many other things to worry about just then. People often died suddenly in the eighteenth century. But it is probable, at the very least, that this final seal upon an episode already half buried, but at one time more purely radiant than any he had ever known, added a further load of bitterness to the darkening spirit of Mademoiselle de Rousset's once relatively debonair correspondent.

He answered, after a long delay, indifferently. A few further letters were exchanged, mainly on business topics. At last, in 1782, silence supervened on both sides. A solitary enquiry from the lady, in the following year, for news of her captive hero elicited no response. By January 1784, the unhappy Egeria was dead, in what circumstances it has not yet been possible to ascertain. There is some evidence not only that she was consumptive, but also that she had been over-working in the marquis's interests, helping his wife to keep his affairs in order and to maintain her steady siege of the Government on his behalf. It would be absurd to surmise that she died of a 'broken heart.' The intensity of the phrasing of her earlier letters can be more plausibly ascribed to vanity and 'literature' than to a real obsession. But the last months of the only thoroughly 'decent' woman friend de Sade can be said to have ever had must have been melancholy ones.

There was another eminent gentleman in the prison at Vincennes who wrote a good deal. The marquis used to see him regularly at exercises on the ramparts and took a dislike to him on account of the privileges he seemed to enjoy. One day, in June 1780, there was an altercation.

De Sade, who was being taken back to his cell after a walk, approached the other, who was being escorted from his for the same purpose, and hissed between his teeth:

"I should be obliged for your name, Sir. I propose to cut your ears off as soon as we both get out of this place. The favours you receive are no doubt a sign of the criminal partiality for you shown by that sodomite de Rougemont."

The gentleman addressed looked him up and down haughtily.

"My name, Sir, has never been associated with the dissection and poisoning of unfortunate young women. I shall have pleasure in writing it on your back with my cane, unless they break you on the wheel first. My only fear is that I may be obliged, before I can attend to your chastisement, to go into mourning for your execution."

The vicomte de Mirabeau was, in fact, a distant relative of the marquis de Sade, who was probably unaware of the fact. But at this period there was little sign in the young man of the extraordinary political genius that was to dominate so many of the noblest minds of the revolutionary period that began in 1789. In 1780 Mirabeau was better known for his erotic escapades and his frequent imprisonments for such reasons than for eloquence or administrative ability.

His literary activities in his cell at Vincennes were more concerned, just then, with concocting a series of indecent 'Letters to Sophie' and other obscene works than with political treatises, though he was just beginning, at the same time, to study history and philosophy.

The two men, in some respects rather alike, never met again. But the marquis remembered their single encounter when he wrote in *Juliette,* III, 98, some years later: "Mirabeau wanted to be a libertine, just so as at least to be something. But he is nothing and never will be anything so long as he lives." A characteristic footnote to this passage adds: "Not even a legislator! The delirium and folly of 1789 are well proved by the ludicrous enthusiasm this vile spy of the monarchy inspired. All we remember of the unscrupulous blockhead today are his knavery, his treachery and his ignorance."

The impulsive author certainly underestimated, perhaps envied, the great but admittedly somewhat raffish revolutionary. Few people, however, are proof against prejudicial opinions formed at a single meeting in difficult circumstances, when high words passed. And de Sade was peculiarly intolerant, by nature, of rivals: he could not bear to think that Mirabeau, though pock-marked, was handsome, bold, violent and clever, in any degree approximating to the flamboyant style of the marquis de Sade. Worst of all, perhaps, was the mastery of invective, where little remained to choose between the competitors.

Mirabeau was released from Vincennes Prison in 1782. By that time the marquis had already decided to employ his time to better purpose than quarrelling with everyone in sight. He was reading much, writing, probably, more. He ran through the works of such sceptical philosophers as Voltaire, Vauvenargues, Montesquieu and Machiavelli. He studied ethnology, history, music, the Latin, Greek and Italian classics, the medieval tales of chivalry and even, for a time, metaphysics. Apart from the 'Journal' and necessary letters — his idea of necessity in this connection was extensive — he seems to have already begun to write more pieces for the stage, a form of composition in which he had often indulged at La Coste, both in prose and in verse, sometimes combining the two in a single play.

He used his pen till he could no longer hold it, or till his eyes grew sore. Then he took to the books. It was the existence of an anchorite and a polymath. That well-knit, urgent body of his degenerated. He practically forgot it. His ferocious sensuality mounted to the brain. His temper worsened steadily as the strain of living as an almost exclusively mental entity wore down his self-control, never a very prominent trait in any Provençal, let alone this particular specimen.

He would sometimes fly at Renée physically when she came to see him, feeling that he could not endure her ineptitudes and conventional phrases a moment longer. At last, in September 1782, de Rougemont had to forbid her to visit her husband in case she got seriously hurt. The poor woman, like so many well-meaning persons of less than average intelligence, undoubtedly possessed the faculty, maddening to the tragically preoccupied, of saying and doing things out of season. When he talked of injustice, persecution and ruin, she would recommend warm underclothing and an occasional dish of apricots. When he was pleased with the work he had done on one of his comedies, she would praise one by someone else which she had recently seen produced. When he enquired about the safety of his property she told him that 'everything was quite all right' and added in the same breath that one of his precious manuscripts had disappeared.

So it went on. One can well imagine the proud, embittered captive, who passed his days perforce, now, in the company of so many of the mighty dead, being primly enjoined to keep smiling at the destiny which was tearing his fettered soul to pieces and to trust in the diplomatic tact and eloquence of the speaker, who, in his view, could hardly tell one word from another or a friend from an enemy. It is no wonder that this doubly tormented apostle of unrestricted freedom of behaviour more than once, in a frenzy of exasperation, tried to silence so inapposite a counsellor for ever.

This alternate monotony and agony of negation dragged on until February 1784, a few days after the death of Mademoiselle de Rousset. The futile correspondence, the desperate scenes, the stratagems and subterfuges, the codes with lemon juice, the calculations, the endless lists of requirements, the plunges into the mystical philosophy of numbers, the solitary orgies of baffled lust and fury followed one another, blended into one another, like the apparent eternities of a nightmare. There were intervals of utter absorption in reading and taking notes, of hard thinking on sociological and political subjects, of the theoretical construction of utopias and of plans for the destruction of contemporary civilization. But these grew more and more exhausting, roused in him more and more the rage of a caged eagle.

Meanwhile, certain changes, pregnant with future action, were taking place in the ideas of the men who ruled France. One consequence of a minor administrative move influenced the lonely mind of the marquis de Sade, at this period, to take a new direction.

The policy of Louis XVI, or at any rate the policy, to which he saw no objection, of his advisers concerned with the administration of the law, worked far less arbitrarily than that authorized by his predecessor. Under Louis the Great and Louis the Well-beloved, prominent people were regularly locked up simply and solely because they had offended a Court favourite. Under Louis XVI this happened much more rarely. Consequently, some of the numerous State Prisons in France, by the middle 'seventies and early 'eighties, began to seem superfluous.

In February 1784, it was decided to close the gaol at Vincennes and transfer its few inmates to the Bastille, which had plenty of room for them. The marquis de Sade was accordingly escorted, on the last day of the month, to more commodious quarters in this four-square, gloomy structure, dating from the fourteenth century, with its eight frowning towers.

Here the prisoners were divided into two main classes, those, like the marquis, detained on grounds of precaution or by way of admonitory correction and those who lay under presumption or proof of guilt. The former were subject to no investigation or judgment and were held 'at his Majesty's pleasure.' Most of them enjoyed a certain degree of comfort and freedom. Visitors were admitted. Exercise and even games were allowed. Food was abundant and good for those who could pay for it.

De Sade was allotted one of the best rooms in the whole place, an octagonal chamber, fifteen feet in diameter and twenty feet high, on the second floor of the tower ironically called the Tower of Liberty. The barred window gave a view of the rue St. Antoine. There was a curtained bed, a table and two chairs. The new tenant had the bare, whitewashed walls, covered with crude drawings and inscriptions by former captives, decently veiled by draperies.

He found that, in addition to these amenities, prisoners were permitted to receive, not only any visitors they pleased in the large interior courtyard, but also, actually, newspapers. Madame de Montreuil, whose almost lifelong ambition to see her son-in-law safely behind bars was now satisfied, saw to it that his meals were of high quality. He himself took care that she should not forget this extremely important matter. His letters to his wife, at this time, are full of impatient requests for this, that or the other solid or liquid delicacy.

The marquise was now authorized to visit her husband twice a month, presumably in the expectation that his temper, in those almost luxurious conditions, would improve. She generally stayed three or four hours and always brought with her either household stores, clothes, books — these latter elaborately specified to her beforehand — writing materials or special titbits in the way of eatables or wine. A warder was at first always present. But later on the prisoner, after some weeks of exemplary behaviour, managed to have this formality cancelled.

He then renewed against the unfortunate Renée, not only his verbal accusations of connivance with Madame de Montreuil, but also his assaults. On one occasion her screams brought a couple of turnkeys to the scene. They were, by their own account, which may be taken with a pinch of salt, just in time to save her life. The visits of the marquise, after this affair, were, naturally, prohibited.

Correspondence took their place. The cipher lessons were resumed. Finally, permission was again granted for personal interviews. But now the presence of a warder was insisted upon. The marquis, however, had begun to lose interest in the practical matters, the administration of his estates, the education of his children and so on, which Renée wished to discuss. He even grew indifferent to the progress of her endless plans for his release. He was becoming more and more absorbed in literary work.

His labours amounted, during the next three or four years, to four major productions. Their titles were, first, *The 120 Days of Sodom or, The School for Libertines;* second, *The Portfolio of a Man of Letters,* in four volumes; third, *Oxtierna, or, The Misadventures of a Libertine,* a play in three Acts; and fourth, *Aline and Valcour, or, The Philosophical Novel.*

The 120 Days of Sodom, which took the author only thirty-seven days to write, in the autumn of 1785, working between seven and ten every evening, is the most important of these four works. It is perhaps the most important that de Sade ever wrote, as not infrequently happens in the case of the first large-scale performance of a subsequently prolific author. The manuscript was not printed until 1904, when the Berlin psychiatrist, Ivan Bloch, writing under the pseudonym of Eugen Duehren, published a strictly limited edition of a hundred and eighty copies. He considered the book, he writes, "of capital significance in human history."

This view has been vigorously disputed. It is true that the German doctor was a francophobe and inclined to take de Sade's sweeping denunciations of French society under Louis Quinze at their face value. It is also true that other works by the marquis are superior to this one in literary style. But Bloch's opinion was firmly founded upon the remarkable degree to which this novel anticipates the work of Krafft-Ebing and Freud in its meticulous classification of the vagaries — the author listed six hundred of them — of the sex instinct. Krafft-Ebing himself pales into insignificance beside de Sade's masterpiece of scientific investigation. But this eighteenth-century treatise on sexual psycho-pathology not only exceeds the work of any purely scientific sexologist of later times in imaginative, speculative and intellectual power, but also, four years before Mrs. Radcliffe and eleven years before 'Monk' Lewis, exemplifies for the first time the 'black' or 'Gothic' type of romantic 'thriller,' deliberately setting out to horrify the reader.

The author begins by informing us that towards the end of the reign of Louis XIV four wealthy and influential debauchees, aged between forty-five and sixty, pooled their available capital of two million francs in order to give themselves up to a hundred and twenty days of dissipation.

They represent four groups of that 'authority' which de Sade so detested, the aristocratic, the religious, the financial and the legal. Each has previously married the daughter of one of the others in order, writes the marquis, 'to consolidate the bonds of the intimacy between them.'

The duc de Blangis, a man of immense physical strength and stature, has murdered his mother and raped his sister. After killing his wife he married the mistress of his brother, an archbishop, and had a daughter by her whom the prelate subsequently married. The archbishop is a slightly built, somewhat effeminate and extremely excitable swindler. Durcet, the financier, is a fat little fellow with homosexual tendencies, a white skin, prominent hips and a weak voice. De Curval, the judge, resembles a skeleton covered with hair. He is a homicidal maniac and an expert on poisons.

Constance, Durcet's daughter and the duke's present wife, is a slender, dignified brunette, inclined to modesty on occasion. Adelaide, de Curval's daughter and Durcet's wife, is a little blonde, fond of solitude and 'mysteries.' Julie, daughter of the duke and wife of de Curval, is tall and rather stout, with poor teeth and a pathological hatred of water. She drinks heavily. Aline, the archbishop's wife, daughter of his former mistress and Blangis, is an altogether more shadowy figure than these vivid, if mostly appalling, protagonists.

The group decides to give four suppers every month, each to cost ten thousand francs. To the first of these banquets sixteen young men between twenty and thirty and sixteen boys between twelve and eighteen are to be invited. The second is to be attended by 'girls in good society,' the third by the vilest prostitutes that can be found and the fourth by twenty virgins between seven and fifteen years old. Each Friday is to be consecrated to female homosexuality.

In addition to these guests four elderly women, experts in erotic perversion, are hired to give, in turn, five lectures daily. The first, Duclos, deals with a hundred and fifty common aberrations; the second, Charville, a 'Lesbian,' with a hundred and fifty 'double or multiple perversions'; the third, Martaine, with a hundred and fifty criminal vagaries involving the sex instinct, and the fourth, Desgranges, with a hundred and fifty based upon torture.

The feminine lecturers are provided with girls and boys 'of good education,' ten a day, who are used to illustrate the discourses, which last altogether thirteen days.

These extraordinary gatherings take place in the duc's lonely castle, situated in the middle of a Swiss forest. The lecture-room adjoins the dining-hall and is of semi-circular shape. The platform is occupied by the lecturer and its steps by the human 'apparatus.' Next the platform are two hollow pillars, equipped with instruments of torture. Here those who behave unsatisfactorily are duly punished. In the basement a large vaulted chamber contains "the most terrible contrivances ever imagined by the most ferocious ingenuity and the most refined cruelty."

On the 29th of October — a week after the marquis began to write the story, probably, and therefore the date when he reached this point in it — everyone assembles in the castle. All the exits are walled up. Each day's routine is drawn up as follows:

    10 a.m.   Visit boys
    11 a.m.   Light lunch with girls
    3–5 p.m. Dinner
    6–10 p.m. Lectures and erotic spectacles
    10 p.m.   Supper and thereafter, till 2 a.m., orgies.

Obscene language only is permitted in the castle. On Sunday evenings boys and girls who have behaved badly are punished. At the end of the one hundred and twenty days most of these young people are summarily massacred.

This deliberate parade of atrocities is the fruit of a frustrated mind driven in upon itself by a permanent grievance against society. Fortunately for the student that mind was of unusually robust and acute quality, had plenty of worldly experience, a savage sense of humour and, most important of all, possessed that aristocratic disdain of furtive half-measures and prurient suggestion, which are far more dangerous to innocent enquirers than blunt statement.

Nothing is more revealing, in this connection, than the author's own style.

"Among true libertines," he writes on an early page of *The 120 Days*, "the fact is recognized that the senations communicated by the organ of language are the most agreeable and the most vivid in their effect; accordingly, these four rascals of ours, desiring the deepest and furthest possible penetration of pleasure into their hearts, conceived a somewhat singular notion. The idea was, first to be surrounded by everything best calculated to assuage, through lubricity, the other senses, and then to hear, in minute detail and in a logical order, a description of all the various deviations of the subject, in all its branches and related fields, in a word, to use the libertine's vocabulary, all the 'passions.' Few people are aware of the extent to which these may be varied when the imagination takes fire; the wide range of difference observable between all the other obsessions and tastes of humanity is here even further extended; to define and isolate these deviations would perhaps be one of the noblest, as well as most interesting, labours to be undertaken in the sphere of morality."

After this indication of the typical rake's insistence upon elaborate preparation, by speech and contemplation, before consummation, the marquis scornfully, or perhaps slyly, adds:

"I should advise the pious reader, here and now, to put the book aside, if he does not wish to be shocked, for he has already noted that most of the subject-matter will be far from chaste in character and we have no hesitation in retorting, before he continues reading, that the telling of it will be even less so."

The duc's opening admonition to those who will form the raw material of erotic experiment and example is also characteristic.

"Weak and fettered creatures," he cries, "fated only to serve our lusts, consider the situation, reflect upon what you are and what we are and tremble. You are no longer in France: you are in the midst of an uninhabitable forest, beyond lofty mountains whose passes were blocked immediately after you had traversed them. You are confined in an impregnable citadel: no one knows you are here. You have been spirited away from your friends, from your parents; you are already dead to the world and you only still breathe because we need you for our pleasures. And of what nature are your present masters? Scoundrels of unlimited and known depravity, who have nothing divine in them but their lubricity, nothing of the law but what is in their guilt, nothing of restraint but what is in their debaucheries; they are godless rakes, unprincipled atheists, the least abandoned of whom is stained by innumerable crimes; in their eyes the life of a woman — a woman say I? — of every woman on earth, rather, is of no more value than a fly's. Few of our excesses, I can assure you, will not disgust you. Submit yourselves to them without protest and endure them with patience, humility and courage. If some of you prove so unfortunate as to succumb to our intemperance, let these play their parts bravely: we none of us live for ever: and the luckiest chance that can happen to a woman is to die young. . . ."

The discourse is as precise as if by Molière in its rendering of a shallow and brutal caricature of the solemn eloquence of the contemporary pulpit or administrative assembly: it is just such a speech as a coarse ruffian, once expensively educated and knowing just enough of what education means to bedevil those who lack the advantage, might make to his dupes, if he were bully as well as trickster. It was not for nothing that the marquis had trained his pen in writing for the stage. He seems himself to recognize the success of the portrait of the duc. For he adds just here, in parenthesis:

"There may be no such touch of delicacy in crime as in virtue, yet it is not more imposing, has it not always a sort of grandeur and superb character about it, which always has and always will attract us more than the dull and emasculated aspect of virtue?"

He is asking us to admire and shudder at his monster, to agree that nothing *could* be more monstrous: and at the same time he urbanely excuses us, as a man of the world and an expert in psychology, for our reluctant admission that we do find villains of the out-and-out sort more fascinating than heroes.

It is all very patronizing and subtle and simultaneously difficult to ignore. Such passages explain, in part, why de Sade in time came to be called, perhaps had been called by a few ever since his first exercises in complex licentiousness, the 'Divine' marquis.

He proceeds to become even more confidential and colloquial with the reader, impudently assuming the latter, as Baudelaire did after him, to be as great a libertine as himself.

"No doubt many of the deviations to be now described will repel you, that goes without saying: but there will also be some that will enchant you to the point of paroxysm; and that is all that is necessary. If we had not mentioned and analysed everything, how could we have guessed what your own taste was? It is your business to concentrate on the latter and omit the others; and if everyone does this, gradually everything will be accounted for. This is the tale of a magnificent banquet with six hundred different dishes. You will not want to try them all: but you will have a very wide choice; and you ought to be grateful to, not critical of, your host. Select some and ignore the rest, without inveighing against the latter simply because they were not just right for you. Consider that they will be agreeable to others and be philosophic about it. As for the diversity displayed, you can rest assured that it is not exaggerated. Examine any passion that seems to you the same as another, and you will find that they are different, however slight the difference may be, and that this difference precisely indicates the essence of the type of lasciviousness in question . . . each is marked by a stroke in the margin, underlining the appropriate name of the passion treated."

Nothing could be more scientifically persuasive. One is conscious, all the time, of a mind which, under only slightly more favourable conditions, could have innovated in optics or botany with as much success as, at any rate, the contemporary mind of Goethe. Moreover, the marquis, it is evident, would have made a first-rate schoolmaster in any of the recognized subjects of the curriculum.

The session at the duc's castle is opened by Madame Duclos. Each day she examines five 'common perversions.' Discussions, interruptions and various kinds of byplay occur during the lecture. She is followed in the same way by her three colleagues. Scarcely a sentence is legally quotable today.

We are told that at the end of the celebrations only sixteen out of the forty-six persons, including the 'monsters' and their wives, who had taken part in the proceedings, survived.

In the intervals of these 'serious' works the marquis despatched secretly, through his wife, articles for the public Press. In these he accused his supervisors and the Montreuil family and their friends of all sorts of petty persecutions practised upon him. These fabrications — for there was little or no foundation for them — were merely to keep his hand in. They amused him by their effect upon the reputations of prominent people who were walking about in liberty while he languished in gaol. He found it entertaining to be a perfect nuisance to everyone, both inside the Bastille and out of it, while he remained a prisoner. It is clear, nevertheless, that he was on the whole treated with great indulgence by the authorities all this time.

An attempt was made by his family, in the autumn of 1786, to get him to sign a power of attorney in connection with the administration of his estates. It evidently gave him the greatest pleasure to refuse absolutely even to see the lawyers charged with explaining the matter to him. He wrote in October, with obvious enjoyment, in the third person, to Balthazar de Sade, his uncle, a Commander of the Order of Malta — to which the marquis's son Armand had, incidentally, been admitted in 1784 — through the Governor of the Bastille, maliciously adding the name of Madame de Montreuil to the double superscription. The letter reads:

"M. de Sade, finding that all the considerations which have been brought to his notice concerning the preservation of his property are of the greatest possible cogency, and feeling, in common with his respected uncle, the imperative necessity for appointing some person to control the arrangements proposed, urges that no one is better qualified to exercise such control than himself, the comte de Sade" — such became the marquis's official title on his father's death. But he never used it except in formal communications — "and that the causes of his retention in prison are of no greater weight than those which render such detention injurious to himself, his wife and his children; he accordingly begs the Commander de Sade to include in the memorandum to be addressed to the Minister all the arguments set forth in his previous demand, deducing from them the need for his presence upon his estates" — all these possessive adjectives refer, of course, to the marquis only — "and to relieve him from the burden of the *lettre de cachet;*" — i.e., the King's private order under which he was held — "after so long a detention and in view of such weighty arguments the Minister is too just a man to refuse the Commander's request. This reply is the last which the comte de Sade will offer upon the subject."

The letter may well have been concocted with the aid of a legal friend. But, even so, the marquis's characteristic directness and forcibility of expression, far rarer in those ceremonious times than they are today, glitter through the clumsy language of litigation, as does his sardonic humour, his aristocratic dignity and the real bitterness of his frustration. His resolve to continue being a nuisance is equally obvious.

·The family revenged itself by tightening up the captive's routine. No more visits were to be allowed, no special privileges permitted, for the future. All letters written by the marquis would be copied in the Governor's office and only the copies despatched. This precaution was intended, of course, to prevent further recourse to lemon-juice and other invisible inks.

In the following month (November 1786) the prisoner began to suffer from attacks of giddiness, followed by prolonged lassitude and the expectoration of blood. For a time he was given up by the doctors. But eventually, after months of intermittent suffering, he made a complete recovery. "These scoundrels are always tougher than decent people!" remarked the deputy Governor regretfully.

It is interesting to find that this expert in sensations was given opium as a palliative at the time of his illness, but showed no particular inclination for it, though its excitatory effects upon the sensual imagination were already well known in Europe. The marquis was, in fact, just one of those people who, though they often find it necessary to stimulate the imagination of their friends, stand in no need of such stimulus themselves. It is quite probable, for example, that he never took an aphrodisiac in his life, fond though he was of administering such drugs to others.

He was restored, then, by June 1787, to his usual robust health, after a long convalescence during which he showed all his old hectoring spirit. On the 23rd of that month, at eight o'clock in the evening, he sat down to compose a new novel.

A preliminary note reads:

"Two sisters, one, extremely dissipated (Juliette), has a happy, rich and successful life; the other (Justine), extremely strait-laced, falls into a thousand traps, which end by causing her ruin."

He had by now realized that the *120 Days* were over-strong meat for a first publication. No one but professed debauchees would read the book. His present idea was to reaffirm, more effectively and to a wider public, his thesis of the raptures and roses of vice — Swinburne got this phrase from reading the novel the marquis was now about to write — by disguising himself, first of all, as a conventional moralist. The misfortunes of 'Justine' would be presented as a warning to all good Christians of the wickedness of the world. It was going to be great fun describing these calamities, for the horror and despair of innocent people had always been the most powerful stimulants to his 'satanic' imagination. As for 'Juliette,' she would play a secondary but repetitive part, simply showing again how dreadful really vicious persons could be and how often they seemed to achieve material success. Such triumphs, the moralist would add, were, naturally, of no consequence at all compared with the eternal flames of hell which awaited those who enjoyed them.

Opportunities for irony would be immense and no one could attack the book for immorality. One could always follow it up later by the *120 Days,* from the author's point of view a much more serious and sincere work.

He laboured so continuously and gleefully at this new project that his eyes began to give him trouble. The sea-water prescribed by the prison doctor did them no good. But in a fortnight, nevertheless, actually on the 8th of July, the manuscript of the 'philosophic tale,' as he called it proudly, was finished.

By 1788 the marquis had drawn up a catalogue of the works composed by him to date. They included, in addition to those already mentioned, some account of which will be given later, no less than thirty-five pieces for the stage, six short stories, *The Recreations of Florbelle, or, Nature Unveiled, The Memoirs of the Abbé of Modore* and *The Adventures of Emilie de Volnange.* These productions were all either destroyed when the Bastille was stormed in the following year or else burned by the police who discovered them.

A fragment of the notes for *Emilie,* however, survives. It reads as follows:

"Senarpont had deflowered his sister at the age of seventeen, becoming, by her, the father of Emilie. Consequently, Madame de Valvore is only 32, not 35 years old, as you say. Correct this. Emilie, really the daughter of Senarpont, passed as the daughter of M. de Valvore. She hates her mother, is sorry she only has one, would like to murder two of them. Remember this point when you make her find a second mother. The mother had saved Senarpont's life and the brute had forced her to act as a prostitute in every brothel in Paris. When he married her to M. de Valvore he did so in order to dominate and tyrannize over the household. M. de Valvore knows quite well that Emilie is Senarpont's daughter. She had helped to torture her mother and has drunk her blood. She eventually kills her by the Chinese torture of removing the seven skins of the body.

She eats her heart, so it is clear that the mother does not escape and dies in Senarpont's castle. These details are to be found at the end of the 10th copybook of the *Memoirs of Valvore*. Add, at the end of this copybook, all the points necessary to explain the mystery of Emilie's birth."

In the margin of this fragment appears the note:

"Since the birth-date has not been corrected, Emilie, too, must not be made too young at the time of her death: otherwise the period covered by her story would be too short."

It is evident that the marquis was nothing if not a methodical writer.

The other works which survive from the period 1786–1788 are the melodrama *Oxtierna, or, The Misadventures of a Libertine,* the first version of *Justine* and *Aline et Valcour.*

The play was written in prose. Its plot, as summarized by the dramatic critic of *Le Moniteur* on its production by the Molière Theatre in October 1791, is quite exciting enough for Verdi or Mascagni.

"Oxtierna, a rich Swedish nobleman and a determined libertine, has violated and carried off Ernestine, the daughter of Count Falkenstein: he has her lover imprisoned on a false charge: he takes his unfortunate victim to an inn, a league from Stockholm; the innkeeper, Fabricius, is an honest man. Ernestine's father manages to rescue her; she plans revenge on the brute who has dishonoured her: she writes a letter, ostensibly from her brother, to Oxtierna, challenging him to a duel at eleven o'clock at night. Her father also sends Oxtierna a challenge. The latter so arranges matters that his two antagonists, Ernestine and her father — for it is the girl who really intends to fight him — each take the other for the guilty nobleman. Father and daughter, disguised, engage in mortal combat. Their duel is, however, interrupted by Ernestine's lover, whom Fabricius has enabled to escape from prison. The young man kills Oxtierna in a second duel and marries Ernestine."

This rigmarole, leading up to a favourite idea of the marquis's, parricide, and containing a typical Sade hero-villain, in Oxtierna, is no worse than many a story which has held the stage both in his time and in ours, to say nothing of the nineteenth century. It is written, incidentally, with all the verve and sense of the theatre of which the author was a master and contains some fine passages of invective. So far as language is concerned, it could certainly pass a Continental censor to-day.

Justine, as composed in 1787, is described by the marquis himself, in a note on the manuscript, as

> "a work of an entirely new character. From end to end of it vice triumphs and virtue is humiliated. We must wind up by reinvesting virtue with all its due prestige and making it as attractive as can be desired. After finishing the book, no one will be able to do anything but detest the delusory triumph of crime and esteem the humiliations and misfortunes undergone by virtue."

The idea was a brilliant one, for the accepted formula for novel-writing in those days, as in these, was the triumph of virtue and the discomfiture of vice. The marquis's naturally combative disposition, as well as his true Frenchman's intolerance of sentimentality, inclined him to reverse the usual procedure, while his worldly prudence warned him that the 'moral,' nevertheless, must be the same as heretofore. In the end, of course, his intoxication with the 'imposing' elements of crime carried the day. *Justine,* for all its formal intention to edify, turned out to be a far more vivid delineation of the delights of atrocious behaviour than of the satisfactions of retaining one's sense of decency. The heroine's feelings are described perfunctorily. The acts of her tormentors are recounted with extreme relish. This first version is not nearly so full or so obscene as the final one, composed under the ferocious stimulus of the Revolution. For the moment it will be sufficient to note its general character, returning at a later stage to give some further details of it.

As for *Aline et Valcour,* it has already been mentioned as in part autobiographical and as an epistolary romance written under the influence of Richardson. Its interest apart from these elements is slight, the narratives being for the most part frigidly conventional even when indecent. Any respectable author of the day might have written them to the dictation of a lecherous ruffian holding a pistol to the scribe's head. The 'philosophy' referred to in the alternative title of this work consists merely in the sophisms with which the numerous villains of the piece justify their conduct, though there are some passages of political and sociological reflection. These, however, scarcely rise above the level of a popular newspaper of the time.

The 120 Days of Sodom, already described, is the major production of this epoch in the marquis's life. With it, as indeed with the rest in their degrees, he becomes something more than a raffish protagonist in the sexual field. His actual 'crimes,' to date, had been little or nothing more than could be expected of such a personage, with a dash of semi-scientific curiosity concerning biology and psychology, which he shared with many of his contemporaries. But in the last few years of imprisonment and persecution he had begun to rationalize his resentments and ardours. The mind had taken charge. His future 'crimes' would be cerebral only.

CHAPTER SIX

Citizen Sade

THE marquis had already predicted, in 1788, the coming social up-heaval. He had even identified it as the fall of the monarchy to an attack by the masses of the people. During the period of literary composition, as an aristocrat confined in the Bastille under a *lettre de cachet* of Louis XVI, he had written, in *Aline et Valcour:*

> " 'Listen,' Zané" — the French king of an imaginary country on the Gold Coast, visited by one of the heroes — "addressed me with the excitement of a fanatic. 'You are undoubtedly the last Frenchman I shall ever see. De Sainville, I still wish to belong to the nation which gave me birth. . . . Oh, my friend, let me tell you the secret I never intended to reveal to you till we had to part; the deep study I have made of all governments and particularly of that under which you live has made me almost a prophet. The examination of a people, the careful investigation of its history since first it began to play a part on earth, easily enables one to foresee what will become of it.
>
> O Sainville, a great revolution is brewing in your native land! The crimes of your kings, their merciless exactions, their debaucheries and their incompetence, have sickened France: she has had enough of despotism, she is about to break its fetters. When she is again free, this proud part of Europe will honour with her friendship all the peoples which govern them-selves as she does.' "

An outcast often sees more of what is going on than an established member of a community, particularly if the former is by nature an enemy of the latter. The preliminary rumours of rebellion, the cheers, the shots and the gallopings of hoofs in the streets, could already be heard through the thick walls of the Bastille during the early months of 1789. The newspapers, for those who could read between the lines, were full of omens. De Sade listened eagerly to the gossip of his gaolers. He began to look forward to a social change which might be of advantage to him as an author, might even, if he played his cards carefully, procure his release. He hoped little from the marquise now. She was losing heart, getting old and lazy, thinking, in these days, more of her children than of her unsympathetic husband.

The marquis was no eager democrat. He awaited the forthcoming explosion with cynical contempt, but with serious calculation of the personal profit to be possibly derived from it. His almost feudal disdain for the 'people' enabled him to foresee, as he put it, that "God will be the first victim of the Revolution and virtue the second." A new public might come, even this year, to listen complacently to the apostle of the splendours of immorality.

He set to work, forthwith, to revise and expand *The Misfortunes of Justine*. He now called it *The New Justine, or, The Misfortunes of Virtue*. The style, he decided, must be different, for the new public in view. There was to be less hypocritical bamboozling, more realism, more analysis, more science, in tune with the 'revolutionary' outlook of the coming era. He determined that, this time, Justine should miss nothing.

She begins, in the revised version, with escape from a priest who plans to violate her: she falls out of this frying-pan into the fire of a shopkeeper, Dubourg, who is even more lascivious than the priest. He succeeds, finally, in raping her. Her landlady robs her and introduces her to a bawd, Madame Delmonse, a 'Lesbian.' The latter, repulsed in her licentious advances, accuses Justine of theft and has her clapped in prison. A fellow captive, a woman named Dubois, sets fire to the gaol. Sixty persons are burned to death. But Justine and Dubois escape. While the former is obeying a call of nature she is seized by brigands and forced to join the band. She flies from the brutal orgies of these criminals with a merchant whose life she has saved from them. He rewards her services, as soon as he finds himself alone with her in a wood, by knocking her down, violating her and leaving her unconscious. On coming to herself she witnesses a scene of pederasty between a young gentleman and his lackey. They take her home with them and she is given employment by the gentleman's mother, a virtuous lady upon whom her son has both incestuous and murderous designs. He forces Justine, in the end, to kill her benefactress. The girl then escapes from this den of infamy and puts up at a boarding-house in a small town. But she finds that it is a training-school for prostitutes of both sexes. She runs away with the headmaster's daughter, but the latter is caught and dissected alive. Justine then meets a maniac whose specialty is making women pregnant, delivering them himself and subsequently drowning the new-born children. After evading this monster she is nearly killed in a monastery whose inmates are all 'sadists.'

She then reaches Lyons, narrowly avoids assassination in an extremely sinister hostelry, falls into and out of the hands of a perversion-ridden white slave dealer, then is hurled, by another man whose life she has saved, into a ditch full of corpses and has yet another narrow escape from an ecclesiastical dignitary who spends his time beheading the women he has 'ignobly outraged.' After being unjustly condemned to death, Justine, on her way to execution, meets her sister Juliette again.

The latter is enjoying the greatest happiness and prosperity. She soon obtains Justine's release. After hearing her sister's story Juliette tells her own, in the first person.

She was first corrupted by the abbess of the convent in which the two sisters were educated. She became a prostitute immediately on leaving, but in the grand style. She then set to work, by robberies, poisonings and procurings, to obtain even more money. Her crimes and travels are prodigious, her wealth colossal, her cynicism boundless. We are told that Justine was eventually struck by lightning and killed, while Juliette passes away peacefully in her bed, many years later, as a countess.

This work, the best known and the most often quoted of all those by de Sade, can be described as intolerably diffuse, utterly incredible, monotonously nauseating and, in spite of some vividly conceived and realized incidents, infernally — in the literal sense of the word — dull as a whole. Yet this is the only thoroughly pornographic book in the world which contains proof of a brilliant intelligence in the author. There is much penetrating observation, well digested learning and striking originality of thought to be found in it, especially in the part of the novel devoted to Juliette's adventures and conversations.

The marquis's literary labours were interrupted, in April 1789, by the turnkey's tales of what was happening outside the walls of the Bastille. It seemed that huge crowds, ragged and bare footed, were encamped around the city of Paris and were attempting to force the gates. The urban populace were in sympathy with these provincials and were growing dangerously restless.

An ugly political journalist with a bad stammer but a violent manner, Camille Desmoulins, was deliberately exciting them. Two leading industrialists, Henriot and Reveillon, were particularly unpopular. The latter had said that any workman's family ought to be able to live for fifteen sous a day and still 'have a watch in his pocket.'

On the night of the 27th of April the houses of these two plutocrats were stormed and sacked by a furious mob of malcontents, whose chief concern appears to have been the wine cellars. The orgy of plunder and intoxication went on all the next day and night.

Other demonstrators, encouraged by this performance, attacked other houses, upset gentlemen's coaches, robbed foot passengers in the streets. The few police were almost helpless against this rising tide of amateur criminals. Two regiments of cavalry were summoned from Versailles to deal with the trouble. The rioters climbed the roofs, and rained down tiles and other missiles upon the dragoons, who were ordered to open fire. More than a hundred of the citizens were killed. Some of them had been mere spectators of the fighting.

The revolt was suppressed for the time being. But obviously it was by no means over.

The marquis, intensely interested, for purely selfish reasons, in this news, took action at once. During the night which followed the first quiet day he prepared a number of cardboard posters. They bore, in large red letters, such legends as:

PEOPLE! COME AND DESTROY THE VILE BASTILLE! CITIZENS! COME TO THE AID OF THE OPPRESSED! ARM YOURSELVES, BRAVE FRENCH-MEN, COME TO THE SUPPORT OF THE VICTIMS OF TYRANNY! WE PRISONERS SUMMON YOU AND ARE READY TO RECEIVE YOU! FIVE HUNDRED WRETCHED CAPTIVES WILL DIE IF YOU DELAY THEIR RESCUE!

Actually, at that time, there were no more than nine prisoners, including the marquis, in the Bastille. Four of these were forgers, two were counts and two were common lunatics. The advertiser, however, was not concerned with such petty details. He concealed the placards, which were flexible, under his clothing when the time came for him to take his daily exercise on the ramparts. He found no difficulty in hanging them, at moments when the warder's back was turned, over the muzzles of the cannon pointing from the battlements.

A crowd soon collected in the rue St. Antoine. But by that time the marquis was back in his cell. The Governor of the Bastille, when the display of the posters was reported to him, ordered their removal and made the most rigorous enquiries as to how such an offensive feat came to be performed. But he never discovered the culprit, who was actually able, once at least, to repeat the exploit, in spite of the redoubled vigilance of the warders.

It is of course not to be imagined that this incident was responsible for the famous raid, more than two months later, on the prison. The Bastille was not, on that 14th of July, stormed out of sympathy for the handful of swindlers, aristocrats and madmen who were confined in it, but to enable both supporters and resisters of the Revolution to get at the weapons which the gaol contained. Some citizens wished to defend themselves, others to be free to pilage with less interference.

The Governor, naturally enough, put a stop to all exercise on the ramparts. The marquis instantly flew into one of his violent rages. He set fire to his cell, as a start. Then, about a month later, he actually escaped from it, getting as far as the foot of the tower, where he began struggling with the sentries. He was conducted back to his quarters with a musket barrel at his ribs.

The punishment for this breach of the regulations was three hours' solitary confinement in one of the dark and damp little underground dungeons of the prison, where so many Frenchmen of bygone days had starved to death or died under the teeth of enormous rats.

De Sade, on his release from this unpleasant experience, was on his way upstairs when he happened to catch sight of the Governor. Immediately, he halted, shook his clenched fist at the officer and in a furious voice roared out:

"I'll have you hanged by the people of France for this, you ——"

"My dear Count," returned the Governor, with great tranquillity, "if you won't listen to reason and will persist in repeatedly throwing the whole gaol into an uproar, I shall really have to order you to be shot."

This threat was, of course, not meant to be taken seriously. Nor did it intimidate the captive, who retorted between his teeth:

"We'll soon see which of us two it will be who will be first bled to death like a stuck pig!"

The marquis certainly had an uncanny gift for prophecy. Only a few weeks later the Governor's head would be paraded, on a pike, in the rue St. Antoine.

The prisoner, back in his cell, had by no means come to the end of his resources. A few days later he seized a large metal funnel with which he was in the habit of emptying his slops out of the barred window into the moat below. Placing this object to his lips he bawled through it over the sill:

"The Bastille prisoners are being murdered! Hurry, to the rescue! Or we shall all be killed!"

This episode took place on the 2nd of July. De Sade followed it up by hurling into the street papers in which he described the torture of his fellow captives.

The Governor began to be seriously alarmed, for the temper of the populace remained ugly, and highly inflammable. He consulted his Minister. That functionary instructed him to remove M. de Sade, the most obstreperous of his charges, to the Hostel of the Brothers of Charity at Charenton le Pont, a south-easterly suburb of the city.

On the night of the 3rd–4th of July the marquis was driven from the Bastille in a closed carriage. The police inspector, Quidor, held a pistol against his temple.

"Move or speak, and I'll blow your brains out!"

The prisoner remained quiet. But even so the drive, though it took place in the small hours, made the inspector feel anxious. More than once a riotous mob tried to hold up the vehicle. But at last, about daybreak, it managed to get through to the Hostel.

Next day the marquis's cell in the Bastille was searched. After an inventory had been taken of a library of some six hundred volumes, including ten manuscript books, and of some valuable furniture, pictures and clothes, the door was sealed.

At Charenton the inmates were mostly epileptics and idiots. The good monks were terrified of the new arrival, whose reputation was well known to them. They let him do pretty much as he liked. He was mainly occupied, for some time, in trying to get his wife to retrieve the property left at the Bastille. But Renée had by now fallen completely under the influence of her implacable mother. Madame de Montreuil had advised her, in view of the uncertain political situation, to retire, once more, to a convent and recommend her soul, and the marquis's, if she thought there was any point in it, to God. From her secluded retreat the marquise did nothing but write inconclusive letters to various functionaries, who saw clearly enough that she was no longer interested. The times were, in any case, too stormy for family business.

By October she had fled, with her children and many other people of means, not interested in politics, from the convulsed capital. Otherwise, such was the lawlessness of those days, she would have risked not only robbery, but ill-treatment and even death. Fortunately, she did not go to La Coste, but to one of the Montreuil country seats. The marquis's favourite château in Provence was sacked and burnt by the peasantry in the following year.

By the time the Bastille had fallen and the unlucky Governor's head, as his unruly captive had predicted, carried round the walls on a pike, when the supremacy of Louis XVI and his Government was no longer recognized, when all duly constituted authority in France was at an end and the whole country seething in an uproar of contradictory orders, violence and rapine, the worthy Brothers were glad enough to be rid of the imperious M. de Sade. He left the Hostel on the 1st of April, 1790, a Good Friday, the anniversary, almost, of the Rose Keller incident. Ten days before, the National Assembly had decreed that all *lettre de cachet* prisoners should be released.

The marquise, on hearing that her formidable husband was once more at liberty, took steps to let him know, not only that she was not prepared to meet him, but that she was arranging for a legal separation. During the long interval since she had last visited the Bastille her blind affection and loyalty had at last been undermined. She was no longer young. In fact, she had reached an age when women often lose their grip on the world of men and affairs. Her character, in any case, had never been a strong one. And her mother's single-minded hostility to the marquis had been exerting a relentless pressure upon her innate conservatism for nearly a generation. Piety now took the place of what passed in Renée for passion. The marquise de Montreuil de Sade, as she now significantly signed herself, had fought her final battle for normal domesticity, and lost.

Her unregenerate consort, free for the first time in twelve years, felt that he himself, as well as the times, had changed. He was fifty, had put on a lot of weight, coughed continually, was half blind after these long years of little but reading and writing and suffered from indigestion, headaches and rheumatism. Incidentally, he was almost penniless, for his property in the Bastille had gone up in flames or been stolen, La Coste was a ruin, his wealthy wife had cut off supplies and entered a suit for divorce against him, his former friends were all either dead or destitute, his lawyers and other agents silent, all his relatives grimly uncommunicative.

He looked up an advocate whom he knew slightly, one M. de Milly. This acquaintance consented to feed him and give him a bed until he was in a position to fend for himself.

The ex-prisoner tackled Gaufridy first. He notified that urbane but slippery gentleman that he now intended to take over the management of what was left of his estates himself. Then he wrote a tactful letter to his infirm and rich aunt, on the de Sade side. This communication contained, as usual when the marquis corresponded with his own family, a good deal of hearty abuse of his relatives by marriage.

"When I married into (the Montreuil tribe) I acquired a good few pauper cousins, some Pont Neuf hawkers and a couple of other relatives who had been hanged . . . these ruffians are still trying to compass my ruin, since they can no longer keep me shut up. They want to separate me from my wife and get her dowry back. . . ."

He goes on to paint a picture of plundered and deserted old age, puts down his transfer to Charenton and his losses in the Bastille all to the machinations of these 'wicked rascals,' upon whose heads he calls down the vengeance of heaven.

An extremely polite letter to the new Chief of Police follows, with a description of the lost manuscripts. These papers, however, were never recovered.

To one of the few friends he had left in Provence he writes that he does not propose to visit his estates there just yet, in case he is hanged on one of the 'democratic gibbets,' a jocose observation which need not be taken too seriously. The real 'democratic' danger had now shifted again from the countryside to the cities, for many of the large army of servants which the old landowners had maintained had been reduced to destitution by the hasty extermination of their employers and were now ready to go back to the former system of 'exploitation.' The marquis's real reason for remaining in Paris was simply lack of money. He adds frankly that he is glad the old régime has gone, for it had done nothing but make him miserable. He continues:

"Valence, Montauban and Marseilles have become theatres of horror where, day after day, performances are given, by cannibals, of dramas in the English style" — this is probably an illusion to the widespread contemporary French view that the English, in their plays, cared for nothing but massacres like that in the last Act of *Hamlet* — "which makes one's hair stand on end. I used to say to myself, years ago, that this charming and gentle nation of ours, which once devoured the toasted loins of the Maréchal d'Ancre" — an Italian favourite of Louis XIII murdered by guardsmen in 1617 — "was only waiting for the chance to burst into flame" — (*s'électriser*) — "so as to prove that in its permanent state of suspension between ferocity and fanaticism it would adopt its natural tone at the first opportunity.

But it's time to stop all this. One's letters must be prudent these days. 'Despotism' never used to open so many of them as 'Liberty' does."

This note to a fellow aristocrat gives a clear enough picture of the marquis's feelings, midway between contempt and relief, regarding the political and social situation at that date, May 1790, when he had been about a month at large. As for more private matters, he writes to Gaufridy ten days later:

"I am living with a delightful lady who has herself been the victim of misfortune and who is therefore capable of compassion for other such unhappy ones. She has wit, talent and lives separated from her husband, as I from my wife. She treats me with unlimited generosity. She is married to a President of the Grenoble Parliament, M. de Fleurieu, and is forty years old. I add this last detail to enable you to perceive that with myself at the age of fifty, which makes ninety years in all between us, there can be no harm in our association."

By June, or less than ten days later, this playful mood had changed, apparently, to sombre despair. The meeting with Madame de Fleurieu had been a bit of luck. But now the old frustration was closing down on him again. He writes to the same pathetically trusted correspondent, who took care to keep **Madame de Montreuil** apprised of what was going on:

"You have no idea of the infernal and cannibalistic proceedings those people have been conducting against me. If I had been the basest of mankind, no one would have dared to subject me to such barbarous treatment. In short, it has cost me my eyes and my lungs and made me so unwieldly corpulent that I can hardly move. It has extinguished all power of feeling in me. Nothing now attracts me. There is nothing I care about. The world, the loss of which at one time I was so insane as to mourn, now strikes me as unspeakably tedious and dreary. . . .

There are times when I should like to become a Trappist. I can give no guarantee that I shall not disappear one of these fine days, without anyone knowing what has become of me. I have never been such a misanthropist as since my return to live among men. If I seem strange to them, they can be quite sure that they produce the same effect on me. I was extremely busy during my detention. . . . I would have had fifteen volumes to get printed when I came out. Of these I now have scarcely a quarter. Madame de Sade, with unpardonable carelessness, allowed some to be lost, others to be confiscated. The result is that thirteen years' work has gone for nothing. . . .

Since then, that sensitive and delicate-minded lady, Madame de Sade, has kept me at arms' length. Any other woman would have said, 'He is unhappy. Let us dry his tears.' Such sentimental logic makes no appeal to her whatever. It seems that I have still not lost enough: she intends to work my ruin. She has lodged a plea for separation. In taking this incredible step she will end by rendering plausible all the vile slanders which have been spewed out against me and by heaping disaster and contumely upon her children and myself. And she is doing all this simply in order to be able to live or rather 'vegetate delectably,' as she puts it, in some convent or other, where no doubt she receives consolation from a confessor who will also smooth for her the path of crime, dishonour and disgrace" — the marquis, now thoroughly into his stride, seems, in his furious haste, to have written 'honour.' But of course he meant its opposite —

"into which her behaviour is leading us all. If the woman had taken the advice of my most deadly enemy" — Renée had, indeed, it is almost certain, taken her orders from Madame de Montreuil — "it could not have been more mischievous and dangerous.

You will, my dear Counsellor, readily understand that this separation, by its sequestration of monies forming part of my wife's dowry and only payable out of my estate, will cause my ruin, which is precisely what those beasts want.

Ye Gods! I had supposed that seventeen years of calamity, thirteen of them spent in prison, in appalling dungeons, might well atone for a few indiscretions in my youth. You see, my friend, how wrong I was. . . ."

One never knows, with the marquis, just how sincere he may be in committing his ideas to paper. Like other impulsive and gifted men, he often let his pen run away with him into absurd exaggerations and even misrepresentations. The reader will know, by this time, in glancing through the correspondence here quoted, just where to sprinkle the salt. Nevertheless, the grievance and the melancholy described were both genuine enough, if less soul-destroying than they would have been in a cooler head and heart, perhaps even less atrocious than the marquis wished his friends to believe. The ravings of an eloquent egotist are not always to be written off as verbiage. Sometimes there is a core of real sorrow and oppression beneath them.

The legal separation between Renée and her husband was ratified, with considerable despatch, on the 9th of June, 1790. The marquis was directed to pay his wife alimony to the tune of 4000 livres a year. The news threw de Sade into such a paroxysm of new rage and despair that he made a scene at Madame Fleurieu's house which terrified that agreeable lady. She asked him to control himself. He cursed her. She left the room, indicating that he must find someone else to look after him.

At this low ebb in his fortunes a woman again, as so often before, came to the rescue of the stout, balding, choleric but still irresistible little man. The mysterious fascination which the fundamentally un-sentimental marquis de Sade exercised all his life long over all the educated women he ever met, even if most of them, in the end, had to give him up, had not decreased with the ruin of his physique and the emptying of his purse.

Marie-Constance Veinelle was well named. She remained devoted to the marquis until his death and it was lucky for him — *veine* in French meaning good luck — that he met her when he did. She was a former actress, thirty years old, the divorced wife of a business man, Balthasar Quesnet, then in America. He had left her with their infant son, Charles, and a slender income. Falling entirely under the spell of her new lover, she took him at once into her house.

He tells Gaufridy that he is very comfortable there. "There is not a word of love." Marie-Constance is a good-natured, decent, cheerful sort of creature. The marquis seems to have paid her something for his room, attendance and food, for he was by now in receipt of certain emoluments for literary work.

His first publisher, a certain Girouard, not quite realizing, perhaps, with whom he was dealing, asked the 'new' author to 'pepper the stuff well.' The old hand passed on this story, with grim relish, to his 'faithful' correspondent, Gaufridy. He writes:

"I gave the fellow enough to poison the devil himself."

The manuscript was the first version of *Justine,* sub-titled *The Misfortunes of Virtue.* In point of fact, as finally printed, in 1791, it is nothing like so pornographic as its successors. Either the mar-quis was pulling Gaufridy's leg — in the same letter he solemnly begs the lawyer not to read *Justine* — or else Girouard changed his mind after seeing the text. The book starts with a verse motto:

> "Nature inspires our tastes bizarre,
> I paint them only as they are."

Once at least this volume was ordered by a lady in the country who supposed, from the title, that it must be a collection of sermons.

These literary activities brought de Sade into contact with pro-fessional colleagues, more than half of whom, as always in France, wrote for the stage as well as for the Press. He became friendly with the actor Boutet de Monvel. The new atmosphere of political rhetoric in favour of 'liberty' and 'the people' created a boom, as it did a hundred and twenty years later in Russia, for theatrical business.

The marquis's prose melodrama in three Acts, which has already been mentioned, *Count Oxtierna, or, The Results of Libertinage,* the title being slightly altered and the manuscript signed only with his initials, DAFS, was accepted for production by the Théâtre Molière and duly shown on the 22nd of October, 1791. The reception was at first enthusiastic. But there were second thoughts.

At the beginning of the second Act a spectator called out: "Curtain!" The curtain was obediently, in conformity with good 'democratic' practice, lowered more than half-way. Other spectators, however, bawled: "Curtain up!" This order was also complied with. The second faction then demanded the ejection of the first interrupter. A riot ensued. Some hissed. But most of the audience applauded the piece. The author was summoned and revealed himself as 'Citizen Sade.'

The dramatist had previously approached the Comédie Française. But he could make nothing of this proud institution, which rejected three of his plays one after the other. Correspondence followed. But it did not improve the situation. Eventually the persistent author was given a five-year pass to the theatre in question, but nothing more. Some of his other pieces were accepted by different houses. But they never reached the stage.

Oxtierna ran only two nights at the Molière. It was accorded a third and last performance, in which de Sade himself played the part of the sympathetic Fabricius, on the 13th of December, 1799, at the theatre of the Société Dramatique of Versailles.

Soon after the marquis had taken up quarters with Madame Quesnet he 'joined the Party,' in other words became a member of the local revolutionary 'cell,' that of the Place Vendôme, near Madame Quesnet's house. This organization was officially styled the 'Pike Section,' with reference to the favourite weapon of the insurgents. Robespierre subsequently entered it.

Citizen Sade, like most born aristocrats, knew how to make himself popular. He represented himself, with great eloquence and success, to the group, as an ex-victim of the old régime. By the middle of 1792 he had actually been elected Secretary. He was frequently sent, as delegate of the Section, to the meetings of the Convention. To this body he expounded at length, in his usual vigorous and lucid style, his social philosophy. By the following year he had been made President of the Pike Section, and a person of considerable importance in the general life of the capital.

In this office he had the exquisite pleasure of presiding when his once wealthy and influential father-in-law, M. de Montreuil, the somewhat henpecked consort of the marquis's remorseless foe for thirty years, appeared before the Section, sweating with anguish, to solicit, with abject humility, the honour of admission to its ranks. De Sade tells Gaufridy, with lofty scorn, that he raised no objection. If he had, the unhappy 'Papa Montreuil' would no doubt have been torn to pieces, like so many other in like case, on the spot.

The scene would have been such as the Section President had often described with the greatest delight, on paper. Private vengeance as well as literary taste urged him to give a signal for which no 'good revolutionary' would ever have rebuked him. That he did not do so in the case of this poor wretch proves nothing if not that, by this time, the marquis's 'sadism' had become purely cerebral and that he shrank definitely from its illustration in practice. The President remained, from the conventional point of view, a 'rascal,' but, from any point of view, in theory only. His mildness on this occasion is almost enough, by itself, to disprove the popular legend of the 'monster.' Fortunately for his reputation, it was only Monsieur, not Madame, who pleaded before him that day.

A police document of this period, dated the 7th of March, 1793, six weeks after the King's execution, describes "Louis Sade, writer, aged forty-nine" — this figure should be fifty-three — "five feet two inches tall, hair nearly white, round face, bald forehead, blue eyes, nose and mouth of average size, round chin." It is not an impressive portrait. That of Oscar Wilde in his latest years may come to mind.

But police descriptions are seldom flattering. One can only be relieved that the 'corpulence' was omitted. Perhaps a more active life, since release from prison, had made it less conspicuous.

At the end of 1791 the marquis had confided to Gaufridy his profession of political faith. He was no Jacobin-extremist — the small shopkeepers' party — he wrote. He was loyal to the King, but an enemy to the abuses committed in his name. Some clauses in the new Constitution were to his taste, others not. He favoured the restoration of aristocratic honours and dignities, since their reduction did no one any good. He considered that the King should stand at the head of the nation, but constitutionally, with two Chambers, on the contemporary English model, of Lords and Commons, to hold him in check.

These eminently reasonable views did not prevent Citizen Sade, later on, from becoming a fervent admirer of Citizen Marat, for whose portrait in the Section's assembly hall he composed an adulatory quatrain.

The picture of the once terrible marquis, during this period, known to historians as the 'Terror,' can only be drawn in the most sober colours. He was the mildest, the most benevolent of revolutionaries, an inspector of hospitals, a labourer at technical reports, a listener to grievances, a sentimental orator. He saved a number of friends far more aristocratic than M. de Montreuil from the guillotine, by having them sent, for so long only, it is true, as their funds held out, to sanatoria on the pretext of serious illness. He was, he said more than once, in principle against the death penalty. He objected to putting it to the vote at Section meetings. As a philosopher, he observed, he considered that the sanctity of human life was a mawkish myth. As an anarchist, however, it was his opinion that massacre should be left in the very efficient hands of Mother Nature.

This was going too far. On the 6th of December, 1793, Citizen Sade was arrested at his lodgings in the rue Neuve des Mathurins, together with his mistress, Madame Quesnet, and taken immediately to the Madelonnettes Prison in the Temple quarter, charged with 'moderation.'

CHAPTER SEVEN

Danse Macabre

HE writes that at the Madelonnettes he was obliged to sleep in a latrine for six weeks. He was then moved to the Carmes Prison, where he shared a dormitory with six invalids, two of whom died during the week he was there. His next gaol was at St. Lazare, the centre, at that time, of a counter-revolution, with which he had to be extremely careful not to exhibit sympathy. He finally reached an 'earthly paradise,' the convent-hospital of Picpus, a 'splendid building with a delightful garden' and charming inmates.

Times were indeed changed. This is the first occasion, in all de Sade's long years of confinement, upon which he expresses approval of the place of incarceration. Unfortunately, his first agreeable impressions had soon to be very definitely qualified.

Shortly after his arrival the guillotine arrived too. It had been transferred, perhaps partly to intimidate the counter-revolutionaries, from the Place de la Révolution to a position immediately beneath the windows of the convent. The author of so many imaginary beheading scenes and the social theorist who was against the death-penalty 'in principle' found this proximity disturbing. To make matters worse, the 'delightful' garden was commandeered as a cemetery for the headless corpses of the executed, some of whom were the former 'charming' inmates of the 'splendid' building itself.

The name of Citizen Sade was duly inscribed upon the fatal list of 'public enemies.' But, before he could be led out to meet his death, Robespierre had met his. The extremists fell from power. Ten weeks later, on the 15th of October, 1794, the experienced captive was liberated. He had spent three hundred and twelve consecutive days in the prisons of the Republic.

The faithful Madame Quesnet again set up house with him. Her guest, in order to show his appreciation of her devotion, had a document drawn up by the local lawyers by which he recognized the lady as, in view of her comparatively tender years, not his wife, but his daughter. It is possible, indeed, though hardly probable, that their relations, by this time at any rate, were purely those of mental companionship.

Aline et Valcour, or, The Philosophical Novel, was now published by Girouard with sixteen illustrations. The book was probably written before *Justine* and is a relatively tame production, as already mentioned. The publisher, by the way, had now been guillotined for royalist conspiracy and the business was being carried on by his widow. The story, in the epistolary form popular at the time as the result of Richardson's *Clarissa,* relates that the two virtuous lovers, Aline and Valcour (or, perhaps, Louise de Montreuil and Donatien de Sade) meet with a 'monster' in the person of Aline's father, the President de Blamont, some of whose personal traits remind us of Madame de Montreuil, wife, actually, of a 'President,' whose more amiable character is shown in Aline's mother, by a typical Sadian inversion.

De Blamont wants to marry his daughter to a rich old debauchee, Dolbourg, a high Revenue official, whose mistress is the virtuous Sophie, believed by Blamont to be his elder daughter Claire. But she is really Claire's nurse's daughter. From this point on stories within stories, for instance, the very long one of Valcour's life before he met Aline, complicate the narrative. Its involutions are too tedious to summarize here.

There are compensations, however. Valcour's letter to a friend on hearing of Aline's death is a really moving piece of prose, the pathetic outburst of a broken heart. It reminds us that the 'wicked' marquis had once in his life at least felt a deep and true emotion. The portrait of Aline, too, is full of the delicacy and charm which might have been expended upon the theme by a far more sentimental writer. We reflect, once more, that Louise de Montreuil must have had a genuinely enchanting presence to inspire the grim author to these rhapsodies.

For the rest, this certainly over-verbose production contains practically no obscenity, and only a very little poisoning and flagellation. Instead, we are treated to the exposition of a very large number of theories of government, morality, education, economics and, of course, sex relations. Some of these ideas are sensible enough and have been advanced, usually in vain, both before and since the marquis's time, in later days, often as if they were quite new.

Aline et Valcour was followed, in 1795, by *Philosophy in the Boudoir, or, Education by Libertines.* This work provides a kind of polemical pendant to *The 120 Days of Sodom.* It expounds, in the abstract, the author's views on such subjects as vice and virtue, God and Nature, law and progress, parents, female duty, marriage, maternity, murder, theft, love, friendship, gratitude, charity and sodomy. These topics are treated in a series of essays and aphorisms, given the form of instruction imparted to a girl, Eugénie de Mistival, by an older woman and a man, with the object of corrupting her mind. The marquis's own opinions are put into the mouths of the two 'teachers,' while he is careful to imply what horrid people they are.

Philosophy in the Boudoir, despite the magnitude of the ideas it discusses, is the shortest of de Sade's works. There are in all only seven dialogues. The principal characters are Madame de St. Ange, aged twenty-six, a physically attractive, amoral, highly sensual personage, Eugénie, a pretty girl of fifteen, with a definitely receptive and lascivious temperament, and M. Dolmance, a cynical debauchee of thirty-six, who really dominates the talk. A minor figure is the Chevalier de Mirval, aged twenty, who is the brother of Madame de St. Ange.

The whole action of the book takes place in a single day and is mainly theoretical conversation. The most interesting of the notions put forward are that religions are the cradle of despotism, that we should only ridicule, not massacre, those who disagree with us, that we can't love our neighbours even if we want to, that equality before the law is an absurdity, since men are unequal in character, and that few and mild laws are best for humanity. Capital punishment should be abolished. But deliberate murder, i.e. not the killing of another human being on a sudden impulse, which the author considers a peccadillo, should be penalized merely by making the culprit uncomfortable.

There are four major crimes, says Dolmance. These are calumny, theft, sexual crime and murder. Their treatment must depend on the circumstances in which they are committed. All private property, for example, he remarks, fifty years before Proudhon, is merely the result of robbery. Yet it would be ridiculous to lock a man up for owning a watch or a house which others cannot afford to buy. As for the man from whom another steals the watch or the house he is merely, as Samuel Butler triumphantly announced nearly a hundred years later, as if it were a new discovery, a fool. Women should have exactly the same freedom in sexual behaviour as men. And, to return to the subject of murder, really the thing is sometimes positively necessary.

We may regard all this as nothing but ingenious special pleading if we like. But in pure logic there is nothing wrong with it. Some of it is brilliantly original in conception. Most of it is extremely well written. One of the marquis's outstanding literary gifts is his thorough mastery of forensic argument. The book is indispensable to those who wish to understand what this 'monster' and 'madman' was capable of intellectually.

In the autumn of 1796 La Coste, or what was left of it, was sold to the deputy Rovère, who had shown Citizen Sade political favour in the recent past. The marquise, who held a mortgage on the place, had first to be paid off by her infuriated husband. But he duly proceeded with the sale. In July of the following year he visited for the first time for many years, possibly with a similar object, his other property of Mazan in Provence. He took Madame Quesnet with him on this occasion, returning three months later.

But Paris was now too expensive for the restricted means of

'father and daughter.' They retired a short distance to the north-west, to St. Ouen, near Pontoise. Here they bred chickens, geese and rabbits. But the farm did not pay and the amateur smallholders had to return to Paris, where new misfortunes awaited them.

The Convention had just issued a decree sequestrating the estates of aristocrats who had emigrated. By some mistake the marquis's name was included in the list of those who had left France. His lands in Provence were taken over by the Government. This disaster left him worse off than he had ever been in his life before. Marie-Constance had to go out to work. It became impossible for the couple to continue living together.

De Sade found a garret in Versailles, where the cost of living was lower than in Paris. He took Madame Quesnet's little boy to stay with him there and changed his name to that of the child, a simple 'Charles.' He 'walked on,' or acted as prompter, at the local theatre. The privations he now endured, possibly due, in part, to the sacrifice of his own needs to those of his 'grandson,' began to affect his health. He had spent two months in hospital before the clerical error which had landed him at this rock-bottom of poverty was rectified.

In 1797 *The Story of Juliette, or, The Prosperity of Vice* was issued, being the sequel to *Justine* and bearing, unlike the latter work, the author's real name. He badly needed the money which reputation as a pornographer would bring and, as the republican régime plunged on down the path of 'democracy,' all sorts of scabrous writings were now finding their way into print with impunity.

In this publication Juliette, after being initiated, by the nuns at her convent-school, into the mysteries of feminine homosexuality, passes on to pederasty under the auspices of the local archbishop and his vicar. Her subsequent adventures are largely unquotable. But a few incidents may be referred to as typical. One of her exploits is to visit a hard-working and deserving family of peasants, partake of their simple hospitality and then surreptitiously set their cottage on fire. She takes care that the whole family are burned to death, except the father, who is allowed to survive, in order that he may contemplate the horrible extinction of his loved ones and the utter ruin of his means of livelihood. When Juliette triumphantly tells this story to an Englishwoman of views similar to her own, Madame de Clairwil, the latter criticizes her severely for having omitted to cause the peasant himself to be arrested for murder and arson.

Madame de Clairwil belongs to a secret club, called 'The Society of the Friends of Crime.' For a considerable time she accompanies Juliette on her lurid career, keeping her up to the mark to such purpose that in the end this incredible representative of perfidious Albion herself falls a victim to the mania for poisoning people in which she has trained her pupil.

Juliette only quails once. It is when a minister of France propounds to her a scheme for starving two-thirds of the population of the country to death and taking possession of the property thus made available for himself. She has her ups and downs, but is always equal even to occasions when all seems lost. She manages to marry a most respectable count, poisons him and sets up as a card-sharper in Italy. Entertained by a gigantic cannibal, whose furniture is composed of human bones, she poisons him too, leaves for Rome, sets all the hospitals and charitable institutions in the Holy City on fire, lectures the Pope and becomes his mistress.

A long story ensues, one of the best told parts of the book, which is put into the mouth of Madame de Clairwil's husband, a wandering brigand, whose swindling expeditions take him to England, Sweden, Russia, Turkey and back again to Italy. Everywhere he commits murders and robberies of the most heartless description.

His wife and Juliette now proceed to Naples, where they indulge in orgies with the King and Queen and throw Princess Borghese into the crater of Vesuvius. After clearing their royal hosts out of almost the whole treasure of the kingdom, the two ladies leave for the north again. Juliette now murders her friend and with the proceeds of this crime starts a really magnificent brothel in Venice. She is ejected from the State by the authorities, but returns at last to Paris with a huge sum of money and, after murdering her little daughter, settles down to enjoy herself in a less unconventional manner.

It must be confessed that this book is very dull in parts and that all the characters, including many prominent people, such as the Pope and the King and Queen of Naples, who were living at the time of publication, are entirely inconceivable as human beings. Nevertheless, here again the marquis, alone among deliberate pornographers, gives evidence of an intelligence well above the average. The sheer inventive power displayed, with scarcely a sign of labour or fatigue, is amazing. The actual narrative hardly ever flags. Many of the scenes are vividly and forcefully realized. The talk is sometimes prosy, in the fashion of the time. But it is often dazzling in its ruthless penetration and percipience.

This is on the whole, however, the most unsavoury of the marquis's works. The reasons are not altogether to be sought in his state of mind at the time of composition. He was determined to make money. Competition was severe. He believed that, if he outdid everyone else in obscenity, he would rise to the head of the army of pornographers in Republican Paris and get away with it by pretending, as Citizen Sade, to be only imitating DAFS, the unspeakable author of *Justine*.

He was simultaneously continuing to besiege the theatre, but in vain. In this field his rivals were men who thought of nothing else, professionals wholly devoted to their public careers as dramatists and much more adroit than this amateur at gauging what audiences would and would not stand in the way of intellectual elevation or 'wickedness.'

At the beginning of the year 1800, when Napoleon Bonaparte had already been elected First Consul, and times were again changing rapidly, de Sade published his first non-pornographic novel, *The Crimes of Love, or, The Delirium of Passion, Historical and Tragic Tales Preceded by a Theory of the Novel.* The work contains eleven stories, each contrasting virtue and vice. One setting is England. Another has the same initial plot and chief character as *Oxtierna,* but an unhappy ending, in which Ernestine is killed in the duel with her father and her lover is executed, while Oxtierna survives and reforms.

The tales are on the whole all either somewhat tedious, and absurd, or else unpleasant, though none of them are definitely obscene. The theme of incest is repeated rather too often. The artificiality of style and sentiment which is the besetting sin, not only of the marquis, but of all authors at any time who are less than the best of their generation, is again and again apparent in this collection.

But the introductory essay on the theory of fiction is excellent. The learned ex-prisoner of the Bastile rapidly surveys the history of the novel from the Greeks to Ann Radcliffe. His moral is that no one should write novels unless they have (*a*) experienced real misfortune or (*b*) travelled extensively, preferably both. He takes this opportunity to deny again, in the strongest terms, that he is the author of *Justine*. He hints, as strongly, that the crude 'realism' of *Juliette* is highly salutary as compared with works by other people —perhaps he was thinking of his enemy Restif de la Bretonne— which showed vice 'wreathed with roses,' conveniently forgetting that he had used similar expressions himself about the raptures of crime. "My desire is," he wrote in this preface, "that vice should be seen naked, should be dreaded and detested, so I show it in all its horror." He was to swear later, when taxed by a hostile journalist, that he had never written an immoral book.

The fact was that the marquis was now turning more and more from pornography and melodrama to politics. His new idea was to save 'democracy' by attacking its most recent tyrant, the Corsican adventurer who was aiming at the crown under the cloak of the republican virtue of ancient Rome.

It was hardly possible, in 1800, to foresee that the First Consul was going to put not only France but half Europe in his pocket. If the marquis, who was nothing if not a man of the world, though also a man of proved courage, had foreseen it, he would probably have thought of some other way of improving his financial position.

As it was, in July of that year an anonymous pamphlet appeared entitled *Zoloe and Her Two Acolytes, or, Certain Decades in the*

Lives of Three Pretty Women. A True Story of the Last Century by a Contemporary. This squib had been printed by de Sade at his own expense, for no publisher would look at it. The names of the characters were hardly disguised and the portraits of them in words were so precise that the originals were painfully obvious. Zoloe was Joséphine de Beauharnais, wife of the First Consul. She had married him while an exceedingly merry widow and had given him more than sufficient grounds for divorce since then. But now that he was on the up-grade she was sticking to him desperately. Laure, Zoloe's friend, was Madame Tallien, who had married the outstanding revolutionary of that name, the successor of Robespierre, in 1794. But Tallien was now in England and his wife was living with a wealthy banker, M. Ouvrard, as one of the uncrowned queens of Parisian society.

The third 'pretty woman,' Voldange, was Madame Visconti, another prominent society lady. Of the men concerned, D'Orsec — an anagram for *'corse,'* the Corsican — was Bonaparte, Sabar was Barras, a prodigious debauchee who had been one of Joséphine's lovers before she married Napoleon, had indeed been partially responsible for arranging the marriage, and was one of the five Directors who controlled the French Republic. Fessinot was Tallien. Barmont was Alexandre de Beauharnais, Joséphine's first husband, guillotined by the Jacobins during the early course of the Revolution.

This piece of politically inspired scurrility is neither very interesting nor very amusing. The orgies are a bore, the characters, except Napoleon's, unconvincing. It is clear that the marquis appreciated the main traits of the Consul's mentality. Probably they were common enough gossip at the time. But, as a whole, the squib misses fire. It was unworthy of the author and could have been composed by any one of a hundred political journalists of the day, if they had had the courage to embark on such a thing.

Bonaparte, very sensitive to this kind of attack at the delicate point in his career which he had now reached, was naturally furious. The author was identified, his publisher bribed to set a trap for him. De Sade was arrested on the office doorstep with a copy of *Justine* under his arm and imprisoned, for the last time, the same day. He was taken to the gaol at Sainte Pélagie. It was the 3rd of March, 1801.

The rising despot, to make sure of his man, had his name re-entered on the 'black list' of *émigrés,* from which it had been erased two years before. This step meant, of course, re-confiscation by the State of all the marquis's assets. The ostensible reason for the detention at Sainte Pélagie was, however, 'pornography and insanity.' Napoleon Bonaparte thus started the legend which has lasted into our own day.

The prisoner still denied the authorship of *Justine.* When confronted with the manuscript he had been carrying at the time of his arrest, he swore he had only copied it from the original of another writer. But the evidence on the other side was too strong for this defence. Paintings illustrative of the text of *Justine* were found in the marquis's bedroom. *Justine and Juliette* had been printed together between the dates 1791, that of Justine's anonymous appearance, and 1797, that of the issue of *Juliette* alone, signed by de Sade with his full name.

The police, therefore, convinced that they had caught a dangerous subverter of morals as well as an opponent of the existing régime, kept a strict eye on their new captive. *Justine,* in spite of its fewer horrors, was always considered worse for the ordinary citizen than *Juliette,* no doubt on account of the implied moral in the earlier tale that one could not avoid degradation simply by being good.

The turnkeys at Sainte Pélagie found that this elderly and distinguished-looking author showed a decided inclination for the society of the younger prisoners in his corridor and insisted haughtily upon conducting obscene conversations with them. He was accordingly transferred to another gaol, at Bicêtre, where such temptations were not so easily come by. Charles Nodier, also a writer of some talent, who had too, like de Sade, been sent to Bicêtre for a skit on Napoleon, once saw the famous little marquis walking along a passage there.

"I only noticed at first," he writes, "his enormous obesity, which prevented the grace and elegance of movement that had evidently at one time been his. His tired eyes still showed occasional traces of fire and intelligence . . . he was obsequiously polite to everyone, affable and conventional in his discourse."

It seems that this vision dates from April 1803, when the marquis was being transferred from Bicêtre to his former place of detention at Charenton. It may, however, have taken place at a slightly earlier period, in the Sainte Pélagie prison. The evidence is contradictory.

The reason for the change to Charenton, which was now being used purely as a lunatic asylum, was that de Sade's relatives preferred him to be known as a madman rather than as a criminal. It is clear from Nodier's testimony, as well as from the tone of the incessant petitions which the marquis addressed, at this time, to the Government, that he was already senile at this date. He was writing nothing but silly letters.

The evidence of Ange Pitou, the royalist singer, confined at Sainte Pélagie between 1802 and 1803, is to the same effect. Pitou, who reminds one now of James Boswell, now of Samuel Smiles, was a maddening optimist, whose idea of consoling the afflicted was to treat them to an exhibition of clownish capers and idiotic grins, coupled with snatches from popular operas, in order to assure them that he, personally, was feeling fine. Nevertheless, the grim pornographer said nothing very terrible to him, as would certainly have been the case in the former's prime.

Bicêtre had been called, under the old régime, a 'Bastille de la canaille,' or, as we might say, a 'thieves' kitchen.' It became, in 1801, a combined gaol and hospital, with no less than three thousand inmates. The emphatic but rambling protests which de Sade made at being considered a suitable member of this community gave colour to the convenient opinion that he was sufficiently out of his mind to be taken to an actual asylum, where his excitement and indignation could be conscientiously regarded as mere raving.

Charenton was a model establishment for its day, far ahead of similar institutions, at that date, in, for instance, England. It was kept scrupulously clean, possessed a good kitchen, a numerous staff, an enormous garden, reasonable heating arrangements, a library, a recreation room well supplied with the apparatus of indoor games and comfortable furniture. De Sade, however, still continued the complaints which had now become second nature with him. No one took the slightest notice of them.

The marquis, as usual, betook himself to the fountain-head. He tackled the Director personally. He found, to his surprise, that this gentleman, a former priest, did not merely regard his post as a more or less convenient way of enriching himself, but actually took an interest, not to say a pride, in his work. He listened with attention to this exceptionally polite lunatic's conversation, steering it unobtrusively away from the subject of release to the question of the amenities provided in the asylum.

A chance remark apprised the Director, whose name was de Coulmier, that his new patient was interested in the theatre and greatly lamented the fact that he was no longer able to attend it. Drawing him out on this topic, de Coulmier discovered that the fellow had written plays himself and could talk learnedly about the art of stage production. The idea, so familiar to modern alienists, of psycho-therapy through organized occupational work, began to form in this exceptionally intelligent Director's mind. At least it would divert these troublesome people from airing their imaginary grievances, he thought.

After some preliminary fencing, both with de Coulmier and the central authorities, a regular theatre was installed at Charenton, with room for an audience of two hundred. A ballroom was also rigged up. De Sade threw himself, with abrupt enthusiasm, in his usual hectoring style, into the organization of both dances and theatrical performances. He bullied the manipulative staff, mercilessly drilled the cast, stood no nonsense from its wilder members, sent for actresses from the smaller theatres of Paris and summoned influential friends from the drawing-rooms of the capital to attend his productions.

Gradually the novelty of witnessing plays performed by lunatics began to attract the fashionable world. The stern master of ceremonies at Charenton started ordering scenery and sending out invitations on his own responsibility. De Coulmier saw no objection. He was delighted with the new docility of his charges and lost no opportunity of emphasizing it in his reports to headquarters. He was so grateful to the marquis for the prestige which Charenton was now acquiring that he even agreed to a private arrangement by which Madame Quesnet, as an ordinary guest, was given permanent accommodation at the asylum, in a room next to her 'father's.'

But trouble, as on every occasion that the marquis's luck began to change, was at hand. On the 22nd of February, 1805, the jovial resident physician of the institution, M. Gastaldy, died of apoplexy. Dr. Royer Collard succeeded him, in spite of the protests of the Director, who represented to the authorities that Charenton now had no need of official doctors. Collard was a pompous, humourless and puritanical old gentleman, a born tyrant and a deeply dyed conservative.

He soon told de Coulmier that he considered the dances and stage-shows all nonsense, if not worse. Moreover, he had got wind of de Sade's previous reputation and objected strongly to his having anything to do with the other patients. He even urged that the marquis should be removed altogether from Charenton. The family were able to get this last proposal negatived. The dispute, however, was prolonged. Collard stood practically alone in his condemnatory attitude. But he managed to get the heart taken out of the business.

De Sade returned to his letter writing. The addresses were divided about equally between his lawyers, his relatives and Government officials. He refused to give up control of his property, badgered the authorities with 'proofs' of his mental competence, public services and general innocence. A personal letter to Napoleon, on the 17th of June, 1808, refers to his son, Louis-Marie, now an Army officer in Spain, complains in dignified fashion of his own ill-health and begs deferentially for final release from his undeserved confinement. Unfortunately, an exceptionally violently worded missive from

Collard to the police on the subject of the marquis followed six weeks later. Hope continued to be deferred.

Collard stuck grimly to his obsession. He wrote almost as many letters to the police as did his victim. De Coulmier, a much more reasonable but also a much weaker character than his doctor, wearied of the endless controversy and began to give in. The result could not now long be in doubt. Yet it was not actually until May 1813, that the cynical Fouché, then acting as Napoleon's deputy for home affairs, at last signed an order forbidding all theatrical performances at Charenton.

The marquis had lost his last battle in this world. He grew apathetic even in his correspondence and took to wandering about alone, in the park attached to the institution. He muttered to himself, uttered empty laughs and curses, would, it is said, pluck roses, bury his face in them for a moment, with ecstasy, then tear them to pieces, soil them and throw them away.

On the 30th of November, 1814, he complained of pains in the chest and became feverish. Dr. Ramon, Collard's deputy, diagnosed asthmatic congestion of the lungs, i.e. what we should now call pneumonia, and held out no hope of his recovery. The second son, Armand, for Louis-Marie had been killed in Spain in 1809, was sent for and remained at his bedside, with Madame Quesnet, for the next two days. The end came on the 2nd of December at ten in the evening. The short but heavy corpse was buried in the cemetery of the asylum. All the manuscripts subsequently found in his bedroom were burned by the police.

In 1806 he had given elaborate instructions, which were all eventually ignored, for the disposal of his body. They read:

"My body shall be kept forty-eight hours in the room I die in, placed in a wooden coffin not to be nailed down till expiration of the forty-eight hours. Meanwhile, a message is to be sent to M. Lenormand, Timber Merchant, 101 Boulevard de l' Egalité, Versailles, asking him to come with a vehicle and take my body to the woods on my property of La Malmaison, Mance, near Epernon, where it is to be placed, without ceremony, in the first thick copse on the right of the said woods, coming from the old castle by the wide avenue which divides the woods. The ditch cut in this copse is to be opened by the Malmaison farmer under M. Lenormand's supervision. The latter will remain present until my body is placed in the said ditch. He may have with him any of my relatives and friends who, without any kind of ceremony, may wish to render me this last proof of attachment. When the ditch has been filled in, acorns shall be sown over it, so that later on the ditch may be wholly covered with earth and the copse as thick as before, while the traces of my grave may disappear from the surface of the earth as, I flatter myself, my memory will become effaced from the minds of men, except those few who have remained devoted to me and whose memory I bear with me, in gratitude, to the tomb."

This half-melancholy, half-scornful, but perfectly sane document, pathetic in its nostalgia for a locality which, perhaps, the marquis had but seldom visited, and in its consciousness of an almost universal hostility, proves that de Sade, eight years before his death at least, still retained his aristocratic dignity. The last sentence is probably not to be read so much as a sign of contrition and repentance for past sins, as in the light of a contemptuous dismissal of the world that had treated him so shabbily and was even to treat him shabbily, in its disregard of this last request, after his death.

He left an annuity to Madame Quesnet, together with all his furniture, books and papers. His estates, by an agreement dating from 1811, were already in the hands of his children, Armand and Laure, for the marquise had died at Echauffour in 1810.

The marquis de Sade was neither a scoundrel nor a madman. He was, to begin with, a typical French aristocrat of the eighteenth century, only differing from the average specimen of his class and time, characterized by a fastidious pride, a reckless gaiety and a thoroughgoing scepticism, in the intensity of his preoccupation with his sexual feelings, a temper not only hotter but more capable of permanent destruction of equanimity than most, and the tireless activity of a mind exceptionally clear, unsentimental and enterprising.

He was forced into lifelong official companionship with a woman he despised at a time when he had just become deeply attached to one he might otherwise have adored for the rest of his life. The fire of resentment thus kindled ate down to the very bottom of his heart, driving him to something like a hatred of the whole human race. His high sexual endowment caused him to exploit this vindictiveness, during the first years of marriage, in a rage of lubricity.

Yet the 'crimes' for which he then began to be persecuted by the police, who were in their turn given no rest by his implacable domestic enemy, Madame de Montreuil, amounted to very little, viewed from the general moral platform of the time. His temper was soured and his grievance rendered permanent by what he regarded as these unjustifiable interferences with his liberty.

When they culminated in long-term imprisonment at Vincennes and in the Bastille his artificial isolation from society led him, as it would lead any man with a mind and a tongue, to rationalize his feelings. He had always been exceptionally articulate, though he was not, strictly speaking, either a born intellectual or a born writer. He was far from possessing a basically contemplative temperament. But he was intensely inquisitive, self-reliant and egotistical. He had the bent towards order and scientific analysis of most educated Frenchmen, together with the fiery imagination and ruthless realism of the typical Provençal.

The rationalization therefore proceeded less on purely philosophic and literary lines, though he used those words often enough in describing himself and his works, than first in classification and secondly in vivid illustration of the human energies which most interested him both by native inclination and owing to the restrictions placed upon them in his own case by his incarceration. Even a cold-blooded man, in such circumstances, will brood upon and exaggerate desires which cannot be satisfied. The hot-blooded marquis externalized, monstrously distorted and wildly magnified them, in a flood of words inspired by purely cerebral excitement.

On his release he played at politics and tried to make money by sensational writings, just as many a far less intelligent man was doing at the time, to counter poverty and friendlessness. But the dissipations of long ago and the privations of more recent date had undermined him both physically and mentally. Already, by 1790, he was not the man he had been in 1778 by a very long way. That road had been haunted by phantoms of despair, assuming the lineaments of monsters of depravity, the representatives of a system of merciless exploitation, which he had persuaded himself intellectually the human race deserved but which he was himself incapable, out of sheer good breeding and the fundamental good nature of most men born to privilege, of attempting to impose upon it.

The psychological story ends with a grotesque ballet. We see the magnificent iconoclast, the lordly apostle of anti-social paradox, the magisterial romanticizer of grandiose crime, the lieutenant of Satan, Moloch and Mammon, slinking about Paris with his obscene manuscripts, dodging policemen, bragging and strutting, a comically obese, bald figure, almost a dwarf, in front of bored Governors, Directors and specialists in lunacy, threatening his pitiful theatrical casts, all more or less insane, grandly receiving, in his threadbare finery, fashionable gossip-mongers in search of a new sensation at a madmen's theatre, writing, by turn, diffuse begging and menacing letters, lecturing Collard and de Coulmier, finally declining into a dishevelled shuffler, a myopic and asthmatic septuagenarian, drifting alone along garden paths; ready, at one moment, to drink in the scent of roses with a feeble parody of his old sensuality, at the next to trample them underfoot with an equally feeble caricature of his old, all-conquering scorn.

Greater men have fallen into worse states at the end of better lives. The marquis de Sade did not lead a 'good' life, nor was he a 'good' man. He was, perhaps, nearly a great one. At any rate he was as unhappy as all great men have always been, whatever they may consider it good for us to suppose bout their struggle with life. Neither an active villain of any consequence, nor a case for the alienist, de Sade was simply a man of enormous sexual energy who had atrocious luck and reacted accordingly. That he incidentally, in the very process of this reaction, gave both serious artists and serious scientists matters for reflection which have changed the face of society and modified human nature itself, while the politicians have been fighting their wars and making their money, is the real reason for taking another look at this ultimately melancholy figure a hundred and thirty-seven years after his lonely and discomfited death, encountered, like that of so many other benefactors of humanity, in circumstances of lamentable poverty, obscurity, humiliation and contempt.

Book II

The Chevalier

Wehe der Nachkommenschaft, die dich verkennt!
J. W. VON GOETHE: *Götz von Berlichingen,* ad fin. 1771.

CHAPTER ONE
Sultanas in the Library

THE fall of Napoleon marks the end of a brilliant social and intellectual era in Europe. People were to be brilliant again, but not in knee-breeches or narrow, gauzy skirts. For the moment the mood was one of sober, not to say melancholy, reaction. Magnificence went out of fashion. An age of industrious, yet mentally rather restricted men and women set in. The European world had had an overdose of glory and wished to put its house in order.

It was now no longer a Frenchman from Corsica, but an Austrian, who dominated the scene and represented the stabilizing forces at work in the continent. Prince Metternich believed himself to be in sympathy with 'liberal' ideas. But he was determined to stamp out 'revolution.' Inevitably, and particularly since his sovereign, the Emperor Francis I of Austria, was a hidebound absolutist, Metternich's system led to repression, not only of violence of action, but also of freedom of thought. With the birth of censorship, political reformers went to prison and those unacknowledged social legislators, the poets, into exile. Art and literature, wit and imagination, began to decay, together with the less refined rebels against the dead level of respectability.

The last great poet who thought and wrote in German, Johann Wolfgang von Goethe, died in 1832, four years before the next German-writer who was to attain European fame, Leopold von Sacher-Masoch, was born. Goethe, too, had been a rebel in his time. But he had made his terms with the changing social conditions of his old age and its new political ideals. He died a calm optimist.

The men of vision, however, who grew up under Prince Metternich, took a different view of the society in which they had to live.

The family of Sacher was of Spanish origin, being descended from a certain Don Mathias Sacher, who had followed the Emperor Charles V to Germany in the sixteenth century, married a Czech lady and settled in Prussia. Some two hundred years later the Sachers moved to Galicia, a district at that time forming the northeast corner of the Austrian Empire, bounded to the north by Poland and to the east by Russia, its southern limits being marked by the Carpathian Mountains.

Leopold Sacher, Chief of Police of Lemberg, the capital city of Galicia, and recently created a Chevalier by the Emperor Francis I, was married to a lady belonging to the ancient and noble Polish family of Masoch. Two years after his son, Leopold, was born he obtained the imperial permission to quarter his wife's arms with his own and to be known in future as Leopold von Sacher-Masoch.

The population in this part of Europe was then and still is one of the most mixed in the world. The basic peasant stock, variously called Ruthenians, Ukrainians or Little Russians, had at this period endured centuries of servitude. It was, consequently, wild and backward to the last degree. It was mingled with Poles and largely exploited by Polish landowners. In the towns Jews predominated. The next most numerous nationalities were Germans, Hungarians and Czechs. Austrians formed the official aristocracy. This kaleidoscopic society of dramatic contrasts, deep-seated rivalries, passionate prejudices and exotic eccentricities was an exciting one to live in, maddening in its chaotic character or fascinating in its complexity, according to taste.

Little Leopold's Polish mother employed a Ruthenian nurse, Handscha, to look after him in his earliest years. This young woman was a typical representative of her race, handsome as a wild animal, fierce and illiterate, but deeply imaginative, a teller of dark and bloody stories, in which the main elements of life appeared to be frenzied eroticism and ruthless cruelty, the primitive foundations of a rich and vigorous, but tragic, folklore.

The boy, however, as soon as he could read, was taught French as well as Polish. The fairy tales of Perrault introduced him to a more tender type of romance and gave his literary talent, which showed itself very early, a second direction. By the time he was eight years old he was already composing highly sentimental and melodramatic accounts of spiritual and material adventures.

He was a dark-haired and lean-faced child, rather tall and thin for his age, with deep, black eyes set far back in a pallid countenance, and a big, straggling mouth. His mother soon noticed that he was nervous and excitable. But there were sturdy traits in his temperament, too. He loved to roam about the countryside, like a hunter, with the toy gun which his father had given him. He rather enjoyed the frequent storms which he encountered there in spring and autumn. He began to form an ultimately enormous collection of tin soldiers, cut out uniforms for them from the illustrations in his books and carefully pasted this paper clothing on to his miniature warriors. In the elaborate wars which he and his brother Karl conducted with these armies he showed an aggressive and subtle intelligence.

At this period, then, little Leopold, whose domestic background was aristocratic and fairly luxurious, had already developed an urgent curiosity about the more mysterious and sinister aspects of this world, so long as they had, too, a certain splendour and an element of fantasy about them.

There was a personage living in the house at Lemberg who seemed to him to incarnate all his ideals of high and dangerous romance. This was his paternal aunt, a certain Countess Zenobia, of Slav extraction and of a commanding personality which is perhaps more common among the women of her race than elsewhere. She was a tall and handsome woman in her middle thirties, with an extravagant taste in dress and a somewhat insignificant husband. Leopold adored her and she was amused by his adoration. She let him fetch and carry for her, help her with her frequent changes of costume and generally dance attendance on her.

On one occasion, when he was adjusting the Countess's slippers for her, he dared to kiss the embroidered leather as he fitted it over her elegant instep.

"Ha! You little devil!"

Zenobia laughed. But she instantly followed the laugh with a vigorous kick in the face. Leopold tumbled at her feet, rubbing his cheek ruefully. But he found that he was even more delighted by the pain than by the snatched kiss. It riveted his attachment to his aunt. Thereafter, she could hardly ever get rid of him.

One afternoon, when she was out, he entered her bedroom and hid himself in the wardrobe, for the pleasure of plunging his face into the scented silks and laces that hung there and embracing the gowns as if they were so many material Zenobias. Suddenly, the door opened. His aunt entered, followed by a strange man, much younger and better-looking than the Count. Leopold, motionless, his eye glued to the keyhole of the wardrobe, held his breath.

Zenobia slipped off her fur mantle, donned a *kazabaika,* an embroidered house-jacket of the kind fashionable at that time and place, and pulled the young man down beside her on a divan. They kissed and caressed each other, the Countess decidedly taking the initiative. Leopold's big mouth fell open and his huge eyes grew rounder and rounder.

But as he watched these familiarities, which were rapidly becoming more and more reckless, the door of the bedroom again opened. The Count entered. For an instant he stood still, petrified with astonishment. Next moment, Zenobia sprang to her feet. She flew at her husband and struck him in the face. He turned and fled. At the same time the lover darted out of the room by another door. Then Leopold, trembling with excitement, accidentally caused the wardrobe to creak. His aunt dashed at his hiding-place, dragged open the door of the closet and, with a shout of fury, hauled him out by the scruff of his neck. In a second she had thrown him, face downwards, on the carpet, knelt on his shoulder and delivered a rain of blows, with her open hand, on his posterior.

The adult Leopold, long afterwards, in giving his wife an account of this affair, added that the pain was terrible, but that it enraptured him. He went on to say that after the receipt of this castigation he made his escape, but returned a few minutes later to listen at the bedroom door. He was then fortunate enough to hear the sounds, first of an altercation between husband and wife, then of a thrashing administered by the latter to the former with a whip, which seems to have been, very conveniently, lying about somewhere in the room.

It is more than probable that the mature Leopold allowed his luxuriant imagination full play in this lurid narrative. He considered, at the time, that his wife needed education in these matters. No doubt there was really some foundation for the tale. He may have spied on his aunt and caught her with a lover. The Count may well have been somewhat feeble-minded or worse, about his formidable consort's adventures. But the details, as Leopold subsequently passed them on, for his own purposes, are almost certainly invented. Even in Lemberg in 1845 a woman of the world, living with her husband in the house of a near relative, full of servants and children, would scarcely use the conjugal bedchamber as a place of assignation, even if she were in the habit of thrashing her husband in it. To believe Leopold in full, one has to assume that Zenobia must have been so utterly reckless in her pursuit of perverse pleasures as to be quite out of her mind. The deliberate staging of an adultery behind unlocked doors in the circumstances described would be merely insane, whatever the motive. And we do not hear that Zenobia was afterwards taken to an asylum.

But there need be no doubt of the Countess's existence, of her imperial appearance or of her tyrannical disposition. These phenomena set Leopold's feverish imagination aglow, before the age of puberty, with a fire that was never to leave the depths of his mind and that was destined, towards the end of his life, to blaze upwards with catastrophic effect.

It was probably in the year after this episode that the Polish landowners of Galicia rose in revolt against the Austrian Government. The conspiracy of February 1846 was directed from Cracow. The

Galician Poles were exiles from their own country. But nationalist sentiment had been exasperated by the abortive revolution of 1830, in Poland itself, against Russia. Austrian rule, though less oppressive than Russian, was not sympathetic to its subject minorities. The women, as usual in Slav countries, were to the fore in this plot. A feature of it was the fantastic plan for the strangling of their Austrian dancing partners at a great military ball in Lemberg. Wires were to be fitted to the necks of the officers as an incident in a sort of allegorical masque, then applied in grim earnest.

Unfortunately for this appalling scheme, a day or two before the date of the ball one of the Hapsburg family died, the Austrian Court went into mourning and the officers were forbidden to attend social functions.

Nevertheless, the revolt was duly inaugurated. The Polish nobles of the countryside mustered their retainers and began to move against the capital. In Lemberg itself shooting began in the streets and barricades went up. Leopold von Sacher-Masoch, the Chief of Police, had his hands full. His house was fortified and his family forbidden to go out.

But now the Polish peasants, less interested than their masters in national autonomy and quick to seize the chance for revenge, with Government approval, on their hated compatriots, to say nothing of the sudden widespread opportunities for plunder, attacked the half-deserted castles and manor houses, ambushed isolated bodies of the revolutionaries and, assisted by the barbarous Ruthenian shepherds and other lawless persons, began to inflict upon the rebels those indiscriminate massacres, hangings, burnings, burials alive and other indescribable tortures which have always marked a proletarian revolution.

When the Austrian regular troops at last arrived, there was little left for them to do but to crush the rebellion as ruthlessly as it had been planned. In a few weeks it was all over. But the stories of atrocities remained in circulation for a long time in Lemberg. Little Leopold missed few of them. He became an avid listener, a fascinated reader of the crude novelettes that now began to be published on this subject, a spellbound gazer upon their cruder illustrations.

He had not yet done with experience of the details of popular disturbances. In 1848, the year of revolutions all over Europe, his father was transferred to Prague, the scene of one of the bloodiest. The son used to tell his friends, in after life, that he had been out on the barricades, as a boy of twelve, with a girl cousin named Miroslava, some years older than himself. She wore a beautiful fur jacket, he would say, and carried pistols in her belt. She ordered him about, shouted commands, he hastened to obey. Amid these scenes of death and destruction he conceived a passionate adoration of her.

He may have, like other adventurous little boys, roamed the dangerous streets in those days. It is also true that women, from both the official and revolutionary sides, took part in the fighting and he must have admired their martial glory. As for the more intimate details, they may or may not have been wishful thinking. At any rate, it seems certain that he was given a puppet theatre as a present at that time, in which he was in the habit of representing plays of his own composition about the Galician and Czech revolts.

Leopold's lifelong passion for the stage, in which trait he resembles the Marquis de Sade, dates from this epoch. He now read not only Molière and Scribe and Gogol in their original tongues, but also Schiller and Goethe, for he was at last learning German, the language in which he was to make his literary reputation.

People with strong and wayward personal emotions nearly always become devoted to the theatre, where clashes of character move more swiftly to more exciting climaxes than they normally do in real life. In general, though the exceptions are obvious enough, the primarily philosophic or intellectual artist is contemptuous of or at least indifferent to the glamour of the footlights. The keener vision of such temperaments discovers the colour and fire of life in more abstract media. But the specifically romantic genius, that of a de Sade and a Sacher-Masoch as well as that of names of less equivocal repute, soon finds that life as it is generally lived is a miserably poor relation of that revealed by the raised curtain of any sort of a theatre.

Leopold went to school in Prague and, unlike many boys, including the Marquis de Sade, who subsequently attain literary eminence, he was given excellent reports, which were rewarded by permission to stage private theatricals at home. The subject set for the school leaving certificate was 'The Influence of Music on Human Character.' Leopold may have wished that 'the Theatre' had been substituted for 'Music.' But the essay he wrote, said the headmaster, in awarding him the prize, might have been signed by a first-rate professional writer rather than a schoolboy of sixteen.

His father, however, like so many fathers of brilliant sons in those days of political reform, wished him to study law in preference to the arts of literature and the drama. Leopold obeyed without much reluctance. He felt, in the first flush of his youthful intellectual arrogance, that he could take this or any other technical discipline in his stride, and still devote his deepest instincts to a less prosaic subject.

At seventeen he was already in love with an actress, a Czech named Kolar, of whom he characteristically wrote, at a later date:

> "She was a woman of the typical Slav sort, with nerves of steel. She could kill the man she hated and turn him who loved her into her slave. She always played dominating parts, Tsarinas and Sultanas, and wore their magnificent, gold-embroidered furs. She was the Omphale and the Semiramis of the Slav world."

He got to know this 'empress' by writing to enquire whether she would allow one of her female pupils to take a part in one of Goethe's plays, which he was staging at home. Kolar was gracious and helpful, but only professionally. Her sexual interests did not include boys of seventeen, however gifted and charming.

The death, at this juncture, of Leopold's fifteen-year-old sister, Rosa, affected him deeply, really turned him, he said later, into a serious student and writer. His impulsive and passionate temperament drove him, on this occasion, into the very depths of ordinary human sorrow. He was to show as infinite a capacity for utter absorption in simple enjoyment, as well as in emotions upon which most of his friends looked with sheer amazement.

In 1852 he began his study of law at the University of Prague. The following year the Chief of Police was transferred to Graz, in the district of Styria, to the south of Austria. Leopold pursued his studies at the university in that city to such purpose that by 1855, when he was still only nineteen, he was granted the degree of Doctor of Laws. By the following year he was lecturing on German history in the university. His appearance at this period is described by a contemporary as follows:

"A slender and graceful young man of very boyish aspect and a certain frank simplicity of behaviour, he showed no trace of presumption or pretentiousness. He had an extremely intelligent face, wonderfully beautiful eyes, dark hair, a pale complexion and was rather careless in his dress."

Another who knew him then writes:

"The main trait of his character was a certain cheerful sensuality. He was extremely indulgent to other people's failings, generous and good-humoured to a fault. He seemed to think of nothing but study and work, except when playing with his paper-uniformed soldiers, a game which occupied him for hours at a time and often led him, in his enthusiasm for it, to turn the whole house upside down."

The preoccupation with tin soldiers was a reflection of the young historian's professional studies, which he took very seriously. The attempts of the Emperor Charles V to unify Europe interested him particularly, not only as a political philosopher but also on account of the connection of his ancestor, Don Mathias Sacher, with that sovereign. He went to Vienna to consult the Court and National Libraries for evidence as to Charles's career. He found some new material there.

In 1857 appeared the first work by Leopold von Sacher-Masoch, entitled *The Rebellion in Ghent under Charles V.* The author, armed with his fresh data, had challenged current ideas on the subject of this revolt and wrote in a brilliant, antithetical style more suited, perhaps, to fiction than to scholarship. Amateur critics compared him with Macaulay. But his academic colleagues were either grimly silent or briefly contemptuous.

It was known that Leopold was only twenty-one, had a passion for the stage and some wild ideas about universal freedom for everyone, such as all young men with brains have entertained at one time or another. Nor did the experts, few of whom ever condescended to read novels, approve of the way in which their junior used the German language. The authorities, in general, decided to ignore him.

The acclamation of less exalted circles was encouraging. But Leopold came to the conclusion that he had better give up the ungrateful task of putting life into the dry bones of history. His colleagues seemed to like it dry. For one of their complaints was that in his work the "apparatus" of erudition was missing. He decided to devote his talents, in future, to more purely imaginative productions.

He looked back, for the setting, first to the days of his childhood in Lemberg, to the tales of Handscha and to the strange inhabitants, Jews, Slavs or mixtures of the two, of the Galician countryside.

Galicians, even today, are some of the most extraordinary people to be found in Europe. The records of philosophy and of art, of the worlds of learning, commerce, politics, picturesque adventure, social intrigue and cosmopolitan swindling are full of their famous or infamous names. Yet almost all of these well-known contributors to human history began life in abject poverty, with every conceivable disadvantage. Few of those who regularly refer to them are aware of their origin. For in the majority of cases the Galician destined to get into the newspapers is a citizen of the world, unidentifiable with any particular corner of Europe, by the time he is twenty.

Leopold had the born novelist's flair for the unexpected personality. He delved deeply into the reasons why a Ruthenian shepherd should be, in his normal life, a pattern of ancient Roman stoicism, without ever having heard of Cato or Seneca, while ready, at a moment's notice and often incomprehensibly, to assume the character of a repulsive and terrifying demon.

He found, in the first place, that there were as many religious sects in Galicia as in England, but that they were all very much stranger in their practices and beliefs. There were the Doukhobors, a kind of Quakers, who rejected all man-made laws and positively enjoyed martyrdom; the Skoptsi, who regularly castrated themselves; the Jewish sect of the Karaits, who despised other Jews on philological grounds; Mennonites, who resembled Plymouth Brethren; Armenians, Greek Orthodox believers, Protestants, Catholics and above all swarms of strictly conservative Jews, whose lives involved an endless series of ceremonies and tabus, mostly of a very gloomy description.

All these sects went in for the defiance of conventional secular law and order in one way or another and were consequently much exposed to Government persecution, which, as usual, merely intensified their peculiarities and their stubbornness. Some of the underground offshoots had their definitely sinister side, which profoundly fascinated Leopold. There were, for instance, the 'soul-takers,' who sacrificed other human beings in order to 'save' their souls.

Their agents were often women. For the female Galician, like the female Pole, is liable to exceed the male in unscrupulous daring, subtle dissembling and merciless bullying. Galician folklore accounts for this unusual state of affairs by representing that God sent the human spirit to their country in the form of a bee. All the women rushed at it and took its spirit away. Nothing was left for the men.

Leopold assures us that he knows of cases in which a young, rich and extremely elegant lady, belonging to the sect of 'soul-takers,' has suddenly arrived, alone, in a large town, and caused a great sensation by her attractions and eccentricities, though refusing to allow her numerous admirers any intimacy. Then she, just as suddenly, disappears. After a time, one of the men who have paid court to her receives a note inviting him to visit her in a distant part of the country. On arrival, he is seized, imprisoned, tortured and preached at until he begs for death. In her presence, to the sound of hymns, he is subjected to slow torments which only end with his life.

Such tales, such characters, such existences seemed to the young historian, in their mixture of sentimentality, extreme intelligence and atrocious barbarity, inexhaustibly suggestive of the real nature of that intimidating cross-section of the human soul which, as a novelist and a Slav, he was bound to consider the most absorbing mystery on earth.

His study of it was prolonged. It was not until the middle 'sixties that he began to use this material for pure fiction. Until then it was mingled with history, as in *Count Donski* (1859), dealing with the Polish revolution in Galicia in 1846, and *The Emissary* (1860), concerned with the Viennese insurrection of 1848 as a setting for a character resembling his aunt Zenobia. He achieved a certain reputation with these works, but still only among a comparatively small set of youngish people.

By 1860 Leopold had given up his post at the University of Graz and was devoting himself, professionally, to literature alone. Socially, both his father's position and his own charm and literary prestige allowed him to enjoy the best that Graz had to offer. This included romantic young ladies. But Leopold could not find one to suit him. If they were not either stupid, insipid or abjectly sentimental, they seemed to have no time for him. The nearest to the 'sultana' type appeared to prefer older men or at any rate young men more dashing, frivolous or conventionally handsome than Leopold was.

It was rather disappointing. But literature, definitely, was not. Here one could invent one's own ideals, hard-headed but passionate noblewomen, used to authority and fond of it to excess, who stopped at nothing to satisfy their lust for dominion and symbolized it by never leaving off their furs and always having a dog-whip, a horse-whip or a knout within easy reach. He had pictorial representations of such super-females, one in Polish national costume, with her cat-o'-nine-tails, and one, colossally nude under her furs, with a horse-whip, stamped on his notepaper.

The main lines of Leopold's character were now, in his early twenties, laid down for good. It only remained for them to develop. His basically Slav mentality had committed him to a fierce idealism, with a great capacity for devotion and self-sacrifice. He was also fundamentally an artist rather than a man of action and it therefore came natural to him to personify his abstract ideal as a woman, a repository of love, rather than as a man, a model to imitate in fighting for the satisfaction of his desire.

But the strain of oriental savagery in the Slav could not be content with a madonna, an image symbolizing only maternal calm and refuge. The mother-figure had to be such as to command respect by inspiring a primitive emotion, that of fear. The virago, the termagant, the Valkyrie, the stormy cloud-rider, not the heavenly, philosophic resident above the clouds, no Beatrice, but a Brünnhilde, must be the only effective commander of this kind of poet, who is at his best, not in the contemplative tranquillity of recollection, but in a fine frenzy.

It was but a step from this general intellectual and artistic outlook to the particular concrete wish for humiliation in love. It was but a step from that wish to one for the physical stimulus of pain as the indispensable preliminary to pleasure.

As has already been suggested, Leopold was not the first man in human history to feel in this way. The exquisite delight of helplessness in sexual passion had been known from the earliest dawn of civilization and perhaps before the dawn. Physical discomfort had been found to provoke lust even more powerfully than physical well-being, which always had a tendency to loss of energy. But it must be emphasized that Leopold, unlike the sybarites of all times and places, was driven by an impulse at bottom spiritual, not carnal. The typical hedonist inevitably comes to be a sceptic, if not a thoroughgoing cynic. Leopold's mind instinctively rejected both the indifferent and the scornful attitude to life. He remained all his days an enthusiast, a builder of utopias.

The obverse of the medal, his shy reserves, his gentle simplicities, his intuitive understanding of children and animals and his sympathy with and generosity towards all sorts and conditions of men, but especially the unhappy, his entire lack of prejudice and arrogance, all prove the same point. Such traits are not characteristic of the mere sensualist, an irretrievable egotist by definition. Leopold von Sacher-Masoch was never a debauchee, either deliberate or unconscious. He was a lover of humanity and therefore one of its predestined victims.

CHAPTER TWO

Anna von Kottowitz

THE social circles in which Leopold moved at Graz, in 1861, comprised official and diplomatic families, those which surrounded the University and the rather less formal world of literature and journalism. The members of the latter, if they knew how to behave themselves decently on occasion, had a certain prestige among at least the feminine members of the first two. It was a poetical age. That is to say, it was a time in which poets, writers and artists generally had considerable influence in society. They were mostly detested by male careerists in business and politics, who considered them irrelevant nuisances. They were patronized, however, though with strict reservations, by the learned. And women, with a good deal less reserve, often found them an agreeable change from their conventional husbands and fathers. In Central Europe, in the 'sixties, a young man with creative talent might be quite lionized, if he had good manners and were not too particular.

Leopold had not the kind of good looks or the type of disposition which appeal to the average young woman. His appearance was not virile and he was fundamentally shy, though he could be very charming if he liked. But he had a graceful figure, an intensely serious way of using his eyes and could tell the most extraordinary stories, full of blood-curdling episodes, about love affairs in remote places and times. There were ladies, usually some years married, who thought him much more attractive than cavalry subalterns.

Among these feminine moths was the wife of a certain Gustav von Kottowitz, a doctor of medicine who used his profession chiefly as a means to erotic adventure. The other conspicuous traits in his character were hypocrisy, cupidity and cowardice. He was, in short, a smooth scoundrel, but not very dangerous to people who had their heads screwed on the right way. That of his wife, Anna, was, unfortunately for herself, a little loose.

She was in her middle thirties, and the mother of two young children, when Leopold, then twenty-five, was presented to her. But Anna, as became the wife of a connoisseur, looked more like an odalisque than a matron. Her languorous and opulent beauty, always expensively dressed, for her tastes were extravagant to a degree, seemed perfectly designed for entirely straightforward love-making and for nothing else. Anna took full advantage of this happy circumstance and the doctor had no objection. For he knew that if it came to a show-down she could reproach him, to say the least of it, with far more scandalous infidelities than her own.

Anna's psychology was as simple as her beauty. She had little personality or will-power, was good-natured and sentimental, sporadically prudish, fundamentally lascivious and greedy, but too timid and unenterprising to impose her appetites in difficult circumstances. She was really crassly selfish, but loved to pose as the helpless victim of others, especially of her husband. The mentality, in fact, of this magnificently seductive animal hardly existed.

But Leopold only saw the magnificence. He was twenty-five, he had only just managed to get rid of a dull cousin whom his parents wanted him to marry, he was bored to death with designing young girls and their fulsomely hypocritical mothers, he had never met anyone so like the sultana of his dreams as Anna. This splendid maturity, he felt sure, was the one inspiration he needed to release the confused ideas that were surging within him, of a life that should be to the life he saw around him as a fine orchid to a coarse weed.

Anna, for her part, understood vaguely from friends as frivolous as herself, that this rather effeminate-looking young man with the deep, dark eyes was the son of wealthy and important parents and received large sums of money for the articles he wrote in the newspapers. Fluttering her long lashes at him, she made the flattering and characteristically banal remark that he seemed to be the candle round which every silly moth, like herself, came to singe its wings.

He shook his dark head vigorously.

"No, no, gracious lady. And if it ever were the case, it is altered now. It is you who are the candle, I the poor moth."

His vibrant tone, his intent eyes made the empty phrase ring like a solemn bell. Leopold's command of the vocal resources of rhetoric had already begun to be remarkable. He was a born actor in the sense that his lightest word always seemed to mean something more than was immediately apparent. Later in life he was to become a supreme master of the art of verbal persuasion. He could not so much argue anyone out of anything as bewitch them out of it. But the early exhibition of his powers, as time went on, proved quite enough for the already half-won Anna.

She confided to him, at subsequent conversations, that her marriage had been a disastrous mistake and that now she had nothing more to look forward to in life but the probably vain hope of meeting a friend who would 'understand' her. This hackneyed gambit was eagerly accepted by her new acquaintance. He was by nature warmly sympathetic with other peoples' troubles. And now he was spurred by the belief that he was on the threshold of a dazzling experience.

Anna was so impressed by his patience and devotion that she allowed him to be seen with her in public rather more than would be normally prudent. He also became a constant visitor at her house and made the acquaintance of the equivocal doctor. The two men appeared to get on well together. But Anna now meant business. She did not wish, this time, to have the usual brief affair with a man so much younger than herself, who would soon tire of her. She intended to take him, and his financial resources and prospects, as a permanent stand-by, even if it led, ultimately, to divorce.

As a preliminary, she told Leopold on one occasion that Gustav was beginning to be 'jealous.' He appeared so delighted with this entirely imaginary information and so ready to accept its implications, that she ventured to follow it up, a few days later, with a further invention.

"Gustav told me yesterday that you are not to come to the house any more."

He frowned, then laughed.

"What nonsense! I shall ask him what on earth he means by such an absurdity."

Anna looked uncomfortable. She had expected a less vigorous, a more tenderly protective reaction, from this peculiar young man. But, on reflection, she concluded that the die was now cast. She remained confident in her ability, since Leopold really seemed so fond of her, to wriggle out of the lie somehow, if it should ever be discovered.

Nevertheless, she made a half-hearted attempt to dissuade him.

"Oh, don't do that, my dear friend. It's not worth while. We can meet elsewhere —— "

"Oh, but I shall certainly ask him for an explanation —— "

"Well, if you insist. But —— "

He changed the subject and paid her a smiling compliment. She was too lazy and too pleased with the more familiar turn of the conversation to protest.

The letter in which Dr. von Kottowitz replied to his young friend's astonished enquiry reads as follows. It is dated the 16th of October, 1862.

"I have never forbidden you to come to my house and so there is no question of my having insulted you. I should, however, be glad to have a talk with you, with a view to clarifying the position as it affects my private family life, in a perfectly friendly way. I should prefer the interview, since it concerns my private interests, to take place without witnesses and I am rather surprised that you should wish it otherwise. If my wife really told you in public that I had forbidden you the house she must take the consequences."

The doctor's attitude is clear behind the carefully chosen phrases of this letter. As was usual with him, his view was subtle, ignoble and anxious about the main chance. His idea was to blackmail both Leopold and his wife 'in a perfectly friendly way,' without open scandal.

It is not quite certain whether the verbal interview took place. But evidently the matter was further discussed between them, either by word of mouth or by correspondence, for the husband writes again about a month later, in the same sense but now dexterously assuming, what was probably not yet the case, that adultery had already taken place.

"I will say no more about the past, which has already been sufficiently discussed, except that you have been misled as to my feeling for my wife and that as a result of this error your own feelings reached the height which you now represent as unconquerable and that you then used your friendship with my wife to inflame her interest in you to the point of passion. It is no use now crying over spilt milk, but at least the consequences of what has taken place, the unspeakably disastrous future, we must make some effort to ameliorate . . . is it not worth while trying, for all our sakes, to see whether it is still not possible for us all three, from now on, to regard that fateful episode calmly and be content with the new relationship that now subsists between us?"

He ended with the impudent suggestion, which cannot have been meant seriously and was probably only put in as a prop to his tearful pose of an innocent, loving and injured partner, that Leopold should take himself off abroad for a time. It is obvious enough that the doctor's real object was a three-cornered *ménage* in which he, like any other bully, would hold the whip-hand.

Leopold had other ideas about whips. He answered brusquely, in the highest of spirits, by challenging Dr. von Kottowitz to a duel. Fond as the former was of being terrified by the opposite sex, he was never afraid of men.

The doctor, however, as he explained at great length in his reply, was not a fighting man. He declined, in so many words, to meet his opponent.

Even Anna could not stand this pusillanimity. She agreed to abandon her unworthy husband, and incidentally her unfortunate children, to go and live with Leopold. The latter, completely enslaved by his new mistress, took a house for her and settled down to some of the hardest professional work of his career in order to find the money to lavish on her extravagant tastes.

At first he enjoyed himself immensely. Editors were accessible and generous. They were delighted with the stories of theatrical life, published as a collection in 1863 under the title of *Imitation Ermine,* which he wrote at this time. Anna, moreover, had a full share of the love of teasing natural to her type. When she found that nothing pleased her lover better, she was quite ready, out of pure malice, to go to extremes. Whips and birches came into play. Real torture was discussed at exhaustive length, if not practised. She even, one day, proposed beheading him. It was decided that nothing could be more satisfactory, if it were not for the inconvenient after-effects of this operation.

Leopold was careless about money himself. But after a time he began to find his mistress's expenditure on luxuries which had nothing to do with his fetish — sweets and other feminine fripperies were just as interesting to her as furs — absurd and embarrassing. He delicately and tenderly hinted at this opinion. She flew into a rather vulgar fit of temper.

He was delighted with this exhibition of fury, the first genuine 'sultana' mood he had seen in her. After this, he took to deliberately provoking such tempests and subsequently cowering under them. One day, beside herself with exasperation, she let fly at him with her open hand, hitting him a really hard blow in the face.

Leopold staggered, grimacing. At once she fell on her knees beside him, terrified herself, and begged his pardon.

"No, Anna. Don't apologize. I like it. Do it again."

She stared at his grinning features, dumbfounded. But he knew, by this time, how to rouse her again.

"Tell me, Anna. How much did you pay for that hideous antimacassar you bought at Biedermeyer's?"

She got to her feet, gasping with anger.

"You mean swine —— "

He made a half-hearted attempt to get hold of her wrist. She shook herself free, hit him again, then kicked him. He staged a mock wrestling-match with her, forcing himself to hurt her just enough to disengage a blindly spiteful and violent retaliation. The fight ended, when the scratches and bruises had sufficiently stimulated him, in an erotic embrace.

The lovers now began to understand each other better. Anna, for her part, had no objection to knocking Leopold about pretty regularly, if the pain and humiliation she inflicted upon him resulted in more and more triumphant shopping expeditions. Her natural pettiness of mind rather enjoyed the frequent opportunities he gave her of persecuting him physically. Moreover, her by no means dormant senses were being aroused by the extremely virile character which Leopold was then able to give to the sexual intercourse which invariably followed these scenes.

She began to take an interest in tales of debauchery. On one occasion, after a reading of *Manon Lescaut,* a copy of which Leopold lent her, she declared that she saw no reason why a woman of spirit should not take up harlotry as a profession. Leopold, who was writing a great deal, for money, at this period, showed her some of his more lurid compositions. She seemed greatly taken with the passages dealing with erotic behaviour.

But the young man had now come to see that his Anna, splendid creature though she was, could never be a real 'sultana.' She lacked the true arrogance, the aristocratic touch. Her tantrums could be matched by any fishwife. Her sensuality was coarse, her insolence mere nagging. But he found a new pleasure in the realization that his beautiful 'panther' was a crude gold-digger, with no more moral sense than a barnyard fowl. The shock of finding that he had tied himself to a common trollop excited him enormously, gave him the thrill of a martyr.

He told Anna that he would be frightfully jealous if she were ever unfaithful to him but added that he did not see how he could stop her being so if she wished to be. At first she answered, in conventional terms, that the very idea horrified her. The irresistibly persuasive eloquence with which he then overwhelmed her, full of dazzling intimations of the ennobling effects of moral freedom, and of moral suffering, and of the intellectual refinements with which a true passion could be most worthily exalted, went right over Anna's handsome head. But she gathered that she would have nothing concrete to fear from him if she threw her bonnet over the windmill.

Anna was not the woman to resist temptation if she were not to be seriously punished for yielding to it. She was pretty sure, in any case, now, of the permanence of her sexual power over her lover. She felt instinctively that he would always come back to heel, whatever happened. She pretended to be only teasing when she told him, at last, that she fully intended to 'betray' him one day. But Leopold saw the gleam of concupiscence in her fine eyes and was satisfied. He began to look round for possible 'deceivers.'

The Governor of Graz himself, the Archduke Heinrich, had an eye for a pretty woman. Leopold contrived that he should notice Anna. The great man was distinctly interested. He made discreet enquiries, however, before committing himself. Someone who knew Leopold well informed the Archduke that Anna's 'protector' would be only too delighted if his mistress were seduced by the local crossing-sweeper, let alone a Hapsburg. Heinrich did not care for this aspect of the matter. With regret, he let it be known that his affections were definitely engaged elsewhere.

Leopold shrugged his shoulders. It would have been agreeable to land an Archduke as a cuckoo in the nest. But after all, it was not the rank of the interloper that mattered. It was the simple fact of the seduction that was the important thing. Others would not be so particular as to the terms on which they enjoyed the favours of so outstanding a local beauty.

Graz was full of Polish *émigrés* at this period. Some were genuine members of the expropriated nobility, honest and unlucky patriots victimized by their Russian overlords. But, as their romantic situation excited a good deal of sympathy on the part of the Austrian inhabitants of Graz, both charming ladies and influential gentlemen, a very large number of entirely bogus 'Polish counts,' with fantastic titles, had sprung up in the city to batten upon the bounty of bright eyes and full purses.

Among these was a certain 'Count Meciszevski,' who seemed to Leopold ideal for the private business in view, except that he had, for a Pole, a rather mean and unromantic appearance. He made up for this disadvantage, however, by a very persuasive tongue, which aroused Leopold's professional admiration, and an exceedingly amorous disposition which, according to his own account, had won many remarkable prizes. Leopold thought him worth bringing home to dinner and introducing to Anna, who appeared to be greatly attracted by him, while he, in his turn, ogled her all the evening.

Leopold hoped that events would now take the course he so much desired. But the Pole, when next they met, confided to his new friend, for whose literary, social and financial eminence he professed the profoundest respect, that he was a bit pressed for money. His sacrifices for the fatherland, he went on, with a manly tear or two, had practically ruined him, so that he was quite unable to take his rightful place in society.

The novelist nodded sympathetically. He understood, perfectly correctly, what the other meant. The 'Count' simply hadn't got the wherewithal to make a start with the obviously expensive Anna. The 'protector' determined that it would be well worth while to finance him, for a short time anyhow. He enquired tactfully what the other's business plans were. Meciszevski, to whom this kind of talk was child's play, instantly rattled off the details of a magnificent scheme which would make both their fortunes in a few weeks if only the capital could be found. Leopold, in the end, consented to lend him a considerable sum, half of the amount indicated by the Pole as essential initial expenses.

A few days later Anna confessed, with a great show of contrition, that the 'Count' had become her lover. Leopold appeared thunderstruck. He gazed at her with such an appalled expression in his great dark eyes, turned so white in the face, that she was quite frightened.

He questioned her in a low, dismayed tone as to the details of the event. He had to dig them out of her at first. When they began to come through, his eyes brightened. At last his insistence became quite lively.

Anna saw that it would be to her advantage to invent some lacerating features of what had been in fact a somewhat commonplace affair. She warmed to the task and soon had him kissing and embracing her in an ecstasy of erotic horror, revelling in the idea of a degradation which he now quite forgot he had been the first to inaugurate.

This was all very well. But some six weeks later an unpleasant discovery was made. Anna was found to be suffering from syphilis, at that time an incurable disease. Leopold could not ignore this. First, in a panic, he packed her off to a hospital. Then, after ascertaining that he himself seemed to have escaped infection, he sent a challenge to the 'Count.'

Meciszevski, after expressing his horror at the event and disclaiming all responsibility for it, replied that he could not dream of fighting his 'dear benefactor.' In any case, he added, more naively than Dr. von Kottowitz had explained in similar circumstances, he had a weak heart which precluded him from indulging in such military excitements.

This was scarcely the answer of a 'Polish nobleman.' Leopold began to suspect the social credentials of his 'betrayer.' As son of the Chief of Police, he had easy access to their records. After a prolonged search he came across the description of a 'wanted' man which appeared to conform in every detail with Meciszevski's person and circumstances. The document supplemented this information with the statement that the man in question was known to be a Russian by birth, by trade an assistant in a chemist's shop on the Russo-Polish border. He had robbed his master's till and escaped abroad some months ago.

The impostor was duly laid by the heels, on Leopold's directions, and repatriated to his native land to stand his trial for theft. Meanwhile Anna was recovering for the time being and Leopold found to his relief that no trace of her disease could be identified in his own body. But their association was now obviously at an end. He took leave of her with a regret which seems to have been perfectly sincere. After all, he was still very young, not yet thirty, and the liaison had lasted four years.

He idealized her in later life. He would often describe her superb beauty and 'strange charm' to his friends and lament the 'treacherous betrayal' of this, his first and deepest love. It is quite certain that he enjoyed talking and writing like this. Leopold's truth was always rather poetic than factual. The trait makes his diary, which began to be published in 1869, an extremely unreliable source for the details of his biography, though an infallible guide to his psychology.

The importance of the affair with Anna von Kottowitz lies less in the indubitable fact that he genuinely loved her or in the probability that she was the first woman whom he thus genuinely loved, than in the peculiar circumstances of their life together. Those circumstances involved the first full-scale practice of what the Herr Doktor Freiherr von Krafft-Ebing, who was even then beginning his researches into systematized delusional insanity, eventually decided to call 'masochism,' after reading the accounts of Leopold's career sent to him by well- or ill-meaning friends.

The term has stuck and is perhaps a more convenient one than the more scientific 'algolagnia.' But it is a typical piece of misfortune for Leopold's memory that his name is now connected, not with a particular type of prose narrative or a particular type of social philosophy, in both of which fields he excelled, but with a kind of sexual reaction which was current long before he or any other Christian European was ever heard of and will be current so long as the human race continues to people the earth.

If Anna had lived up to her physique and been as much of a queen mentally as she was materially, if she had been intelligent and generous enough, and as appreciative of Leopold's great gifts, as she was of his money and prestige, Dr. Krafft-Ebing might never have heard of 'masochism' and Leopold von Sacher-Masoch might have lived, like many another distinguished man, his peculiar sex life without having it flourished in his face by his enemies or by those too stupid to understand him, while he still remained alive.

Genuine artists are nearly always unusual sexually, if only by having perhaps more exalted ideas of the function of sex in inspiration than other people. Those who live in a sexual relation with the creators of visions bear a heavy responsibility, if we take the view that there is not yet enough beauty in the world. Such junior partners must not suppose that what is sauce for the normal is also sauce for the exceptional being. Above all, they must be a little less selfish than the average lover.

Leopold, like other passionate and intelligent men, was born to suffer more than the cold-blooded and the bone-headed. He of all men knew well enough that pain is the mother of great production. But there is a point at which pain becomes sheer destruction. He was to reach it before he died, though not for very many years after he had said good-bye to Anna. But if he had never had to say good-bye to her he would probably never have been annihilated, in his lifetime, as a man of genius.

During the years of this first experiment in close and prolonged association with a woman Leopold's character matured. He became more articulate, more certain of what he wanted from life and of what he wanted to give it. But his mind did not change. It only deepened and, so to speak, flourished. Anna had not really satisfied him. Leopold was no more to be satisfied than any other idealist. It was on the crucial psychological side that she failed him. She only looked like, did not actually think or feel like, a 'sultana.'

But for this very reason, as has already been suggested, she hardened and exasperated his obsession. To be so near and yet so far from his aim acted like a violent spur to both his physical and to his moral desires. This situation also accelerated his intellectual and creative ambitions.

It had been necessary to do a lot of hard writing in order to keep Anna in the material luxury to which, with his entire approval in reality, she was so intensely addicted. Apart from ephemeral journalism which, as usual, paid best, he wrote, during this period, as well as the tales of theatrical life already mentioned, a solid historical study, *Hungary's Decline,* giving an unorthodox version of the events leading up to and proceeding from the disastrous defeat of King Louis of Hungary by the Turks at the battle of Mohacs (1526). Leopold's idea was that the King's 'sultana-like' wife, Maria of Austria, played, in the interests of her native country, a much more conspicuous part in the history of her adopted one, during those years, than has usually been allowed.

The acknowledged experts frowned, as they had frowned in 1851, over the *Rebellion in Ghent.*

Nevertheless, this was the first really lively German writing since Goethe. The characters struggled, not only against their own environment, which had been the rule in the novels of the last thirty years, but with their own inmost selves, seen, it is true, largely as the result of their surroundings. He was writing, at the same time, in other stories, of what he knew at first hand, both the settings and the inner conflicts. They had a vivid realism, therefore. And in the Galician tales, particularly, a strangeness that differentiated them altogether from the conventional narratives of the day.

Readers were astonished by the fierce energy of his Slav heroines, for few of them had yet made acquaintance with those of Dostoievsky, even then being foreshadowed in the earlier work of the Russian author. But Sacher-Masoch's 'female demons' were placed, not in any familiar urban environment, but most often in the wild and melancholy landscape of the Carpathian foothills, among an exotic race, half barbarous, half sophisticated, by turns dreamy and shockingly eruptive, familiar with and even obsessed by the dark side of life, furious egotists roaming the nightmare kingdoms of folly, passion and vice.

The younger set in Graz discussed these works very excitedly. The older people were less interested. They could see no depth, little but sensation-mongering, in these accounts, written, to be sure, from the Austrian point of view, of the extravagantly crude behaviour of semi-savages. The author, however, was even then engaged upon compositions which were to compel the attention of professed intellectuals.

The first of these, naturally enough, was a version of the story of Anna von Kottowitz herself and her unusual lover. It was called *The Separated Wife* and concerned the relations of a 'super-woman,' Frau von Kossov, with a man whom she dominated physically, though he was her intellectual and spiritual superior. This book, first published in 1865, is Sacher-Masoch's earliest major novel. It is important for the understanding of his view of the sexual problem. Its evidence proves that he was no 'feminist.' He took neither the French standpoint, that women are delightful and mysterious playthings, nor the American, that they are the main point of reference for masculine accomplishments.

Leopold regarded the fully developed woman as an egotist of so unadulterated a type that she can practically do without a mind. The primitive will to aggression and tyranny takes its place. As a poet, he was attracted by a certain barbaric splendour, 'beyond good and evil' in this behaviour. A few years later the more truly philosophic mind of Nietzsche was to perceive that destruction, wrath and denial, which he, however, regarded as specifically male characteristics, might be accompanied by beneficence, creation and affirmation. Leopold, in his most engrossing sexual experience, had already come to the same conclusion. To put it crudely, when Anna turned him upside down and inside out, he felt all the better for it.

The Separated Wife, nevertheless, shows that, in spite of his profound appreciation of feminine power, equated in his judgment with characteristic feminine beauty, Leopold would never for a moment admit that any woman could be his intellectual equal. Conqueror in the fields of will and physical energy, she cannot even be a competitor, he implies, in those of imagination and logic. She can release them to perform their functions, like a princess smashing a bottle of champagne over the bows of a battleship, which then goes on its way rejoicing. But once she has done that, it is an impertinence for her to pretend any further interest in the launched career.

He could give a lighter turn to these ideas. For Leopold, though as devoid as most Slavs of any English sense of humour, delighted in farcical situations. He had written, about 1860, a story called *Kaunitz,* on the plot of which he afterwards based one of his comedies, entitled *The Verses of Frederick the Great*. 'Kaunitz' is the name of a real person, a former Austrian ambassador in Paris, who once tried to get Louis XV to combine with Austria against Prussia. The French king, in the story and in the play, is ruled by his autocratic mistress, Madame de Pompadour. Frederick of Prussia had permitted himself to be satirical in verse about this typical 'masochistic' relationship. Kaunitz, therefore, was enabled to reverse traditional French policy and arrange the alliance. The tale is told by Leopold with fine appreciation of its ironic features, though his sympathy with Louis is also very evident.

But the four years with Anna von Kottowitz, mentally abject as she was, with all her superb carnality, inspired Leopold to more than stories of temperamental actresses, queens and slave 'furies,' to more even than comedies and an exposition, in fiction, of the view of women to which his name afterwards became attached. It was towards the end of the period of her influence that he came to conceive his *magnum opus,* at which, like Goethe, he was to work, off and on, for most of his life, but which, unlike Goethe, he was never to finish.

The *Legacy of Cain* was planned as a vast work, in six parts, to be nothing less than a complete diagnosis of what the author felt to be the contemporary sickness of society and a statement of the only possible remedy for it. Part I, *Love,* was published eventually, in its entirety, in 1870. All the others remained fragmentary. They were to have been called, *Property, The State, War, Work* and *Death.*

Love contains six stories, of which the first, *The Wanderer,* forms a sort of prologue, to prepare the reader's mind for a new view of sex relations. The rest expounded this view under various aspects, including homosexuality and the monogamous ideal. The masterpiece of these six is the famous *Venus in Furs,* begun under the aegis of Anna, to whom the author showed certain passages in a last attempt to get her to understand what he wanted from her. He failed. Anna read the extracts in much the same spirit as a moronic schoolboy his copy of a notorious novel recently banned by circulating libraries. She was coarsely inflamed by a few sentences here and there. But that was all.

In these circumstances *Venus in Furs* remained incomplete for the time being. It was to come to fruition, eventually, under conditions a good deal more congenial to the indefatigably persistent author.

CHAPTER THREE

Fanny

SHORTLY after the break with Anna a Berlin theatre, somewhat rashly, agreed to produce *The Verses of Frederick the Great* and the author was invited to attend the first night. The piece, as already intimated, was pure comedy, perfectly innocent of political satire. If anyone was made to look silly in it, the butt was Louis of France, not Frederick of Prussia. A hundred years had elapsed since the events portrayed on the stage. But in those days Prince Kaunitz really had persuaded Maria Theresa of Austria to attack the Prussian king. And in the early months of 1866 feeling in Berlin was already running high against the Austrian administration of Prussia's neighbour, Holstein.

In the play the malice of Frederick, a Prussian national hero, was used by Austria as a tool to turn the French against him. The pit groaned and whistled at this untimely reminder of an old hostility which was now repeating itself in the politics of the day. In a few minutes a serious riot had started. The curtain was rung down and the piece withdrawn. Leopold returned in dudgeon to Graz. That summer war broke out between Prussia and Austria, ending in the decisive defeat of the latter at Königgrätz (Sadowa) in July.

The war perhaps turned Leopold's attention once more to history and politics. At any rate, it was in 1867 that a historical study, luridly illuminated by scenes of 'masochism,' was published. It dealt, as had the previous study, entitled *Hungary's Decline,* with the attempt of Maria of Austria, widow of King Louis of Hungary, who fell fighting against the Turks on the disastrous field of Mohacs in 1526, to unite the two countries. She was opposed by John Zapolya, the Governor of Transylvania, who wanted the throne of Hungary for himself, by the fat knight Istvan Verboczy, leader of the middle-class party and by the rich Jewish financier Speranzes.

Zapolya, with Turkish help, obtained two-thirds of the kingdom in the end. But the swaying fortunes of the diplomatic battle interested Leopold, once he had got into the stride of his book, less than they had attracted him a few years previously. He was coming to care far more for the strange intricacies of human character than for the mazes of Court intrigue. All the protagonists of *The Last King of the Magyars,* as this last production (1867) was entitled, are strongly drawn and vividly realized. Verboczy, especially, approaches Falstaff in comic force.

Maria herself is, as might have been expected, a typical 'sultana.' She runs needles into the Turkish ambassador and finally has him sewn up into a sack and thrown into the Danube. A large proportion of the princesses and other female aristocrats of the sixteenth century in central and south-east Europe were headstrong and domineering women, who could be pretty bloodthirsty, or worse, on occasion. Leopold, at this period, obviously preferred these ferocious shadows to the merely enigmatic, if handsome, leaders of contemporary society.

One of these, however, a certain Baroness von Reizenstein, whom he met in 1868, looked, for the moment, more promising. She wrote, under a male pseudonym, as Franz von Nemmersdorf, certain sinister romances which were enjoying considerable popular success at the time.

The Baroness, who seems to have known Leopold well by reputation before she met him, submitted the manuscript of one of these stories to him in his capacity as editor of a magazine which he had recently founded, called *The Austrian Arbour.* In an accompanying letter she stated, with a resolute frankness which delighted him:

"My intellectual and emotional position is in every respect a completely independent one. But please do not assume that I mean by this that I share the Byronic grievance that no one can love me. Love and friendship, if they are as genuine and dynamic as I would have them, tend, if persons of strong character are involved, to result in the driving of an Indian sort of bargain: they hand out gold and receive iron in return."

The letter bore a Munich address. He replied to it at length. A somewhat high-flown correspondence ensued. Soon the Baroness was confessing, in eloquent but unmistakable terms, her love for this unusually communicative editor. Leopold, all his life, seldom had difficulty in convincing distant feminine correspondents that he was the man of their dreams. It was one of the few pleasures that this born writer could enjoy without almost instant disappointment.

At last they met in the flesh, in Vienna, in the late summer. The Baroness turned out to be a good-looking woman of masculine type, very intelligent, downright and capable. But she had two serious drawbacks. Leopold found her to be, at bottom, sentimental rather than 'despotic.' Secondly, she was definitely inclined to take a passionate interest in younger and 'fluffier' members of her own sex.

This lady's idea of making the best of both sexual worlds in a broad-minded sort of way, which did not exclude the encouragement of her editor to join her in the pursuit of other young women, did not appeal to the creator of less equivocal heroines. The budding romance came to nothing, in the end, but an exchange of courteous profundities. Leopold returned to Graz in a mood of frustration which was becoming depressingly familiar to him.

But he could never resist long letters from female aspirants to publication, if they seemed to carry a hint of something more interesting than a vulgar intrigue. In 1869 he received a thick bundle of manuscripts from a certain Fanny Pistor, writing from Baden in Austria and signing herself Baroness Bogdanoff. This correspondent expressed her deep admiration for all Leopold's works, in particular *The Separated Wife,* which she had recently read. She wished to have his 'frank' opinion of her own stories and would welcome a personal interview. The letter discreetly hinted at a 'perfect' understanding of the editor's sexual tastes.

He saw at once that there was no question of literary talent in this case. But he was sufficiently attracted by the phrasing of the letter to consent to meet the authoress.

Fanny bore very little resemblance to the Baroness von Reizenstein. She was neither so handsome nor so clever. But Leopold instantly perceived in her the indefinable look, veiled as it was, at their first meeting, by the usual social conventions, of a predatory and authoritarian sensuality which had nothing to do with convention. The suggestion of an objective and ruthless lasciviousness, altogether lacking in the tender and considerate affection normal between lovers, yet conceived on the grand aristocratic scale, which insists upon luxurious settings and tempestuous scenes, imperious caprice and disdainful aggressions, enthralled him.

The lady, for her part, while by no means of noble blood, was well equipped, psychologically, to understand Leopold. She was far more imaginative than Anna von Kottowitz, far less romantically impulsive and talkative than the Baroness von Reizenstein. She had a kind of direct, primitive simplicity in her fundamentally selfish and cold lust for domination in sexual relations which would theoretically have satisfied Leopold all his life if this type of passion had not been of its very nature as brief as it was arrogant.

They agreed at once to embark upon a liaison to be characterized materially by a prodigality in which furs and foreign travel were to play a conspicuous part and spiritually by the utter subordination of the male to the female partner. This compact was not merely a verbal one. It was mutually signed, sealed and delivered with the greatest formality and precision. The document, crucial for the comprehension of the dovetailing outlooks of both parties upon sexual feeling, reads as follows:

> "Herr Leopold von Sacher-Masoch gives his word of honour to Frau Pistor to become her slave and to comply unreservedly, for six months, with every one of her desires and commands.
>
> For her part, Frau Fanny Pistor is not to exact from him the performance of any action contrary to honour, i.e., which would dishonour him as a man or as a citizen. She is also to allow him to devote six hours a day to his professional work and agrees

never to read either his correspondence or his literary compositions.

The mistress (Fanny Pistor) has the right to punish her slave (Leopold von Sacher-Masoch) in any way she thinks fit for all errors, carelessness or crimes of *lèse-majesté* on his part.

In short, her subject, Gregor, must accord his mistress a wholly servile obedience and accept as an exquisite condescension any favourable treatment she may give him; he recognizes that he has no claim upon her love and he renounces all lover-like rights whatsoever.

Fanny Pistor, on her side, promises to wear furs as often as possible, especially when she is in a cruel mood.

This period of servitude is to be considered at an end after six months and no serious allusion to it will be permitted at the expiration of the period.

Everything which may have happened must be forgotten. The former love-relation will then be resumed.

These six months will not necessarily run continuously. They may be interrupted for prolonged periods, which will begin and end whenever the mistress chooses. This pact is hereby put into force by the signatures of the contracting parties.

Commencing date, 8th December, 1869.
(Signed) Fanny Pistor Bogdanoff.
Leopold, Chevalier von Sacher-Masoch."

A number of points are to be noted in this extremely curious document, by no means the last in this sense that Leopold was to draw up.

In the first place, the limit of six months was probably imposed by Fanny rather than by her partner. She was not the sort of woman to let herself in for an indefinitely prolonged association with any man. The final paragraph allowing for holidays from this rigorous régime was also no doubt insisted upon by the lady, in case she might get tired of it, a contingency which would hardly apply to the gentleman.

It is Leopold, however, who is responsible for the second paragraph. He was at pains, all his life, to point out to his mistresses that his love of subservience was a sexual idiosyncrasy, and did not extend to permitting himself to behave like a coward, a thief or a conspirator against society. In other words, they must clearly understand that when an Austrian gentleman lay at their feet, he did not assume this posture because of a natural bent for base or mean actions, but simply because it stimulated him sexually, a result which the perpetration of a swindle or the evasion of a duty would be far from effecting in any degree whatever.

People, whether men or women, who would not accept this view of the matter were invariably sharply snubbed by Doctor (of Laws) von Sacher-Masoch, who stood no nonsense from anyone in any field but the sexual.

The insistence upon time off for literary composition, the refusal to discuss his work with his mistress and the prohibition of the all-too-frequent feminine privilege of reading a lover's private correspondence, are also characteristically Leopoldian. He had all the mature writer's disinclination for alien, especially female, interference with his professional productions. And he had, of course, a particular reason for avoiding the growth of jealousy on the part of a mistress, since it was only she, in his view, who ought to make *him* jealous. He found nothing more tedious, all his life, than the converse.

The pompous word *lése-majesté,* which strikes a normal reader as comic, was probably perfectly seriously intended, at least by Leopold. He really did wish to regard a mistress as a sovereign power. The intensity of his sexual feeling for her, once it was given its head, which it usually obtained in a very short time, did in fact partake of the devotion of a feudal retainer to his chief. He really would feel an agony of remorse at an inadvertent injury to his 'queen' and consider that he thoroughly deserved the most savage punishment for it. He, Leopold von Sacher-Masoch, was not a member of an old-established imperial autocracy for nothing.

The point, again, as to his mistress's right to be indifferent to him and his own consequent renunciation of 'loverlike' claims upon her is typically 'masochistic.' Whatever disconcerting features there may

have been about Leopold as a lover he never importuned his partner
to prove her love for him and was therefore never odiously complacent about it afterwards, either to her or others. Nor did he ever,
equally odiously, pursue her with his lusts out of season.

The furs had long since become an indispensable symbol of sexual
power with Leopold. Without them, he was impotent in both the
physical and mental senses, for he always had such a garment within
reach of his hand when he was composing, even when the wearer
was absent. This fetish, in fact, unlike those of most men, exercised
its inspiration in spheres where the sex instinct had been wholly
sublimated in the act of spiritual creation. The emphasis upon furs,
then, in the Leopold-Fanny 'treaty,' has much more than a purely
lascivious significance.

Finally, Fanny again seems to appear in the penultimate paragraph, where 'no serious allusion to the period of servitude' is to be
permitted after the six months have elapsed and 'the former love-
relation will then be resumed.' Leopold would have liked nothing
better than to talk about it 'seriously' to the end of time. Nor would
he ever take much interest in 'resuming' a 'former love-relation.' It
is evident that Fanny wished to leave a loophole for a more normal
association in the future. Leopold, like most artists, did not share the
feminine passion for long-term planning. He probably trusted to his
own already well-tested eloquence for dealing with this less congenial proviso when the time came.

Meanwhile, the liaison started under the best possible auspices.
The partners were, of course, to tour in Italy, the land where no
amorous passion, however exceptional, could find itself anything but
perfectly at home. Fanny played her part to perfection, showing an
originality in the details of the project which enchanted Leopold. It
had already been suggested, at the time the 'treaty' was drawn up,
that he should be called 'Gregor,' a typical name for a valet in this
part of Austria. This name had, as we have seen, actually been incorporated in the precious document.

'Gregor,' therefore, was the name inscribed upon Leopold's travelling papers. Everyone they met on their tour assumed as a matter

of course that the dark, shy, delicate-looking man, who rode third-class on the railways, carried the Baroness Bogdanoff's luggage and ran her errands, was a servant. Some of them guessed, quite rightly, that he was also her lover. But this supposition did not cause a very great sensation in Italy in 1870.

Fanny laid down the itinerary. They went first to Venice. Here, as in the case of Anna von Kottowitz, Leopold suggested that his mistress, in order to increase his mental humiliation and torment, and therefore his passion for her, should take a lover. Fanny raised no objection. The idea, in fact, appealed to her aggressive, not to say cynical, temperament. Leopold would have liked, as the necessary interloper, a young, handsome and arrogant Duke, at least. But these were neither very easy to find, even in Venice, nor, when found, did they move fast enough to satisfy the impatient self-tormentor. In the end, a compromise had to be made with one Salvini, a third-rate actor, neither so youthful, wealthy, well-born, good-looking or intelligent as he might have been.

Still, Salvini, who seems to have been highly flattered at his easy conquest of the rich foreign baroness, had a satisfactorily Mephistophelian look, in the Italian manner, about him and a natural talent for insolence and ostentation. Once he understood what these strange alien tourists wanted from him he acted very much better than he ever had on the stage.

Leopold, in order to heighten the exotic colouring of the halo with which he had already invested this mediocrity, always called him 'the Greek.' Greece was farther off than Italy from Graz and possessed, so he had heard, an even larger number of ferocious bandits. It pleased his peculiar romanticism to assume that the fatuous Salvini would really be more at home amid scenes of rapine and outrage in the neighbourhood of Mount Olympus than in a *palazzo* or a gondola.

'Gregor' duly, in his capacity of valet, hovered round the newly united lovers, officiously bringing in refreshments at awkward moments and being discovered in close proximity to the bedroom door when either his mistress or the actor emerged on necessary errands.

On one of these occasions Salvini found him with his eye glued to the keyhole and ventured, cordially encouraged by Fanny, to box his ears. 'Gregor,' apparently in an ecstasy of remorse, but actually enraptured by this hearty gesture of contempt from his 'betrayer,' kissed his assailant's hand with Slavonic effusiveness. This incident had, of course, the effect, desired by all concerned, of redoubling the actor's vulgarity and conceit.

It was an ideal setting for the author's inspiration. He took his full six hours a day elaborating it in the tale already mentioned, *Venus in Furs,* which ultimately became his best known book. It was published that year, 1870, as one of the six stories in Part I, entitled *Love,* or *The Legacy of Cain.* The others were called, *The Wanderer, The Man of Surrenders, Moonlight Night, Plato's Love* and *Marzella. The Diary of a Cosmopolitan* was also industriously continued, and a further instalment issued, in 1870.

But of all this literary activity *Venus in Furs* was destined to live longest. Fanny is therein named 'Wanda von Dunayev,' Leopold himself 'Severin Kusienski' and Salvini 'Alexis Papadopolis.' The keynote of the book is struck in a dialogue between Severin and Wanda on an early page. "In love," he tells her. "There is always the hammer and the anvil." "Aha," retorts the lady. "And you're the anvil, eh?" When he swears eternal fidelity, she replies: "Oh, I could never love a man longer than a month unless I could try him out for a year first."

The astonishment and excitement with which these heretical exchanges were perused by the more sentimental of the library subscribers of 1870 may be imagined. There were others, as Leopold was to discover later, whose indignation was tempered with enthusiastic and not always disinterested curiosity.

A transcription of the original 'treaty' between Leopold and Fanny is embodied in *Venus in Furs.* A second document, however, even more drastically phrased, follows it in the book. Severin signs, at Wanda's request, the following statement, which, perhaps, looks back, rather pathetically, to Leopold's disillusion with Anna von Kottowitz: "Having had enough, for years now, of life and its deceptions, I hereby voluntarily put an end to my existence, in which I take no further interest." Wanda, in other words, can go so far as to kill him, for her amusement, if she likes.

Venus in Furs, naturally enough, relates much more exuberant episodes than actually took place in Venice between Fanny, 'Gregor' and Salvini. Wanda has a number of ferocious negresses at her disposal. These slaves are present at her love-scenes with Kusienski and are often suddenly ordered by her to seize and thrash him at a moment of erotic climax. Alexis Papadopolis has a terrible reputation for cruelty in the campaigns which he has led against the Turks. He is a man of inordinate and bloodthirsty passions and extremely brutal to poor 'Gregor,' who suffers agonies of jealousy on his account.

An incident is recounted in which the Greek, who is hidden in Wanda's bedroom, leaps out upon the supposed servant and almost hammers the life out of him. Meanwhile Wanda, under the very eyes of her unfortunate first lover, packs her trunks preparatory to departing for good with his tormentor. The two of them leave Severin writhing on the floor, in the last stages of mental and physical anguish, and he never sees either of them again.

The real parting between Fanny and Leopold came much more prosaically. Each found that there seemed to be no reason for prolonging the original six months stipulated. The lady had made it clear from the start that she was not a one-man woman. It is probable that her exceptional vitality and pugnacity enjoyed the bullying and the 'deceptions' for most of the time they spent together. But in the end she must have wearied of the perpetual round of dressing up as a 'sultana,' physically assaulting her partner and parading other lovers under her nose. She was not really, after all, a pathological case for treatment by the investigators of 'sadism' but merely a shrewd, domineering, rather spiteful type of female debauchee, who found it piquant to kick and slap the shyer sort of male and enjoyed cheating him to his face. But Fanny was much too restlessly capricious to want to go on being a 'tigress' or a 'hyena' for the whole of her erotic life.

As for Leopold, it is certain that he was, at one and the same

time, an unrivalled reader of women's minds and a determined
builder of his own fantasies in them. One side of his genius saw
through Fanny at a glance. But the other, the creative, the most
essential part of him, instantly took charge. No doubt most imaginative men exaggerate those qualities in their mistresses which the
males in question find most congenial to themselves. Leopold did
more. His personal magnetism, his conversational eloquence, were
such that he was often able to convince the objects of his attentions,
for varying periods, that they had in fact 'the soul of Nero in the
body of Phryne,' as he was fond of putting it.

He failed, in the end, every single time he tried to do this. It is,
perhaps, the tragedy of all artists whose intellectual eye is as keen as
their intuitive one. But with Leopold, owing to his sexual obsession,
the tragedy at last overwhelmed his potential greatness. That time
was not yet. Fanny was, for the moment, just another woman who
had not quite come up to expectations. He was not so terribly disappointed with her as he had been with Anna. Fanny had at least understood him and he was duly grateful for the fact. He returned to
Graz chastened but not by any means in despair.

For the next eighteen months he was mainly occupied, after placing the manuscripts he had brought back with him from Italy, with
the theatre. A young actress of no more than seventeen, one Jenny
Frauenthal, was chosen to play the lead in a comedy of his which
was produced in Graz at this time. She was pretty and conceited. He
was tired, for the time being, of sophistication. She was flattered by
the gravely courteous attentions of the famous and romantic-looking
author, who had such a strange reputation as a lover and had written
such extraordinary books. The couple actually became engaged to
be married after a few weeks. But Leopold could not deceive himself
long this time. Jenny's conceit was not aristocratic arrogance, but
just vanity. Her features were charming and her tantrums and sulks
delightful. But she was not even a wild kitten, let alone a 'tigress.'

As a last resort, to test his feelings for her, he encouraged her
opposite number in the play, the actor Roll, to make love to her off
the stage as well as on it. No jealous pangs, as he had hoped, in-

vaded his heart. With reluctance, for he could see that the girl had become quite fond of him, he broke the engagement suddenly and decisively. Jenny announced herself as heartbroken and the 'deceiver' tactfully withdrew to Vienna. As soon as his back was turned she forgot him.

In Vienna consolation awaited him in the form of the visiting French actress, Mademoiselle Clairemont, who appears to have received the exotic Galician dramatist with open arms. She was not so stupid as Jenny. But she was, in Leopold's opinion, incurably frivolous. Nevertheless, the association between these two lasted some time and Mademoiselle Clairemont eventually presented her latest lover with a permanent reminder of herself in the shape of a daughter. It was the first time Leopold had ever become a father and he was delighted with the child, whom he called Lina. The baby was put out to nurse in an apparently reliable family at Klagenfurt. The mother returned, in the best of tempers, to Paris, where she promptly fell in love again. By the spring of 1871 Leopold had again settled down in Graz, where the chief emotional tangle of his life was already in preparation.

CHAPTER FOUR

Wanda

~~~~~~

HE was now thirty-five years old and rapidly rising to the height of his literary powers. He had behind him, already, three substantial works of historical scholarship, all containing original research and original views of central European history. In addition, he had now published the first part of his *magnum opus, The Legacy of Cain,* which was intended to do no less than diagnose and prescribe for modern society by way of a series of powerfully imaginative and intellectually disturbing tales, thirty-six in all. One of these in particular, *Venus in Furs,* was beginning to make its way all over Europe and even in the United States.

Four further separate novels by him, as well as a large number of shorter stories, had appeared between 1863 and 1869. In the exclusive and sceptical literary circles of Paris, the cultural centre of the continent, he was already being mentioned as the successor, in German literature, of Goethe, since whose death few Frenchmen had taken the slightest interest in whatever might be written in the German language.

He was also a popular and successful dramatist, several of whose plays had been produced with general acclaim, not only in Graz. In that city his social position as the Police Commissioner's son, the charm of his manners and the distinction of his conversation, combined with his somewhat feminine but decidedly not effeminate appearance and the gossip about his love affairs, from which it was evident that he practised what he preached in his novels, had for some time rendered Leopold von Sacher-Masoch a notable personality.

Those who despised him on principle found him difficult to ignore. Those who were intrigued by his ideas or his behaviour passed easily from curiosity to enthusiasm.

He was, therefore, the object of a great deal of attention from young women and from some who were no longer as young as they used to be. The social conventions of the 'seventies, even in Galicia, prevented such manœuvres from taking the franker forms. But the letters he received from anonymous female correspondents took up a larger proportion of his reading time than would be the case with an author in a comparable position today. It was a verbose age. The inhabitants of central Europe are far from taciturn. Sex was then as now the main topic for expatiation between men and women. Conventions were strict, however. To write out one's views, sign them with fictitious names and submit them to recognized authorities was one of the principal pastimes, not to say, passions, of at any rate the German-speaking part of the educated world in those days.

Leopold was by now a practised hand, both as a literary critic and as a fetichist, at recognizing, almost in a moment, whether the communications addressed to him by perfect strangers were likely to interest him. He dropped the vast majority of them into his waste-paper basket. But sometimes a phrase would catch his eye and kindle his volatile fancy. He would then answer the correspondent, always with extreme discretion, for he knew by bitter experience how often such replies are misunderstood, but in such a way — no one was his superior in these delicate subtleties — as would provoke or more gently induce the 'fair unknown' to come out into the open.

He employed this technique with a letter which arrived one morning, somewhat startlingly signed with the name of the fictitious heroine of *Venus in Furs,* Wanda von Dunayev. The epistolary style was fluent, high-flown, but not perfectly literate. He guessed it to be that of a Pole or a Russian writing in German. Emotion rather than intelligence seemed to have dictated it. That was all to the good from Leopold's point of view. Like the majority of clever but highly sexed men he did not care for too much abstract discussion with his partners, though Anna von Kottowitz had taught him that they had to reach a certain level of mental maturity.

The writer in the present case affirmed, as usual, that she had been deeply moved, in a particularly intimate manner, by the general trend of the works of Leopold von Sacher-Masoch and would like them further explained to her, but only by correspondence. She gave Leopold to understand that she was a wealthy and virtuous woman, adored by an innocent young husband. She professed to know that Leopold was himself, at the time, about to marry a Polish actress and ended by warning him that the utmost care would have to be exercised in their (purely epistolary) relations if he wished to be informed more precisely of her opinions on the subject of sex.

It was the kind of letter, in its surface primness and underlying invitation, best calculated to appeal to a sophisticated lover. Leopold felt definitely excited by it. He decided to reply. But he kept his answer brief, though courteous. He said that it was not his habit to engage in correspondence with people unless he knew them personally. He complimented the writer upon her literary discernment but added that, since he was in fact thinking of getting married, he felt in honour bound not to maintain even epistolary relations with another woman unless and until a personal meeting could be arranged. After such an interview, he hinted, he might be of a different opinion.

Two days later 'Wanda's' reply arrived. It was long, tumultuous and extremely outspoken. Now the cards were on the table, he thought. He read it again and again with mounting enthusiasm, hardly believing his eyes.

"You are right," the mysterious 'Russian' told him, "in divining that I resemble closely your *Venus in Furs*. Yet sometimes she seems to draw me to you, sometimes to make you seem a stranger. I want you to belong to me! If our human nature permitted such a thing, I would give many years of my life to possess you without your possessing me. As for what you say concerning the necessity for fidelity to your betrothed, my former letter must have made my attitude on this subject clear to you. I simply desire to intoxicate your senses. I have no ambition to capture your heart."

There was a good deal more in this cynically erotic vein, some of which he recognized as more or less accurate transcription from passages in his own novels. The writer wound up with a number of positively reckless assertions. She was sick and tired, she declared, of her poor husband, though 'of course' he still loved her. Leopold, she almost thundered, must lie one day at her feet, literally at her feet. Yet then she would think of nothing but 'tearing his heart to pieces.'

A normally sexed man of the world, however fond of intrigue, would have recognized this cunningly contrived rant for what it was, the kind of transparent trap that a shrewd prostitute lays, after rapidly sizing up a prospective client at a street corner. In the case of the letter, an average Don Juan of this type would neither know nor care whether it was seriously meant or merely a practical joke intended, for one reason or another, to make a fool of an eminent figure by playing on his foibles.

Leopold, however, was not normally sexed. His obsession had been exasperated by a number of failures to put it into convincing practice. He was half a Slav. His head whirled easily when it was not professionally engaged. He had read of Slav women who really did go on like this, meaning every word they said. He had positive evidence that some women were quite capable of acting as they had spoken in such connections. Finally, he was as ready as we all are to take geese for swans, to magnify the coarse feather of a casual remark that seems to fall in with our deepest aspirations into the noble wing of a realized ideal.

He flung himself, with his usual impulsive prodigality, with the dazzling rhetoric he could always command at will, with the intense emotional heat always ready, at a breath, to turn his heart into a soaring flame, into an impetuous reply. He announced himself to be already her 'slave.' He went on:

"I had thought until today that it was impossible to love a woman simply as the result of reading her letters. Now, nevertheless, I am in love with you. I am in love with your tempera-

ment. It disturbs me to the depths of my being . . . suppose I
told you that I wanted to be whipped by you, that I wanted you
to chain me up? Suppose I told you that I desired intensely to
be utterly yours, if only for a few hours . . . a woman as unusual as you seem to be must possess wonderful furs . . . how
I should love to plunge my face into their scented warmth . . .'"

He reiterated finally, and most urgently, his demand for a personal
interview, no matter where, how or when.

'Wanda,' however, remained obdurate on this point. She answered,
for the rest, in the same strain as before. Leopold began to feel that
this maddening correspodence was a major event in his life. He
thought of little else during the day and for half the night. He exhausted every expedient he could think of, both direct and indirect,
in order to discover the identity of the writer of these 'marvellous'
letters. It was all in vain.

His distress and also the irrational egotism that leads us to confide
to more or less indifferent persons the delight we feel in any unusual
experience, especially of a kind complimentary to ourselves, caused
him to discuss the situation with one of his younger friends, a Jewish
lad of nineteen or so, one Berchthold Frischauer, whom he considered gifted with particular sensitivity in questions of erotics.

"What do you think of this, Berchthold?" he asked the boy one
day, handing him one of 'Wanda's' latest effusions. "It's been going
on for weeks now and I don't know what to do about it. How do
you think I should answer at this stage?"

The serious-minded young student of the heart took the paper and
began to examine it with his usual concentration. Then he frowned.
His delicate features went suddenly blank. He seemed to be staring,
with a positively appalled expression, at a single line of the 'Russian's' not very legible handwriting. As he read on, rapidly now,
merely glancing through the packed pages as though he took little
interest in them, his frown grew deeper and he pursed his lips
angrily.

At last he folded the letter carefully and handed it back to
Leopold, who had been watching him with some astonishment,

as if he were anxious to get rid of it. He cleared his throat awkwardly, stammered a little, then announced in a firm tone:

"I'll see you're not troubled with any more of this kind of thing, Leopold."

The older man stared at him, smiling slightly.

"But I want to be troubled with it. Don't you see how interesting it is? Just imagine! If it were only —— "

Berchthold coughed again.

"Look here, Leopold. It's nothing, it's a hoax, it's beastly. I tell you —— "

"What makes you think that?"

The boy looked down at the carpet, going a little red in the face.

"I know who wrote that letter, Leopold."

"WHAT? YOU KNOW WHO IT WAS —— "

The author, who had been seated at his study table, jumped up and seized his companion by the shoulders, shaking him slightly, the big mouth half open in a grin of triumph, the dark eyes blazing.

"Who? Who? Tell me who —— "

Berchthold shook his head, compressing his lips firmly.

"I'll never do that. *Never* —— "

"But, good heavens, man —— "

Leopold talked for half an hour. But young Frischauer obstinately refused to be drawn. He remained as dumb as a fish, impervious to argument, entreaty and even abuse, for his distracted host finally lost his temper and threatened to put an end to their friendship. Berchthold's only reply to this menace, which he nevertheless obviously felt deeply, was to bow his head and leave the room and the house. Leopold threw himself back in his chair in a paroxysm of impotent anger.

He made several attempts to see the boy again during the next few days. He wrote him letters by turns flattering, apologetic and insulting. But young Frischauer seemed to have vanished from Graz altogether. Leopold could neither find him nor hear from him.

Then a further letter arrived from the mysterious correspondent.

It was signed, as before, 'Wanda von Dunayev.' But the handwriting was quite different. The letter informed Leopold that his original 'fair unknown' was having trouble with her family for some reason which did not, however, appear to be definitely connected with himself. The explanation was incoherent and involved, also somewhat ungrammatical. But the request made at its conclusion was clear enough. Leopold was to send back the letters written to him by 'Wanda' and receive his own in exchange. The whole episode must now be regarded as at an end.

The recipient of this dark communication was stimulated, rather than thrown into despair, by its contents. He saw his advantage at once and replied that he perfectly understood the situation and was prepared to comply with the writer's demand. But he could not dream of doing so by post. That might be dangerous, in the circumstances. He would only hand the letters back, in person, to their writer. Otherwise he considered that he had a perfect right to keep them.

Two or three more letters passed before the second 'Wanda,' who invariably wrote of her predecessor in the third person, would consent to the meeting upon which Leopold remained implacably, though always politely, determined. At last it was arranged that he should come, at eleven o'clock at night, to a certain lamp-post in a certain obscure street upon a certain date and there deliver with his own hand the compromising letters, not to the first 'Wanda,' but to the second, she who now conducted the correspondence on behalf of her 'friend.' At the same time and in the same way he was to get his own letters back.

Needless to say, Leopold was first at the rendezvous, with his packet. All these melodramatic precautions were vastly to his taste. He was resolved to keep strictly to his side of the bargain provided he were thereby enabled to get at least one step nearer to personal, physical contact with the original, the tempestuous, the 'tigerishly cruel' Wanda the First.

After a few minutes of excited pacing and stamping he saw, with a furiously beating heart, a tall, heavily-draped and veiled female figure approaching. As the dark form entered the dim circle of lamp-light out of the surrounding shadows he could perceive that it moved with the step of a young woman, though its proportions, he realized with a thrill of appreciation, were as imperial as would become the most formidable of 'sultanas.'

He raised his hat gravely, trying to penetrate behind the thick veil, through which he could only occasionally catch a glimpse of enigmatically glittering eyes.

She spoke in a harsh, uncertain tone, obviously nervous. But the sound fascinated him by a certain masculine depth it had, contrasting with the evident youth and inexperience of the personality behind it.

"You are the *Herr Doktor* Leopold von Sacher-Masoch?"

"*Madame* — you do me the greatest possible honour — I cannot sufficiently thank you —— "

He began to talk rapidly and fluently, exercising all the charm at his command in the dark, mobile features, expressively gesturing hands and warmly urgent voice. He was feeling all the time that, if Wanda the First was an exciting correspondent, Wanda the Second, in the flesh, even though swathed to the very eyes, was making an even profounder impression on him. The long fur coat she wore, sweeping the ground, was not of the very first quality. But it was good enough to inspire him. He only took his eyes off it to dart a flashing glance at her own, which now seemed closed. Was he boring her or seducing her? He broke off in the middle of a sentence to ask himself this question.

She took advantage of the pause immediately.

"*Herr Doktor,* I must tell you — there are things you must know. But first, here are your letters. Will you please give me my friend's now?"

"But of course, *Madame* —— "

They exchanged packets. Leopold thrust that which the girl handed him carelessly into his overcoat pocket, without even glancing at it. Wanda the Second grabbed Wanda the First's correspondence with slightly comic anxiety and held it tightly clasped against her breast. He noticed with pleasure that the gloved hands were rather large for a woman's.

He struck his own hands together softly, in a rather similar gesture, and asked her, with a reassuring smile:

"Now, *Madame,* you were going to tell me, I think, who — but *who* — is the gifted writer of those wonderful letters?"

As a matter of fact, under the magnetic influence of this tall, fur-wrapped figure with the deliciously hoarse voice, as of an embarrassed boy, and the powerful hands that knew so well how to hold what they touched, Leopold had already begun to lose interest in the answer to this question. He had only put it, really, in order to get her to speak again.

She replied with solemnity.

"I cannot tell you that, *Herr Doktor.* It would be betraying the trust she has in me. I can only tell you that it is *impossible* for her to go on writing to you. Absolutely impossible."

He bent his head a little, trying to assume an expression of disappointment.

"I am desolated, *Madame.* And utterly mystified. What reason can there be? But I can see you will not tell me. Well, I must bow to the inevitable. But you, *Madame,* you at least can tell me, perhaps, something of yourself, can you not?"

She seemed to shudder a little at the eagerness of his tone.

"*Herr Doktor* —— "

"Ah, *Madame,* you are not angry with me, I hope! Tell me now, for I only ask you as a writer, you know how vain we writers are! What did you yourself think of my letters? Were they so terrible?"

His expression was now almost jovial. She answered primly.

"They disillusioned me, *Herr Doktor.* I had supposed that your story, your *Venus in Furs,* was simply a — a work of imagination. I never dreamed you could yourself wish to experience such things. It was a great shock to me —— "

She broke off, lowering her eyes again. He shook his head sympathetically, still smiling.

"You are married, *Madame?*"

"I am."

"Then you must understand me. Now listen, I will tell you." His voice deepened, grew earnest. "I grew up, as a young man, desiring above all things what was beautiful and true, people and things that were superior to the common run of what we see about us and strong enough to maintain themselves for ever upon those heights. My mother is such a person. But she belongs to the past. When I looked into the present I found no such people, but only hypocrites, worshippers of false gods, cowardly and bemused wanderers in the reeking miasma of their affectations, their greed, their malice and their selfishness. I grew to hate the cheap glitter of that tinsel world. But I found that there was, after all, another world, a true one, splendid, and yet terrible. For, since it was both infinitely smaller and infinitely more courageous than the first, the latter hated, feared and persecuted it. I mean that world whose inhabitants grasp life and all its potentialities with both hands, with all their strength, who enjoy it and exploit it, even fiercely, even ruthlessly. The outer world calls them wicked and brutal. But at least they are sincere in their passions, they do not pretend, they acknowledge, they glory in their defiances and their aggressions, they *live,* while the so-called virtuous merely vegetate. I became fascinated by such people. When they were women, I loved them. They have become my ideals to-day, since those of the past are lost for ever."

His thrilling voice ceased for a moment. His burning eyes, fixed upon the woman with a wild intensity, suddenly lost their fire. He added in a much calmer tone:

"Such are my views, *Madame,* of the world in which we find ourselves. They surprise you, perhaps?"

She stared at him, trembling a little.

"Indeed they do. I am amazed at you, *Herr Doktor.* Amazed——"

He clenched his fists.

"Wanda! You must allow me to call you Wanda, for you have yourself chosen the name. Wanda, I implore you, I beg of you, let me write to you. Promise me to answer my letters. I shall die if you refuse. Something comes to me from you. Something that is stronger than myself. I cannot resist it. It is my only hope. Wanda, promise me —— "

He seemed about to throw himself at her feet. In the yellow gaslight his features, pallid and distorted, dominated by the great, darkly glowing eyes, seemed to move stealthily towards her. She shrank back a little.

"No — I couldn't —— "

"Wanda — you *must!* I tell you I shall kill myself —— " His voice rang out loudly in the quiet street. The woman looked nervously behind her. She could see no one in the shadows beyond the lamp-light. No footstep, even distant, sounded on the deserted pavement. But a shutter creaked. The leaves whispered in the few trees that bordered the roadway. The wind rose coldly for an instant, then sank. A light drizzle was beginning.

She turned back to Leopold and saw that he was in the same attitude, his arms bent, his shoulders hunched, his face, which had not changed its rigid expression of entreaty, thrust forward in what seemed an agony of desperate expectation.

She lowered her own head to avoid meeting those intent eyes. "If you insist. But you must understand, I do not approve, I shall never approve of your — your ideas. I shall do my best to persuade you, in your own interests, that they are wrong, wickedly wrong —— "

He drew a long breath, relaxed his whole posture. The strain went out of his white face. His eyes, again, lost their lustre, half closing as his long lips widened in a smile of contentment and relief.

"You have saved my life, *Madame.* I shall write to you of my gratitude and of my — adoration —— "

With a swift movement he caught her gloved hand and pressed it passionately to his lips, for a long moment. Then he stepped back, bowing deeply and sweeping off his hat.

The woman did not seem to know how to respond appropriately to these dramatic gestures. She merely nodded, with abrupt awkwardness, and turned to go. Almost in an instant she had disappeared into the darkness. Leopold stood smiling and motionless for some time after she had vanished, only rousing himself, at last, as the rain increased to a steady downpour.

He spent all the next morning writing to the new Wanda. The other had utterly ceased to exist for him. When, some weeks later, he ran across young Berchthold Frischauer at a party, he had entirely forgotten their last meeting and made no reference to it. The boy himself appeared satisfied with this behaviour and spoke of nothing but his recent holiday in the country and some scraps of literary gossip. Their former relations were resumed, so far as anyone could have relations with Leopold in his present exalted and absorbed state of mind.

He lived only for Wanda's letters. They were by no means so frank as her predecessor's. But they were as inquisitive as he could desire, if less inviting. He responded wtih his usual eloquent enthusiasm. She informed him, on one occasion, that she wished, herself, to write stories. The correspondence, for a time, became almost exclusively professional. Leopold's natural generosity, a hundred times magnified when his passions were engaged, always inclined him to encourage those who merely wanted to pick his brains. He was lavish with advice and promises. Wanda really had, he found, a certain feminine fluency on paper which could be marketed without much difficulty on the introduction of an already successful and influential author. In the course of the year 1872 a story or two by 'Wanda von Dunayev' appeared in popular magazines of the locality.

But Leopold generally wound up his letters with urgent pleas for another personal meeting, cunningly based upon veiled appeals to her vanity and to the gratitude she must feel for his professional help. "It seems to me," he wrote on one of these occasions, "that my talent has really only begun to develop properly since I have been under your influence. The only other woman who ever had that effect upon me was my mother." Both Anna von Kottowitz and the far more inspiring Fanny, the original Wanda von Dunayev, were now for the time being wholly forgotten.

A meeting was finally arranged, in February 1872, at a public masked ball. Wanda appeared with a female friend, both with faces almost entirely covered by the prescribed strip of black cloth. The two women each behaved with the utmost discretion. Leopold was unable to obtain a private interview with either. The whole conversation took place within earshot of and under the eyes of the other dancers. But he was able to gather a much more comprehensive impression of his 'sultana' than he had at the street encounter of a few weeks before.

He realized at once that Wanda was neither particularly well bred nor particularly well educated. Her hands and feet were somewhat clumsy and she carried herself awkwardly. What he could see of her face and figure confirmed the general appearance of a certain coarseness. But her abundant and glossy black hair was really magnificent, her eyes evidently very fine, her skin superb and her build, if not the last word in elegance, at least suggested that robustness and force which Leopold regarded as indispensable in a serious female partner.

He left the ball as much in love with her as ever. For her companion, ten years her senior at least and a rather obvious type of socially climbing but ineradicably commercial Jewess, had left him cold, though he exerted all his charm, without the slightest success, to get her on his side in his endeavours to come to closer quarters with Wanda herself, who had been equally non-committal, in this respect, at the dance.

He caught a severe cold on his way home in the winter dawn, and was obliged to stay in bed for a few days, a fact which was duly reported in the Graz Press. He felt too ill, at first, to write to Wanda. But as soon as he was able to get out of bed and sit by the fire he began to continue their correspondence. He had not yet finished the first letter when one of her own was handed to him.

To his astonishment and delight it contained an enquiry whether he would receive her at his bedside, for she had read in the papers that he was ill and felt anxious about him. He instantly sent off an express note to ask her to call that very evening. He spent the rest of the day in composing an elaborate toilette, making sure that he had all his erotic stimulants ready and rehearsing the details of what he intended to be an elaborately perfect seduction.

He found that he had been far too optimistic, as usual. Wanda arrived punctually, but once more heavily masked and draped. She expressed a not altogether pleased surprise to find him up, lectured him on his rashness and, by implication, on his presumptions. He was contrite, humbly appreciative of her condescension, tenderly respectful. They had a long conversation which he tried in vain to lead into the channels of a declaration.

She would only tell him that she was rather unhappily married to an extremely jealous husband, an Army officer of aristocratic lineage but apparently somewhat limited intelligence, that she wished to live a life of her own apart from this unsatisfactory personage but that this project was materially impracticable as she had no money of her own. She intended, however, to earn enough by her literary talents, which Leopold had been good enough to praise, to enable her to do so and to find among books, works of art and their creators and critics, her true level.

This discourse was heard with sympathetic attention by the convalescent author, who promised to do all that lay within his power to further the scheme. He went on to speak at considerable length, though with every precaution against offending his virtuous guest, of his own most intimate feelings. He began to explain their philosophical basis.

Here the lady interrupted, demanding illustrative detail. He switched adroitly to this subject, with great readiness, but found it a little difficult to comply with his visitor's obviously intense curiosity without arousing her equally intense championship of the proprieties. In the end the discussion had to be postponed, actually in the interests of social convention, the hour being late and the place being a bedroom in the house of a bachelor, who, though so recently an invalid, now appeared to be so very much better.

Wanda retired, still with her mask on and still physically intact so far as her host was concerned. He could only hope that, spiritually, he had made some progress.

This proved to be the case. For, despite his complete recovery from his attack of influenza, the visits now began to be repeated at briefer and briefer intervals, punctuated by more and more intimate letters. The mask, however, remained in position and so did the virtue of the guest, which Leopold was now far too infatuated to pursue except with the greatest discretion.

In April 1872, he explained to her, in a somewhat involved communication, for his mental distraction was now beginning to interfere with the lucidity of his style:

> "I do not wish to be ill-treated by someone who loves me too much but by someone who loves me too little. I find jealousy excruciating and yet I am enraptured if a woman makes me jealous, betrays me and behaves badly to me. Severin (in *Venus in Furs*) gets into a pitiable position. At the very moment when he finds his servitude intolerable, she obliges him to continue in it. For me, to love a woman means to be afraid of her. Most women like a man to be superior to them. I like a woman to be superior to me. I know that I am spiritually superior to any woman. But I require the woman I love to be superior to me by being in complete control of her own sensuality and subduing me through mine. Consequently, my cruel ideal woman is for me simply the instrument with which I terrorize myself."

In this letter he gave Wanda an account of his former mistresses, Anna von Kottowitz and the French actress Clairemont. Fanny, of course, she knew about already from *Venus in Furs*. He was at pains to emphasize the stupid vulgarity of Anna and the cynical frivolity of the Frenchwoman, for he wished the new candidate to beware of these shortcomings.

That summer Leopold's inexhaustible patience and detailed eloquence on the subject of his specialized sexual feelings began at last to have some effect upon his cautious but by now definitely intrigued visitor. She consented occasionally to kiss him, even now and then, playfully, to push him about. She informed him one evening that, for his sake, she had already left her husband and was living with her mother. It was obvious that she now expected him to marry her. He gave her to understand that he would see no objection to this step provided he could be sure that she, for her part, would make the marriage a success by falling in with his ideas on both the physical and psychological sides of their relations. There was to be kicking and slapping, there was to be whipping, there were to be 'lovers' and jealousy.

Wanda seemed, by the early autumn, to have made up her mind. After one or two false starts she succeeded, both in her behaviour when they were alone together, and in correspondence, in putting up a fair show as a modern Catherine the Great, the historical model with which he presented her, accompanying this spiritual gift with others of a purely material character, including, naturally, some valuable furs.

Her gratitude on one occasion took the form of a brief but pregnant note indicating that she was now making real progress, if not as a Fanny, at least as an Anna. It reads:

"Good morning, doggie! Send me the black dress by messenger and be quick about it! Then kiss my furs and think of your mistress!"

The master was delighted with this evidence of his pupil's adaptability. But it was with rather more mingled feelings that he perused a slightly later communication.

"My dear doctor,

If you really love me as much as you pretend to, sign the enclosed paper and add to it a few words agreeing to accept all my conditions and pledging me your word of honour to remain my slave to death. Prove to me that you have the courage to be both my husband, my lover and my dog.

I am not very well today and am lying on the sofa. I should like to see you kneeling at my feet and would like to trample on you. I am ill today, doctor, and I wish you could be ill, too, with me. I am feeling so tired again today and don't know where to turn for support. Why are you not here?"

The enclosure reads:

"My slave!

The conditions upon which I accept and tolerate you as my slave are as follow:

You are to renounce your whole personality unreservedly.

You are to have no individuality apart from mine.

You are to remain in my hands as a blind instrument to execute all my orders without argument.

If ever you forget that you are my slave and do not obey me in everything without exception I shall have the right to punish and chastise you in any way I like without your having the right to complain.

Anything I may concede to you which may please you and make you happy is simply a favour on my part and must be accepted by you as such with due gratitude; I have no duty and no obligation to fulfil towards you. You have not the right to be either son, father or friend, you are simply to be my slave, prostrated in the dust.

Your mind belongs to me in just the same way as your body and whatever may be the degree of your suffering you must, nevertheless, subordinate your sensations and sentiments entirely to my orders.

I am to be allowed to inflict any torture upon you and even if I mutilate you, you must still endure it without complaint.

You must work for me like a slave and even if I became very rich and let you want for everything and trample upon you, you would have to embrace, without a murmur, the foot which crushed you.

I am to be allowed to dismiss you at any time, but you can never leave me and if you ever try to run away, you hereby give me the right to torment you to death in every possible way. You possess nothing apart from me and I am everything for you, your life, your future, your happiness, your suffering, your martyrdom and your joy.

Whatever I ask you to do, good or bad, you must carry out and if I asked you to commit a crime, you would have to become a criminal in compliance with my will.

Your honour, your blood, your mind and your energy belong to me and I am mistress of your life and of your death.

If ever you can no longer endure my tyranny and if its chains become too heavy for you, you will have to kill yourself, for I shall never give you back your liberty again."

It was obvious even to the infatuated Leopold that there was something highly bogus, not to say vulgar and stupid, about this document. He recognized well enough that both letter and enclosure were incurably novelettish in style, the work of a thoroughly coarse and obtuse mind. The clumsy transcriptions of fragments from the wilder passages of his own novels and conversation made him think of a bad actor 'interpreting' Goethe. The enclosure owed a good deal to the 'treaty' which had been published in *Venus in Furs*. But it had been exaggerated to the extent, positively, of caricature. Leopold sighed to think that all his sedulous literary training had simply driven an already silly woman to make an even greater fool of herself.

But Wanda, nevertheless, had got under his skin now. He saw through her transparent manœuvres to trap him into marriage. He knew that it was for this purpose alone that she was carelessly rattling off her crude version of the lessons he had taught her. Wanda wanted to marry a relatively rich and famous man and didn't care in the least how she did it. That was all.

Yet she still attracted him more than any other woman he had ever met. Anna's splendid animality, Fanny's excellent imitation of aristocratic insolence, the Clairemont woman's romping high spirits, could not rival the peculiar mixture of peasant brutality, bourgeois primness and slyness, with proletarian simplicity in the obstinate pursuit of the main chance and nothing else, which distinguished the new, synthetic *Venus in Furs*.

For, finally, it was the purely carnal appeal of Wanda's physique, strongly reinforced by her long resistance to his love-making, that held him decisively at her side, even after he was convinced of her 'novelettishness.' It is never possible to account, by logical analysis, for the power of such wholly material bonds in any particular case. They are never obvious. Even men, or women, for that matter, of extremely sophisticated sensual passions are not simply addicted to the most perfect faces, figures and temperaments they can find. It is nearly always something indefinable, a personal atmosphere, a mannerism, a bodily trait often insignificant in itself, that rivets the chain.

Leopold used to say, long afterwards, that the personal appearance of this incarnate 'Wanda' was 'demoniac.' He seems to have meant that under the heavy, prudish exterior, the normally sulky and evasive expression, the clumsy movements, there crouched, in piquant contrast, a sort of smouldering recklessness, something harsh and barbarous, inaccessible to pity, humour or refinement of any sort, in ambush like a rabid monster or devil, ready, if need were, to stop at nothing for the slaking of its lusts.

This idea was pure fantasy. Wanda did not in the least resemble a demon. She was cut, quite simply, out of the common human mould of undeveloped femininity, obstinate, insensitive, vain, wary and intensely prosaic. It did not matter. Leopold's perverse imagination invested her with what he felt to be a terrible poetry, a hidden essence of the truth about humanity which deeply concerned him both as a man and as an artist.

What chiefly worried him about the new 'treaty' was its insistence, in contrast with that of Fanny, upon the resignation of his 'honour.'

He replied discreetly, in general terms, not mentioning this point, but begging her to agree never to leave him, never to respect, more than himself, the lovers she might take in the future, upon whose numbers he placed no limit, as he had already told her. He added:

"My heart and my mind are equally full of you. I know nothing of you. I do not know who you are. I have not seen your face. And yet you exhale a mysterious force to which I have to submit absolutely, as if it were a supernatural power.

My life belongs to you. Do what you will with it. I cannot define my feeling for you. Think of that and you will understand how ashamed I am when you thank me for the trifling services I have been able to render you.

I owe you a far greater debt, myself!

Don't be afraid. I shall do nothing which may displease you. I do not forget the promise I made you.

You are my fate and I am yours.

If either of us tried to hasten or delay the march of our destiny, the attempt would be vain. Our fate, like birth or death, will be fulfilled when the hour strikes. It would be a failure of loyalty on my part not to tell you all this."

Wanda did not answer this letter, either in person or on paper, for two weeks. When she did at last come to see him she found him nearly frantic at her prolonged silence.

The old arguments began again. He proposed marriage. She declined the offer, unless he would sign the 'treaty.' He refused to do so unless she took her mask off. She refused to do so until he 'signed.'

She was sure of him now. She only wished for documentary evidence that she would be the senior partner.

At last he wrote on the 'treaty': "I give my word of honour to be the slave of Frau Wanda von Dunayev, as she requests, and to submit myself to all her orders." He then signed these lines. But he insisted on retaining the document himself. Wanda sulked. He remained adamant. It seemed as though, at the last moment, the whole project would fall through.

All this time she continued to send him her literary effusions and received them back 'corrected.' She was determined, if the marriage did not after all come off, at least to get some concrete advantage out of her association with the famous writer.

On one occasion she 'ordered' him to send her a whole chapter of his own work to be incorporated in one of the stories she was writing, already practically at his dictation. He retorted, rather sharply, that she must first make some attempt at it herself. Wanda, in her annoyance, had an inspiration, not literary, but very practical.

She went to see him, snatched up a fur wrap and a whip, commanded him to take off jacket and waistcoat and kneel before her. Then she thrashed him, putting into the work all her resentment at the unsatisfactory condition of her plans.

Leopold was transformed, after this scene, into all she could wish. He would marry her, he would write her books for her, he would give her everything he had, material and mental. Now, would she please, *please,* take off that dreadful mask?

Flushed and triumphant, she felt that the great moment had at last arrived. With a melodramatic gesture, she removed the offending article.

He professed to be dazzled by the beauty revealed. But in his diary, that night, he wrote: "Well! She is not beautiful. But she is certainly *piquante* and younger than I had expected." He found out later that she was just twenty-seven.

Wanda retired, still without having 'yielded,' but bearing the precious 'treaty.' A private 'marriage,' without witnesses, was to take place at his house a few days later, on the 15th of November, 1872, his 'name-day,' to be followed in due course, 'when circumstances permit,' by a more formal ceremony. The obstacles at present were the doubtful attitude of Leopold's family, which would have to be nursed, and some momentarily intractable difficulties about funds and accommodation. These, however, both parties were sure, would soon disappear.

The ceremony duly took place, with Leopold in a white tie and tail-coat and his partner in the richest furs he had yet given her. Wine was provided by the host. There was a good deal of teasing. Solemn assurances and symbols were formally exchanged. The bridegroom received a 'punishment' for having forgotten the cakes. The bride confessed to having had lovers before, four altogether, a priest, a hairdresser, a painter and an Army officer. Leopold said that he was delighted to hear it and was vigorously reproved, physically, for this impropriety. Finally, the 'marriage' was consummated with the aid of as many of the stimulants required by the bridegroom as Wanda could remember at the moment.

CHAPTER FIVE

The Labyrinth

DURING the distracting year 1872, filled almost from end to end with
the troublesome campaign for the reduction of Wanda's equivocal
citadel, Leopold had really done very little serious writing. The
achievement, at long last, of intimacy with his new mistress led to
a prolific output over the next few months. Yet it was mostly relatively poor stuff, for two main reasons, which blended into each
other as time went on. In the first place, it now became necessary
for him, as it had been when he was living with Anna, to increase
his income considerably. Secondly, his sexual experiences with the
'demoniac' and on the whole complacent Wanda sharpened and
heightened his erotic predilections till they came to take an inordinately dominant place in his mind even when he was composing on
lines not exclusively sexual.

The result was that throughout 1873 he was turning out a series
of unedifying 'potboilers,' under such titles as *Tales of the Court of
Vienna, The Messalinas of Vienna, Tales of the Russian Court,
Shadows of Society* (these were detective stories of the Austrian
secret police) and *A Female Sultan.* This was the kind of reading
which Wanda herself, in common with the entire lower middle class
of Central Europe, most enjoyed. Since it was, to her, exciting, and
since it paid well, she encouraged and even herself imitated it.
Leopold, just then wholly under her influence, was ready enough
to fall in with her views, particularly as they gave him a chance to
articulate his fetish in plainer language than he had hitherto been
able to use. These lurid publications became immensely popular,

found a host of imitators and set a fashion, which has lasted into our own day. Nothing could have been more unfortunate for the reputation of an author who, at his best, not unworthily followed Goethe in the German novel and had traits in common with Dostoievsky and Turgenev.

Nevertheless, his earlier work had already made its way into more critical circles. He was tremendously excited when, just before the Christmas of 1872, he heard the news that two of his stories, written in the late 'sixties, were being serialized in the *Revue des Deux Mondes*. These were *Don Juan von Kolomea* and *Frinko Balaban*, both with a Galician setting. It was very many years since a German author had been so honoured in the headquarters of European culture.

Wanda wanted to know what this success would be worth in hard cash. Leopold accordingly made a polite enquiry of the editor, with many assurances of his pleasure at the distinction conferred. The reply, signed by the translator, Theodora Bentzin, was brief and to Wanda extremely disappointing. The *Revue des Deux Mondes,* wrote the former lady, was not in the habit of remunerating authors whose work, no matter how often published elsewhere, appeared in those august pages for the first time. The law of copyright did not, of course, exist in its present comprehensive form in those days.

Leopold laughed at his mistress's indignation. He promised to make up to her for this 'swindle' by writing some more about Catherine the Great. He comforted her by pointing out that the piracy in France would almost certainly have the effect of raising his stock elsewhere in Europe.

He turned out to be right. In the spring an invitation arrived from Vienna for him to visit that city, on the most advantageous terms, in order to write up the great International Exhibition to be opened there in May. He was actually offered the editorship of a periodical then being founded in Vienna for the purpose. In these circumstances it was easy for him to arrange to act as correspondent for a number of other newspapers catering for German readers.

Leopold and Wanda, who was now pregnant, arrived in the imperial city a few days before the Exhibition was due to open and proceeded to live in great style there, in the midst of an exhilarating profusion of furs, cats — for which animals Leopold retained a consuming passion all his life — complimentary visits and theatrical entertainments, among which the distinguished author's own comedy, *The Man Without Prejudices,* figured conspicuously. There was a gay meeting with Mademoiselle Clairemont, of whom Wanda had already heard, and who took the leading female part in the play. There were speeches, dinners in Leopold's honour, drives, concerts and dances, at all of which the mercurial inhabitants of the brilliant Austrian capital were in the highest spirits, prophesying endless prosperity for all concerned in the frantically publicized international event about to be celebrated.

The year 1872 had been one of great commercial expansion in Europe, especially for the German-speaking populations basking in the reflected glory of Bismarck's military defeat of France in the previous year. But, as so often happens on these occasions, the financial arrangements made had been inappropriate to the economic situation. Three days after the World Exhibition opened the slump came with terrifying suddenness in a tidal wave of bankruptcies and suicides. Leopold's paper foundered in the general ruin. Money seemed to disappear overnight. The furs had to be pawned, the most expensive of the cats sold. The couple from Graz found themselves in serious financial difficulties.

They managed to struggle on for a few weeks. Then an epidemic of cholera broke out in the city. Panic ensued. Mortality mounted day by day and the streets began to look deserted. Leopold grew hysterical. He examined himself every few minutes for symptoms of the fatal infection. Wanda retired stoically to bed. But the general agitation affected even her stolidity. She gave premature birth to a male infant which only lived a week, to Leopold's utter despair. For almost the only trait he possessed in common with his 'wife,' as she now began to call herself, was a devotion to children.

The position was now quite desperate, in fact. The epidemic was at its fiercest height. Wanda was too ill to be moved. They had practically no money left and no friends who were any better off. Leopold felt he was going mad. He thought more than once of adding to the daily list of suicides. As he grew more and more helpless, more and more dependent upon Wanda, the latter, whose iron constitution, even in the midst of privation and danger, was now recuperating, felt that the moment had arrived for consolidating her union with her 'husband' by a frankness which, while there was still a risk of losing him, she could not bring herself to release.

For Wanda, with all her essential pettiness of mind and automatic, thoroughly feminine, contempt for truth when the acknowledgment of it seemed to stand in her way, did not really enjoy, as clever women often do, the arts of deception for their own sake. She always felt more comfortable if she had nothing more to hide. But she had to be sure, before giving the game away, that the game had no further prizes to offer.

She believed, then, one evening when Leopold was lying beside her in a state of utter abandonment, after a miserable fit of weeping, with his dark head half hidden in her ample bosom, that, since he was now, by his own showing, more completely in her power than he had ever been before, the time had come for a show-down. She had also now grown really fond of him in her limited way, more than half sentimentally maternal. She had come to feel that for all his high-flown talk, he was little better than a child at heart. And it is not worth while to go on deceiving children for very long.

"I want to tell you something, Leopold."

He raised his tear-stained face. He was always ready, again like a child, almost like a professional child, in fact, to hear bedtime stories.

She spoke deliberately, slowly and tenderly, stroking his hair all the time, in her calm, deep, slightly hoarse voice, that, she knew, had always fascinated him.

"I am not an aristocrat, Leopold. My real name is simply Aurora Rümelin. I was never married to an Army officer or to anyone else. I am just a poor girl. My father was a gentleman's servant. He was a bad lot. He drank, and left my mother to bring me up alone. We were desperately poor, half starved. My mother took in washing and sewed all day and half the night. I helped her. I never had any education. At last I got a post in a glove factory, while I was still only a child. Of course I had lovers, as you know. They deceived me. I grew hard before my time. Then I met Frau Frischauer —— "

He sat up suddenly.

"Who? Frau Frischauer, did you say?"

She stared.

"Yes. I met her in the street. She lived near us. Do you know her?"

He chewed his big lips.

"No. I don't think so. But — well, go on."

"Frau Frischauer," Wanda resumed, "was a Jewess and a very clever woman. She lent me books, among others some of yours. We spoke of you. She told me what I thought impossible, absurd stories about your love affairs. She said her son knew you well. I refused to believe her, especially after I had seen you once, in the street, walking with your betrothed, the actress. You looked so grave, so delicate, so gentlemanly, like a — like a seminarist, isn't that what they are called? A theological student —— "

Leopold grinned, running his hand through his thick, dark hair. He shook his head a little and blinked, looking as though he were beginning to enjoy himself.

"Yes, yes. Go on, Wanda. This is really absorbing. What happened next?"

"Frau Frischauer said that you loved anonymous letters. She said she would write you one of a certain sort, which you would be sure to answer. And then, when I read it, she said, I would know that she was right about your being a wicked and immoral man. Well, she wrote that letter and signed it 'Wanda von Dunayev.' You answered it. And she *was right*. I was horribly disappointed and ashamed."

He stroked her hand.

"Poor Wanda! Yes. Of course. And then I was fool enough to show one of Frau Frischauer's letters to — who do you think? Her son!"

"Ah!" Wanda opened her big, dark eyes widely. "So that was it!

He must have gone straight to her and told her to stop it or he would tell the Rabbi. She always said he was very prim and proper, that Berchthold of hers. But she only told me that she had had enough of the whole business and *must* have her letters back. So I —— "

He kissed her.

"So you went and got them back for her like a very brave little Wanda. And so we met. And so the great, the only, the eternal and loveliest romance of my whole life began. Are you sorry now that you agreed to go on with those letters, Wanda?"

He looked radiant, all devotion and exhilaration. She gave him a keen glance under her heavy brows.

"You are not angry, Leopold? I deceived you, you know."

He smiled, shaking his head.

"I am glad you were so clever, my beloved. For I must say, you know, that if I hadn't thought you were a wealthy, married woman, well able to look after yourself, I might not have —— "

She frowned a little.

"Yes. I thought so. But now?"

He reassured her, eloquently. She steered the conversation to the future. He agreed that they must leave Vienna at once, at any cost, return to Graz and get properly married. But it was not until August that they at last managed to get away, and not to Graz, but to a town close by the latter city, Brück, on the river Mur, where Leopold was enabled to rent a former mill for them to live in. But they still remained very poor. A formal marriage, he told her, was out of the question for the time being.

He had begun to work again at *The Legacy of Cain,* for the Vienna crisis had sobered him considerably and he did not feel in the mood, despite Wanda's urgent representations, to start another series of 'Court Scandals.' Part II of the *Legacy* had already made some progress when an event occurred which still further disturbed his impatient mistress's already waning confidence in her plans for their future.

One of the Brück shopkeepers had given Leopold a grey kitten, with which the latter had fallen extravagantly in love on his daily walks through the village. Leopold kept it on his writing-table, petted it all day long and called it Peterl. One morning this charming little creature mysteriously expired. The owner's grief could hardly have been exceeded if Wanda herself had perished. He compared the animal's demise with that of their dead son and declared that these two blows, between them, had affected his mind.

She did her best to keep her temper (Wanda did not care for pets of any kind) and to point out the absurdity of this assumption. But he answered that he was sure he had softening of the brain, for since Peterl's death he could not compose a single coherent sentence. He intended to write one thing, found he was writing another and then forgot what he had originally intended to write. It must be the beginning of the end, he cried wildly, really frightening her for a moment.

This situation continued for some weeks, in spite of all she could do to laugh or scold him out of it. He did no work, complained of appalling dreams and would sit for hours in abstracted silence, the tears streaming down his cheeks. At last, just when her patience became finally exhausted and she had decided to pack her trunks and leave him to get over it alone, he received a fairly substantial sum of money from a publisher and brightened up a little.

She seized the opportunity to raise again the question of a formal marriage. This time he agreed unconditionally. By October they were in Graz. Wanda, as Aurora Rümelin, was introduced to his family, who all detested her at sight. The dislike was mutual. But the proprieties were observed. The marriage duly took place in the church of St. Sang and two days later the parties returned, with some precipitation, to the mill at Brück.

Leopold now seemed in much better spirits. He had shown signs of his old obsession during the marriage celebrations, when he had singled out, at Aurora's mother's house, a tall and stout girl called Adèle Stroheimer, whom he dressed up in Wanda's furs and begged to give him orders about laying the table for the wedding breakfast, professing to be terrified of her 'tyrannical disposition.' At Brück, much to Wanda's disgust, further evidence of this kind was instantly forthcoming.

She had been indiscreet enough to engage as maid a local peasant named Marie, of exceptionally robust physique even for that part of the country. Although this girl's build was rather squat, Leopold insisted on calling her Brünnhilde, compared her with a Valkyrie, but nevertheless lent her his manuscripts to read. He spent hours with her in the kitchen eliciting her opinions on these works.

To Wanda's protests he retorted that the sound common sense of the masses was the only reliable guide for the creative writer and that Molière always used to read his comedies to his landlady before submitting them for production. When, in November, the autumn evenings lengthened and there was nothing to do out of doors, he devised an indoor game which he was to repeat at every favourable opportunity for the rest of his life.

The game was called 'Robbers' and consisted in the ladies retiring to another part of the house while the gentleman promenaded, with the aspect of an innocent but lonely traveller, until suddenly surprised by the irruption of the fur-clad and whip-bearing but skirted 'robbers,' who seized him, tied him up and thrashed him to make him disgorge his money. The game would only end when the victim was reduced to a state of abject helplessness.

Marie was much better at 'Robbers' than Wanda. Vivacious and pugnacious, like most Styrian peasants, she was still young enough to enjoy the rough and tumble for its own sake, without the least suspicion of its sexual significance. She let fly at 'the master,' right and left, with the heartiest cordiality, till, as he told Wanda with the burlesque gaiety of a boy of fifteen, he was stiff and sore all over.

The mistress of the house was not amused. She informed Leopold, at last, that Marie would have to go. The girl's inevitable chatter in the village would certainly give rise to misunderstandings which would make Wanda's own position in the neighbourhood extremely unpleasant. Surely he must realize that. Leopold, with a sigh, acquiesced. Marie went, rather mystified at her sudden dismissal, and was replaced by an ugly and consumptive widow of discreet age.

But even this unprepossessing menial attracted, for a few days, the attention of the incalculable 'master.' The reason was that he had

heard in the village that Lisl, as the woman was called, had been suspected, some years before, of infanticide on rather a lavish scale. She
was said to have got rid of no less than nine unwanted children in
her time. Leopold immediately discovered that she had 'cruel eyes.'
He gave her a fur, and lent her one of his books. But Lisl was too
stupid or too cunning to respond to these advances. Soon afterwards
the arrival in the neighbourhood of an old friend of Leopold's, the
Baron Ferdinand von Staudenheim, sent his thoughts racing off in
another of their favourite directions.

Staudenheim was a big, fresh-coloured, hearty man, fond of open-
air sport and pretty women. His physical age was about forty, his
mental approximately fourteen. He had left his wife and child, with
whom he did not get on too well, in Graz, and was in Brück for the
shooting and a bachelor life for a while. Leopold presented him, with
many encomiums, to Wanda and insisted on his spending practically
every evening at the mill when he came back from hunting.

Frau von Sacher-Masoch, on these occasions, found her husband's
ostentatious and prolonged absences, cautious returns and unending
double compliments to herself and the visitor, rather trying. The
Baron was a gentleman of a type she had not often met before. She
admired him, for he was handsome and friendly, without in the least
taking advantage of Leopold's broad hints and officious devices for
leaving him alone with the mistress of the house. But Wanda had no
intention whatever of sending her legitimate partner into successive
fits of rapture and torment by committing adultery with his friend.
She scarcely yet believed in his repeated assurances that he would
bear her no grudge, quite the contrary, for such behaviour. Like the
majority of women who marry above their original social level she
desperately feared abandonment and divorce and was determined to
give the 'doctor,' as she still sometimes inadvertently called him, no
excuse for returning her whence she had come.

The Baron did kiss her, one fine afternoon, while she was ironing,
with the winter sun on her rosy cheeks and glossy black hair. But
this performance was at Leopold's suggestion and in his presence.
The salute, in the circumstances, could hardly have been other than

chaste and decorous. Wanda took it with what good grace she could muster. But she told Leopold, that night, that she did not care for such antics, which offended her dignity.

"But good heavens, my beloved," cried her husband. "You have a perfect right, by nature, everyone has, to enjoy yourself, whether I am here or not! It suits you to be gay, you are at your best then. It would really do you all the good in the world to take Ferdinand as a lover. He is a perfectly delightful fellow and very susceptible, I assure you. He's only waiting for the word, I'm convinced. Now, why don't you —— "

"I don't want to, I tell you —— " she burst out at him, almost crying. "I respect the Baron. He's not a — not an *adulterer* —— "

"Oh, well, of course, if you feel like that about him —— "

He looked at her so sadly, so reproachfully, out of his great, dark, tender eyes, that she felt a pang of remorse.

"Please don't take it so hard, Leopold. I will try, one day. But not just yet. Not the Baron — please —— "

He sighed deeply.

"Very well, my dear. Very well. I don't want to influence you unduly. But please remember how much it means to me. And do make up your mind soon, won't you?"

She was afraid of antagonizing him and gave him, in a whisper, the required assurance. Soon afterwards Staudenheim was suddenly recalled to Graz on business and did not return.

This incident and a number of others of a similar character, which occurred that spring and summer, caused both parties to this peculiar matrimonial experiment to revise their ideas about each other. Wanda realized that she had to deal with a serious obsession in her husband, not a harmless and rather amusing kink which strong-minded ladies in love often find stimulating. Leopold, for his part, perceived that the harsh strain in his wife's temper, from which he had expected great things in the way of scornful and tyrannical treatment, was merely the usual accompaniment of a coarse-grained nature, and meant that she was anything but a true 'sultana.'

Each partner reacted characteristically to the new reading of the situation. Wanda, who was again pregnant, fell out of love with her husband. She sincerely hoped his children would not resemble him. But at the same time she refused to give up her plan of being the respected and respectable wife of a man of high social and intellectual position, who might be very wealthy some day. To hold him, she would proceed to such lengths only, in indulging his sexual caprices, as she felt sure would not give him any handle against her and would not compromise her own standing with his friends.

Leopold, who lived largely in the moon where his personal feelings were concerned, acknowledged to himself, by no means for the first time, that he had made a mistake. But, since he found himself even more mentally superior to the woman than he had at first supposed, he was perfectly confident of 'talking her round' in time, and with due consideration for her all too normal, from his standpoint, views of the sex relationship.

The time was near when he was to use more drastic weapons to overcome the minotaur of Wanda's stubborn conventionality. But meanwhile he was content to be slyly persuasive, as he circumvented the labyrinthine paths, partly of his own contriving, in which the monster slumbered. He loved intrigues and mazes and flattered himself he had seldom been defeated by them.

Wanda gave birth to another male infant in September 1874. The child, this time, seemed healthy. Leopold had him christened Alexander, Sacha for short, and immediately became devoted to him. The one trait in his character which Wanda now felt she could stand, since it was one that any ordinary woman could comprehend, was his genuine delight in children. She made up her mind, however, to check from the start, if she could, any Leopoldian lines which might develop in Sacha's growing pains.

Two further domestic events occurred this autumn. Leopold's father died and Wanda's husband, to her inordinate satisfaction, inherited the title of Chevalier which he had already used once or twice to enhance the solemnity of those secret documents he was fond of drawing up for his mistresses to sign. A little later, while he was absent from home, a peasant woman called at the mill and, after

some hesitation, explained that the *Herr Doktor* had not been paying her lately for her care of his little girl at Klagenfurt and that the
long and short of it was, she was not prepared to keep the child any
longer.

After some tedious cross-examination Wanda discovered that the
child in question was Lina, now some four years old, Leopold's
daughter by the gay Mademoiselle Clairemont. She knew all about
this affair, which had been, of course, prior to her own association
with her husband. She had been much impressed by the famous
actress when Leopold had introduced them in Vienna the year
before. "Send Linerl here," she told the woman, shrugging her
shoulders. "We'll look after her. There's plenty of room. She can
play with my own boy."

Leopold was delighted when he heard the news. He complimented
his wife warmly on her charity. The compliment was, in fact, deserved. Wanda, with all her faults, was by no means a bigot. Few of
her social superiors, at that date, perhaps, would have done as much
for the living evidence of a husband's wild oats.

With two children, now, to bring up and Leopold's literary earnings on the decline, since the inferior work he had been turning out
lately was injuring his hitherto high reputation, Wanda felt it was
time to take steps to run the household on more economical lines.
Her husband had absolutely no idea of how it was to be done. He
threw money about like water when he had it and allowed himself
to be overreached in every way by anyone who cared to take the
trouble to swindle him.

When Wanda raised the practical question of how they were to
make the most of their slender resources and get rid of the alarming
debts which were beginning to pile up, he at once proposed, very
characteristically, that she should take entire charge of the financial
side of their association.

"I shall give you everything I earn in future, my beloved. I like
being utterly dependent on you. We'll have it legally arranged. I'll
draw up the necessary document and you shall put on your most
imperial furs, my empress, and sign it. Then I shall really be your

slave and shall not dare to call you anything henceforward except, Mistress!"

He had the paper ready in half an hour. Its sonorous periods, interlarded with phrases about 'utter abnegation' and 'complete domination,' indicated that he now renounced in her favour, for evermore, the administration of his income. Wanda felt that this was the most substantial point she had yet scored in her dealings with this incalculable male, fantastically exigent and absurdly indulgent by one unexpected turn after another.

Heartened by this success, she next proceeded to tackle him about the production, as opposed to the distribution, of his earnings. The German-speaking countries were the main source of his fees, since France and Switzerland paid him, so far, only in prestige. For some time German critics had been complaining of the monotony of Sacher-Masoch's heroines. He had shown himself in the past, they declared, capable of drawing all sorts of interesting and convincing characters. But now his tales tended to be overshadowed by a single female figure, an altogether incredible tigress, hyena or she-wolf in human form, who always said and did the same things. They hinted strongly that the distinguished author would soon find himself on the level of the purveyors of blood and thunder for the kitchen and the stables if he did not mend his ways.

She called his attention, with real anxiety, to these articles.

"Leopold, you must do something about this. Or we shall starve."

He gave her one of his peculiar oblique glances, half helplessly appealing, half secretly calculating.

"What can I do? As I haven't yet found my ideal in real life, I am obliged to create her on paper. If you, for instance, had been a true 'Venus in Furs,' as I once hoped you would be, there would be no need for me to bore these good people with my imaginary 'tigresses.' I should have a real one at home. If she would only use her whip properly I should cease thinking about those who might do so."

He dropped his eyes. She stiffened, compressing her heavy lips.

"Very well, Leopold. You shall have the whip, then. You've deserved it."

He looked up instantly, his whole face alive with delight, like that of a ten-year-old boy suddenly presented with the gift he has longed for ever since he can remember.

"My queen!" Then his shoulders rose, his chin sank. He assumed a cowering expression. "Will it be a whip with six thongs? With steel points?"

She nodded, in a silence grim with real anger. That one should have to descend to such absurdities in order to make a man work! It was maddening. Yet one's livelihood and that of one's children depended upon such idiocies. . . .

She rasped out, in the tone of a cook abusing a scullery-maid:

"I'll take the hide off you now, this very instant, you miserable good-for-nothing!"

"Oh — oh — oh —— "

He began whimpering and shuddering, his eyes rolling grotesquely. She strode purposefully to the wardrobe where he kept his collection of stimulants. There really was a whip there of the type he had mentioned, a sort of cat-o'-nine-tails, studded with nails. He had bought it months ago. She had never yet been able to bring herself to use it. But now she would, with a vengeance. The blind rage of the materialist deprived of materials came upon her. For the first time in her life she flew at her husband like a madwoman, flourishing the steel-pointed scourge.

Afterwards, she thought she had overdone it. But she managed to repress the instinctive movement of compassion for the moaning, writhing victim at her feet. The usual erotic scene followed, in which she gradually yielded to his humble entreaties. Physically, he was always able to satisfy her after such preparations. But mentally she felt utterly alienated, as if raped by a hated stranger. No matter. The thing was necessary. Some wives put up with worse, she knew.

Next morning he was in the best of tempers, went immediately to his study and set to work on the next instalment of *The Legacy of Cain*. At luncheon he was radiant, behaved in every respect like a lover in a woman's magazine story. For a few weeks this strange sequence of events was repeated almost daily. His professional industry appeared to be tremendous, his charm overwhelming. Then, again, to her intense dread, he spoke of her taking a lover. "It's all I need now, Wanda. You shall see. I shall be another Goethe. And you will be the first lady in the land."

He had been so reasonable lately that she ventured to argue the point. Couldn't he see that she would be putting herself utterly in his power by committing adultery? Had he so little respect for his 'empress' that he would treat her like a slave-girl, offering her to all his friends? What would people think? It could only lead to their being socially ostracized and ruined, etc.

He stuck out his thick under-lip, looking ugly and sullen.

"All right. If you won't, I shan't write another line, that's all."

He kept his word, neglecting his work and disappearing for days on end into the surrounding country. Once he left her a note which really frightened her. It was on Christmas Eve, 1874. She read, with rising despair, the concluding lines:

"As your love for me has already evidently reached the stage of wanting to see me perish on a dunghill, you will appreciate that it is no longer possible for us to live together on the terms you prescribe. I will leave you the choice of yourself remaining in Brück or going elsewhere. If you decide on the latter course I shall stay here, if you prefer the former I shall take my departure."

It was not the minotaur who was lost in the labyrinth of the Chevalier's intricate perversities. In this bewildering atmosphere of paradoxical illusion and menace only one idea, one course of action, remained stable in Wanda's mind. At all costs she must retain her position as Frau von Sacher-Masoch. She must find some way of holding him without giving him legal grounds for a divorce. It was a fantastic situation. But it had to be faced.

She promised Leopold that she was now ready to take a lover. But she insisted that it must be a lover chosen by herself, not by him. In this way, by thus temporizing, she hoped to bring him to a more reasonable frame of mind.

Cupid and Eros

THE 'Greeks,' as Leopold always called his potential male 'betrayers,' did not exactly swarm in the sleepy little town of Brück. Wanda told him she found the few who existed dull and provincial. She sent more than one of them packing, in Leopold's presence, for 'insolence,' delighting him, in principle, by her aggressive rudeness, though he would have preferred to have it addressed to himself.

He suggested, therefore, that she should spend a few days in Graz, at a conspicuous hotel, and take full advantage of any 'adventures' that might happen to her there. She departed coolly enough, armed with her best furs. But two days later she was back again, complaining of a raging toothache and general ill-health. She reminded Leopold that she was again pregnant and begged him to be patient until the child was born.

He kept his temper. But Wanda could see that he was growing more and more indifferent to her. He began corresponding again with the ladies who wrote to him about his books. She took steps to frighten the most persistent of these blue-stockings. But by the time a third boy was born to her, in November 1875, the relations between husband and wife seemed to have settled into a state of permanent armed neutrality. The infant, as dark as Sacha had been fair, was christened Demetrius. They called him Mitschi for short.

The birth had not been an easy one. Wanda was rather slower than usual in recovering from it. The midwife, a thick-set, cheerful young woman, with a professionally roguish expression, remained in residence at the mill for some days after the event. Leopold, always interested in physiological details, asked her, the very morning after the birth, whether it had not been a pretty strenuous affair.

She nodded, smiling.

"Fortunately, I have strong arms, *Herr Doktor*."

He raised his eyebrows, giving her an intent stare.

"Yes, you look as if you could give a good account of yourself, Frau Zürbisegger. I wonder how you would tackle *me*."

She laughed gaily.

"Oh, the *Herr Doktor* would be too strong for me, I expect."

"Don't be too sure. Let's try, shall we? For instance, if I caught hold of you like this, what would you do?"

"Oh, that's easy."

They had a slight scuffle, punctuated with giggles from the lady, who eventually gave in, but not before the gentleman was quite out of breath.

"Quite good," he told her seriously. "But, you know, Frau Zürbisegger, you would win easily if you wore one of my wife's furs. I am always frightened when I see a strong woman like you wearing furs. We must try again tomorrow. You'll see —— "

"But surely the *Frau Doktor* wouldn't like that, would she, *Herr Doktor*?"

"Of course she wouldn't mind. We'll tell her, anyhow."

After this, Wanda, duly informed of the proposal, to which she felt too weak to object, had to listen every morning to the sounds of a formal wrestling match between her husband and the midwife in the room next door. On its conclusion, the combatants would enter the bedroom and give her an account of the details of the contest.

"The trouble is," Leopold once assured her, as he sat panting on the bed, while Frau Zürbisegger returned Wanda's best fur coat to its peg in the wardrobe, "in wrestling with a lady, one never knows where to catch hold of her. One might commit an indiscretion, you see."

The midwife, over her shoulder, retorted jocularly:

"Don't worry, *Herr Doktor. I* don't mind where you catch hold of me. It's nothing to me!"

"Oh, but . . . "

He seemed ready to talk all day on the subject. Wanda felt obliged to interrupt with a request for professional attention. She was really furious. The fear that the wrestling matches might lead to an actual intrigue considerably accelerated her recovery. A week later she was out of bed. Marlene Zürbisegger was immediately paid her fees and sent back to her husband.

It was characteristic of Leopold that this abrupt termination of the episode did not depress him. He forgot all about it at once.

A few days later he burst out of his study in a state of tremendous excitement, waving the *Wiener Tageblatt.*

"Wanda, Wanda! Just look at this! It's what we've been waiting for for years! Read it, read it . . ."

He thrust the paper under her nose, a trembling finger at one of the 'Personal' advertisements.

Wanda read obediently:

"Handsome, rich, energetic young man would like to meet pretty, elegant young woman, admirer of the works of Leopold von Sacher-Masoch preferred."

"You must answer it at once, Wanda. This is positively providential. Fancy, young, rich, handsome, energetic, knows my books — it's a 'Greek' from the gods — I'll tell you what to put —— "

It was useless to argue. A reply was composed forthwith and posted, together with a suitable photograph of Wanda, by Leopold himself. Within a couple of days a letter arrived containing a photograph of a sufficiently personable, if somewhat fatuous-looking young man, dressed in oriental costume. Leopold gave a positive shout of delight when he saw it.

"A Turk! A Turk, Wanda! Now at last we have got hold of somebody who understands how to make love! WHAT a piece of luck!"

"But, Leopold. Look here. He signs his letter 'Nikolaus Teitelbaum' —— "

She couldn't help laughing. It was certainly a ridiculous name. But Leopold refused to be depressed by it.

"Oh, that's probably deliberate, a pseudonym. Now, we shall have to arrange a meeting at once."

Again she felt too tired, in her convalescent condition, to argue the point. An appointment was eventually made at a hotel in Murzzuschlag, a health resort in the highland district of Semmering, between Brück and Vienna. The weather was fearfully cold. But Leopold gave her, for the journey, a new fur mantle of terrific proportions, a pair of male riding-boots, an astrakhan cap and a dog-whip. The few passengers on the little platform at Brück stared rather hard. As soon as the train pulled out of the station, Frau von Sacher-Masoch threw the whip out of the window and burst into tears.

Next day Leopold received a telegram to notify him that she was returning to Brück that afternoon. He dashed to the station in a frenzy of excitement.

"Well?"

"Well, Leopold. He knew me at once. His mother is a friend of Baroness Kovöcs, who was at our wedding. They have our wedding photograph in their drawing-room at home. He is a very nice boy, Leopold. Very nice indeed. He said he couldn't dream of intervening in the married life of a man for whom he had such deep respect. We talked half the night. But nothing happened. I felt ill, in any case."

He looked at her in silence, with an expression of misery which quite frightened her. To console him, she kept on talking, promised to do better another time. He remained quiet till they got home, then had a fit of nervous hysteria, weeping, imploring her to tell him the truth, putting extravagant descriptions of the scene at the hotel into her mouth. He seemed determined to believe that there had been flagellation, tortures, adultery, mockery of himself, humiliation of the 'Turk,' followed by disgraceful submission to him on Wanda's part. When she indignantly denied all this, he raved at her and threatened to kill himself. She was afraid to leave him alone.

There were calmer intervals, in one of which he explained that he would never dream of divorcing her. He drew up and signed another 'treaty,' declaring that whatever she did had his entire approval and even encouragement. He actually gave her blank sheets of paper, signed with his full name and rank, for her to write what she pleased on them. She kept the papers, but did not make use of them. For she still could not believe that they could be accepted as the evidence of a sane man in the law-courts, if it should ever come to divorce proceedings.

The year 1876 was the worst they had so far spent together. Conjugal relations had been practically given up. The children were periodically ill. Leopold was perfectly incalculable, sometimes his old, tender, charming self, sometimes terrifying her with his appalling fits of mental agony, sometimes dumb for days together. In July she consulted a doctor, who recommended, as doctors will, when they are utterly at a loss, a change of air.

He spent some weeks at a neighbouring spa, Frohleiten, quite alone, and wrote her cheerful letters, telling her that he was doing good work and corresponding with the brilliant French dramatists Meilhac and Halévy, with a view to collaboration. He sent her a cutting from a Swiss paper which compared him with Byron and Mérimée.

But when he returned in October he caught a cold, took to his bed, and the hypochondria and hallucinations began again. Sometimes he would cling to her and implore her to protect him from the devil. Then he would ask her to tell him stories, which must be 'awful' ones. This was not really Wanda's *forte* and she made a mess of it. He interrupted her sentimental meanderings with savage contempt and took a hand himself, frightening her out of her wits with his descriptions of Chinese and ancient German tortures, which he assured her he intended to practise upon himself.

"I could get you to hang me up over the bath, for instance. You would get into the bath and cut my throat, not enough to kill me at once. The blood would drip into the bath and you would bathe in it as I died. Or else you could tie me up with my head in an anthill, on a hot day. Or we might have a 'Nuremberg Maiden' made. That is an automatic dancing girl, you know, made of steel. You put me inside her and when she begins to dance I am cut to pieces by the sharp blades which come out of her arms, breasts and thighs. Then, one can be suffocated, crushed or frozen to death in all sorts of ways. Wouldn't you like to try something like that on me, Wanda, when I am better?"

She promised at least to whip him 'until the blood came,' to put nettles in his bed and make incisions, 'with a small knife,' in his back. But he continued to languish until, one day, Sacha had an attack of dysentery. Almost at once Leopold recovered, to spend hours at his favourite's bedside. When the little boy got better the mother ventured to appeal to Leopold's highly developed paternal instinct.

"What will happen to the children if I behave like a real *Venus in Furs?*"

"They'll be all the better for it. For I shall be in such high spirits, such a good father to them, that you'll hardly know me. When are you going to begin? And what about 'Greeks?' We haven't said much about them lately."

He was incorrigible, had an answer for everything. And the worst of it was, she reflected sadly, that it was just when the children were well and happy, when commissions were coming in regularly and they seemed to be settling down to a normal married life, that he became most insistent upon his 'Greeks' and his 'tortures.' When he was ill he would simply be maudlin about them. But when he was in good health, he made practical plans, wrote letters, looked up advertisements, laid in a fresh stock of 'stimulants.'

The winter of 1876–7 was so bad, affecting the health of the whole family, that it was decided to make a move from Brück and settle, if possible, in Graz again, where the houses were at least draught-proof. Money was still short, however. The best they could do was to take a small house in a leafy suburb, called the Rosenberg. It was a rather squalid little place. But the air was better than that of Brück and the cottage more solidly built than the mill. They moved to Rosenberg in June.

A letter now arrived from a Berlin bookshop assistant, who signed himself Otto Kapf. It was a somewhat illiterate and incoherent epistle, almost illegible, but very flattering. Leopold gathered that Herr Kapf wished to act as his unpaid secretary, would not dream of remuneration, etc., would work night and day for him, consider it the fulfilment of his highest ambition, needed nothing, was utterly devoted to literature, etc., etc.

The distinguished author replied briefly but courteously that he was in need of no such services. But a week later Herr Kapf arrived at the cottage, with bag and baggage. He was a hideous little creature, with shocking manners and an atrocious Berlin accent. Apart from his enormous spectacles, he was the most unsuitable candidate for a secretaryship that could possibly be imagined. His handwriting alone would have disqualified him. His education seemed to be non-existent. It was impossible to discover anything about him which was of the slightest use to anyone. His utter insignificance and unattractiveness were finally sealed by his complete inability to express himself articulately on any subject whatever.

Leopold, however, declined, against Wanda's urgent remonstrances, to kick him out. His vanity was touched by the devotion of the uncouth visitor and though he was obliged to agree with Wanda that Otto could not possibly be considered as a 'Greek,' he seemed to believe that he might be made useful in time. At least, he was neither greedy nor fraudulent. He gave no more trouble, actually, than some decrepit little mongrel and behaved in much the same way. So he was allowed to stay.

After this disappointment — for Leopold only gave up with reluctance the idea that Kapf might, somehow or other, be made to serve as a 'Greek' — an advertisement was inserted in the Vienna *Tagespost,* by Leopold himself, to the effect that a pretty young woman would be glad to correspond with an 'energetic' gentleman.

The advertisement was answered, in suitable terms, by a 'Count Attems.' A meeting was arranged in the wood behind the cottage.

Leopold followed his wife to the rendezvous and concealed himself in the bushes adjoining the agreed spot. Surely a 'Count,' finding himself alone in the middle of a forest, on a beautiful summer afternoon, with a 'fair unknown' like Wanda, would be pretty enterprising?

But when the 'Count' hove in sight he scarcely came up to Leopold's expectations. A weedy little fellow, with commonplace features, wearing a monocle evidently for the first time and grossly overdressed, he spoke in a high, squeaky voice and seemed frightfully nervous. Wanda could not conceal her contempt for his antics. When he caught his foot in an exposed root and fell flat on his face, smashing the precious new monocle, she burst into a loud laugh. After this accident the 'Count' seemed only too anxious to be off and took his leave in a hurry.

Leopold rejoined his wife, in spite of this fiasco, in quite a good temper.

"You were marvellous, Wanda, the way you looked at him and burst out laughing. You ought really to have hit him, though. Or, better still, kicked him. What a pity you didn't bring a whip."

She was relieved at his attitude and hastened to help him make a joke of the whole affair. Nothing more was heard of 'Count Attems.'

Leopold's literary prospects improved this summer. He received a fairly substantial sum from a publisher and the family moved into the centre of Graz itself, where old acquaintances called upon them and a social life began much more to Wanda's taste than vegetating in a suburb. She set herself, as well as she was able, to be a credit to her husband. She did not succeed as well as she believed. But she was too innocent of society and Leopold too contemptuous of it for its snubs to have much effect on their relations.

He had recently published a story, entitled *Plato's Love* — one of the *Legacy of Cain* series — about a Polish 'Count Anatole' who conceived a purely intellectual passion for a handsome boy, found that the 'boy' was really a girl who returned his love, as women will, in a much more material fashion, and therefore decided to see no more of her, lest his 'spiritual' love should be contaminated by a physical element.

One morning a letter arrived couched in the following terms:

"I wonder how far *Plato's Love* reflects your own mentality? What does your own heart say? Would it give love for love? If the desire pictured in your tale is true, you have found what you seek. I am yours because I must be so, 'Anatole.'"

The handwriting seemed to be a woman's. Wanda agreed, adding that 'she must be crazy.' But Leopold, with his usual optimism, felt that the cryptic sentences might emanate from a discontented 'sultana.' He replied, with ardour, though not quite in such crude terms, that he was ready for anything. A regular storm of correspondence now began. Leopold had never known anything like it for length, continuity, eccentricity and the consistently high level of literary expression. 'Anatole' seemed to be a restless sort of being. His letters were posted, almost from day to day, in Salzburg, Vienna, Brussels, Paris or even London.

Wanda, impressed by this peripatetic correspondent's command of the German language, now no longer believed that a woman was in question. She was glad enough of her new conviction, with which Leopold, to keep her quiet, pretended to agree, though his own feeling was quite otherwise. He began, in his usual style, to press 'Anatole' for a personal encounter. The correspondent at first declined, on grounds of 'spirituality,' then at last yielded, but only upon conditions of surprising complexity.

The meeting was to be in a Brück hotel, the Bernauer, on the 13th of January, 1878. Leopold was to book a room there, sit in it with his eyes blindfolded and all lights turned out until midnight, when he would hear three knocks at the door. At the third knock he was to call 'Come in' but not to move from his chair.

This all sounded, to Leopold's delight, very like a woman. He did what he was told. But before midnight one of the hotel servants brought him a letter from 'Anatole.' In three closely written sheets the mysterious correspondent imparted his or her 'dread' at the forthcoming interview. Of course, it's a woman, the recipient told himself triumphantly, stuffing the letter hastily into his pocket.

But a moment or two before midnight, as he sat in the room in the dark, with his eyes duly blindfolded, he heard a distinctly masculine footfall approach the door. Another note, he thought impatiently. Perhaps she's lost heart at the last moment. But the three knocks specified sounded on the door. At Leopold's somewhat disconcerted "Come in!" he knew, though he could not see, that a man had entered the room. A low, musical voice asked where he was. In the pitch dark Leopold got up and guided the visitor to a divan. They conversed in guarded tones.

"You thought me a woman, I suppose?" murmured the stranger.

"Yes. But don't imagine I am disappointed. Far from it —— "

Leopold launched into one of his eloquent speeches. He had already recovered from the shock of the discovery, had changed his ground adroitly and was now planning to make a 'Greek' of his new friend.

The conversation, extremely tactful on both sides, continued until the small hours. Leopold gathered that 'Anatole,' though no longer in his first youth, had never experienced intercourse with a woman. Leopold, for his part, explained that he was married to a woman of great beauty and intelligence, who would give permission, but only at a personal interview, for them to meet again. The dangerous, intoxicating rhetoric for which the author was famous quite turned the other's head. 'Anatole' kissed, on taking his leave, the hand that had written *Plato's Love*.

The correspondence went on and on. But there were no more meetings. 'Anatole' wrote that he was too 'nervous' to endure them. Both husband and wife began to lose patience. At last Wanda, whose curiosity had been thoroughly aroused by Leopold's sedulous propaganda for his new 'Greek,' wrote a peremptory letter. Either 'Anatole' must bring himself to assume normal social relations with friends who both deeply appreciated him or the correspondence must cease.

The answer was a melancholy farewell. Another failure, thought the unfortunate husband, resignedly. But after a silence of several months 'Anatole' wrote again, promising to arrange a meeting shortly and sending 'a thousand kisses to Wanda,' greatly to that lady's astonishment. The correspondence started all over again. 'Anatole' informed the now somewhat weary couple that he would inspect them in the Graz theatre on a certain evening, but that they would not see him. The Sacher-Masochs duly appeared in their box, Wanda in her most resplendent toilette. But though Leopold kept whispering that he was 'certain' such and such a figure in stalls or foyer was 'Anatole' there could be no real certainty in the matter.

Next day a note was delivered thanking the pair for their condescension and asking them to be at the Elephant Hotel, in the dining-room, that evening. Leopold insisted upon their complying with this request also. While they sat at their table a personage in evening dress, apparently a waiter, approached and asked Leopold to accompany him to another room, 'to see the gentleman.' Leopold rose at once and went out. He returned in a few minutes.

"Now, Wanda, you are to go. He's waiting for you. Follow the 'waiter.' Of course, it isn't a waiter really. It's one of his personal attendants. He's someone quite important, I believe. You are in luck at last, my dear. And so am I. How I wish I could look through the keyhole!"

He was in the gayest spirits, almost clapped her on the back. Wanda got up a little grimly, determined to give 'Anatole,' quite politely, of course, a piece of her mind. But when she reached the private sitting-room to which the 'waiter' conducted her, she found the place in perfect darkness. She was addressed in a childish voice by someone sitting on a divan in a corner, and realized that once more the game had gone to 'Anatole.' This was not the big man with the deep voice described so eloquently by Leopold, but a tiny cripple, who talked like 'Count Attems.'

She could scarcely keep her temper. When, at last, she made a brusque excuse to return to her husband, he appeared to be amazed at the substitution.

"I swear it was Anatole I saw, my dear! I can't imagine who the other one can be!"

Next day a visitor called at the Sacher-Masochs' house and asked to see Wanda alone. Fortunately, Leopold was out. Wanda afterwards described to him how she had received an undersized, crippled youth, with reddish, fair hair, pallid, weak features and a melancholy expression. This adolescent had knelt to her in a state of hysterical diffidence, buried his face in her lap and sobbed. He had begged her to forgive him for his presumption, bidden her an eternal farewell, said that he would see her once more in the theatre that evening and would afterwards wait for both Leopold and herself, for 'a last handclasp' in a closed carriage under the walls of the Opera House.

This dramatic event duly took place. When Leopold approached the carriage, two *muscular* arms issued from the darkened window and embraced him. When he withdrew, Wanda's hands were seized in the same firm grip, and kissed. Then the carriage drove rapidly away. The whole scene passed in profound silence.

But even then the last had not been heard of 'Anatole.' Another 'farewell letter' arrived, rather peevishly phrased. It remained unanswered, for even Leopold's appetite for mystification was now satiated. Some months later an enormous manuscript was delivered to him. It purported to describe the whole episode from end to end. The style was portentous and involved to an extreme degree. But he gathered that two friends, both wealthy and cultured men, but one exceptionally handsome and well built, the other sickly and a cripple, had taken it in turns to pursue the correspondence with the author of *Plato's Love*. The manuscript ended with a sarcastic epilogue, evidently written by the more manly of the two partners, which in Leopold's view declined considerably from the literary standard of the material which had preceded it.

"A charming prospect!" wrote this robust 'Anatole.' "I am to put on crimson ermine and white satin breeches and Leopold is to lie at my feet and adore me; I am to torture him, while he begs for mercy. I am to be exhibited to the journalists who come to see him in this weird rig-out of velvet, silk and sumptuous furs, reclining upon a divan, and they will go away and write the most wonderful articles about it. I shall, of course, fall in love with Wanda and she with me, we shall have a gloriously amusing time, and the stupid world, which only believes in what is common, will say of me that I am the lover of both husband and wife. A marvellous life, to be sure! All I should have to do first of all would be to smash my father's unsullied seal to pieces and tear up my pedigree."

Wanda secretly admired this peroration, which she considered the very essence of aristocratic virility and disdain. But Leopold laughed at it, calling it a thoroughly bourgeois production. He had really completely lost interest in 'Anatole' ever since it had become clear that this double personality, so far from being an allegory of Eros as contrasted with Cupid, was a mere case of homosexuality.

What remained of the mystery was finally cleared up in 1881. In that year, while the Sacher-Masochs were staying at Henbach, near Passau in Bavaria, they met a certain Dr. Grandauer, who, on hearing the story, identified 'Anatole,' with great confidence, as the royal friends King Ludwig II of Bavaria, patron of Richard Wagner and builder of fantastic castles, an eccentric giant, and Prince Alexander of Orange, eldest son of King William III of Holland, an almost helpless invalid, who had been found unfit to succeed to the throne and was then living in Paris. Alexander was to die in 1884 and Ludwig II to drown himself two years later.

The year 1878, during which the 'Anatole' affair pursued its desultory and unsatisfactory course, was fated to be one in which Leopold would encounter one grotesque disguise after another of the face of that Eros he worshipped so devotedly. After the male homosexual, the female. Leopold became involved that summer with two notorious Graz Lesbians, girls of good family and education, the younger of whom, known as 'Mignon,' had literary ambitions.

She was not at all Leopold's type physically, being a shy little thing, pretty enough, but with only her big dark eyes and romantic disposition to recommend her. Her friend, 'Nora,' was a big, teasing blonde, complete with cropped hair and cigars, who had no time for Leopold's 'nonsense,' called Otto Kapf the 'son of Heaven' to his face and appeared to have a fatal fascination for feeble-minded females. Leopold gave her up almost at a glance and concentrated upon 'Mignon.' He found a publisher for her stories and invited her to fly to Germany with him.

Wanda, however, soon put an end to this romance, in the most natural way in the world, by innocently describing her husband's sexual perversions to the girls and exhibiting his collection of 'stimulants' to them. This confidential talk had the desired effect immediately. Frau von Sacher-Masoch had certainly been growing up fast during the last few years.

After this particular Eros had veiled his face and turned away, an uncompromising heathen Cupid appeared who for a whole year on end led both Leopold and Wanda into a series of adventures in the end as unpalatable to the one as to the other.

Kathrin Strebinger was the daughter of a half crazy Swiss pastor, of intensely Calvinistic principles and incredible miserliness. She ran away from this boor to Geneva, where she became the mistress of the formidable Henri Rochefort, Marquis de Rochefort-Luçay, a famous French politician, journalist, dramatist, duellist and Communist, then living in exile in the Swiss city. Kathrin was the boyish-bohemian type of female intellectual, physically and mentally as hard and bright as a bagful of new nails, coolly immoral, devastatingly capable, a reckless experimenter in all ways of living, from breaking in wild horses to sampling life as a common prostitute.

She had already had some correspondence with Leopold, in her capacity as translator of his works for the Swiss and French Press and book trade. In April 1878 she wrote to him from Ghent to say that she was coming to pay him a visit. On arrival at the station she flew into his arms and kissed him heartily on the mouth. But he soon found that her sexual attitude was far too casual and prosaic to suit him. He considered her abominably arrogant and slapdash in this respect, despite her precision at her professional work, and resented her open contempt for his little favourite of the moment, 'Mignon.'

Life with Kathrin could not, however, be called dull. Almost every day she told some fantastic story about her lurid past, or embarked upon others in a present which she was determined to render equally lurid. She first seduced, then insulted 'Nora.' She sent herself flowers and erotic telegrams, to be delivered to her in some conspicuous public place, such as a theatre. She broke the heart of a high-ranking Austrian staff officer, a decent fellow, who was really keen on her. She reduced to tears a Baroness who attempted to inveigle her into marriage with a ruined son. She entertained in her bedroom, in her dressing-gown, one of the municipal street messengers. She smacked a Baron's face in a public restaurant for saying he had seen a man come out of her room in a hotel after midnight. The Baron challenged Leopold to a duel. Leopold contemptuously refused to have anything to do with the case. On the first night of a play composed by one of the Baron's friends Kathrin packed the stalls with paid interrupters, who, however, had misunderstood her French accent and clapped instead of hissing. She was not in the least disconcerted by this anticlimax but, on the contrary, told the story all over Graz as an excellent joke. She could never bear malice for longer than a few minutes.

But the most interesting of Kathrin's exploits and the one which eventually led Leopold to decide that he had had enough of her was the case of Sefer Pasha.

This grey-bearded, pseudo-Oriental and lavishly sybaritic collector of antiquities had, it appeared, started life as a Polish Count. He had, however, spent a great many years at the Egyptian Court, where he had amassed an immense fortune by means which necessitated a sudden withdrawal to the neighbourhood of Graz. Here he erected a gigantic castle to house his treasures and became a legend in the district for extravagance and eccentricity. As soon as Kathrin heard of his existence she wrote him a long letter explaining who she, Wanda and Leopold were and that they would greatly appreciate the opportunity of a visit to the castle of Bertholdstein, as the 'Pasha's' residence was named.

Count Koscielski (such was his real title) at once replied that he would be delighted to see all three of these distinguished people whenever they liked for as long as they liked. Leopold, scenting a 'Greek' of the first water, contrived, at the last moment, when the ladies were all ready to set out, to have a raging toothache. Experience had taught him that 'Greeks' were more likely to come up to scratch in the absence of the husband.

He went so far as to send for a dentist to pull the tooth out in the presence of Wanda, robed in her most expensive furs. The dentist of course told him that there was nothing wrong with his teeth. Leopold snapped his fingers impatiently.

"Do as I tell you. Pull it out."

"It will hurt you, *Herr Doktor*."

"Pull it out, I tell you! You are being paid, aren't you?"

The man shrugged his shoulders and produced his forceps. The pain was agonizing. Wanda could hardly bear to watch the operation, which took quite a long time. Yet the sufferer, grimacing, gasping and groaning, never removed his eyes from her face for a moment.

When it was all over she saw that he was pleased with the impassive attitude she had maintained, in accordance with the careful training he had now been giving her for so long. But it was obvious that he was in no fit state to travel. Sefer Pasha was expecting them the next day and must not be disappointed. The ladies departed, finally, without Leopold, who left his wife in no doubt of the part she was to play with the 'ideal Greek.'

It is hardly necessary to add that, after an adventurous journey during which Kathrin's experience with horses came in useful and her reckless daring terrified Wanda out of her wits, it was not the shy, if handsome matron, with her awkward manners and imperfect erudition, who attracted the elderly debauchee, but her brilliant, impudent, brown-skinned and athletic younger companion.

The women slept in separate rooms at the castle that night. In the morning Kathrin informed Wanda, with much hilarity and salacious detail, that she had added their experienced host to her bottomless bag of conquests. Frau von Sacher-Masoch observed primly that she was glad of the fact, for it had saved her, personally, a lot of trouble. But they had better return home that day, she went on, for she was anxious about Leopold's health. Sefer would quite understand the shortness of their present visit, in the circumstances which had already been explained to him.

After some argument Kathrin, who was enjoying herself, as usual, reluctantly agreed to this move and also to represent to Leopold, without details, that all was going well and that the visit would be renewed at a later date.

Koscielski behaved with perfect discretion and indulgence when they all met at breakfast. He renewed his invitation in the warmest terms, making a particular point of his anxiety to see the famous author.

Leopold, when the second expedition was arranged, again contrived that the ladies should precede him for one night. But on this occasion they found themselves allotted the same room, in which, much to Kathrin's annoyance, though she pretended to make a joke of the fact, they were not disturbed. Leopold duly arrived the next day and found much in common with his genial and learned host. But though he enjoyed the latter's highly exotic conversation, he perceived with chagrin that Fraülein Strebinger had stolen his wife's thunder. Once again, a promising 'Greek,' really perhaps, he told himself, through no fault of Wanda's this time, had declined the eternal gambit.

At home, he took the first opportunity to quarrel with Kathrin, telling her brusquely, one day at lunch-time, not to gossip so much. This remark was quite enough for that equally sharp-tongued young lady. After a painful scene, she took herself off to a hotel. For she had no intention, just yet, of returning to Rochefort. About the same time, the deterioration in the tempers of both husband and wife resulted in the dismissal of Otto Kapf. He moved to the house of an eccentric poetess, who had recently been taking an interest in him.

The rest of the year 1879 passed in a dreary round of attempts by Leopold to find more 'Greeks,' every one of which failed him. There were several reasons for these fiascos. Wanda, for her part, was still afraid of divorce, even more so now that the children were growing up. The 'Greeks,' on their side, often suspected the truth, if they had even a smattering of intelligence, since Leopold's ideas about love and jealousy were now notorious. Prospective lovers of Wanda, accordingly, felt that they would be simply made to look ridiculous for his convenience, a reversal of the usual rôles of husband and interloper which did not amuse them.

He was reduced, therefore, to proposing stupid or degraded candidates whom his wife could reject on perfectly reasonable grounds, which he was obliged in common fairness to admit.

The Sacher-Masochs were both glad when, in February 1880, an invitation came from Budapest for Leopold to give a course of lectures in the Hungarian capital. It was really the numerous and powerful Jewish element in the population which was responsible for this gesture. Leopold, who had not a drop of Jewish blood in his body, had never made any secret of his intense interest in and admiration for Jews, who were then, as always, badly in need of highly-placed friends. One of his recent books had been entitled *Jewish Tales* and is still one of the best studies in existence of the European Jewish community. The reception of the Sacher-Masochs in Budapest, for these reasons, was perfervid.

After the lectures, which were a great success, for Leopold talked even better than he wrote, were over, a Jewish family of the name of Suhr invited the Sacher-Masochs to their estate at Ecszed, on the great Hungarian plain called the Puszta, for the summer. Life at Ecszed was typically Jewish, populous with innumerable relatives of every age, sex, extraction, and cultural level. It was punctuated by strange religious ceremonies, fasts followed by gargantuan feasts, visits to other estates, revels with the peasants, encounters with brigands of easily bribable disposition and parties of every description but the vicious. For the simple vivacity of these vociferous people, perpetually in a state of impulsive agitation, did not extend to any but the most primitive eroticism.

Leopold plunged into all this, to him fairly familiar excitement, with the greatest delight and lack of self-consciousness. He was always at his very best with children or childlike persons. He became, almost in a moment, the indispensable centre of every purely secular celebration. It is true that he introduced his famous game of 'robbers' into the outdoor amusements. But this equivocal pastime was here modified to a very innocent version of its original. There were chasings and seizures, but no whippings or 'tortures,' though there might be a mock 'tying up.'

Nevertheless, his obsession with 'Greeks' was really only slumbering, ready at the least favourable sign to raise its, for Wanda, sinister head. That lady was interrupted in her literary labours, for as she did not care much for outdoor exercise she was devoting herself again to this occupation, by an introduction from Leopold to a shy youth from a neighbouring estate, Alexander Gross.

Sandor, as he was affectionately called, had a rather heavy type of good looks and his fair share of concupiscence, but not much in the way of brains, though he was supposed to be studying law at the University of Budapest in his spare time.

He was attracted by Wanda and showed it in his clumsy, inarticulate way. She received him warily, but without antipathy. Leopold's incessant returns to this subject were beginning to get on her nerves and she now, at last, had a good mind to take him at his word. He had recently, moreover, found a new method of bringing pressure to bear on her. He was beginning to hint that if she did not do her duty and 'betray' him, he would take steps to find a mistress who would not be so particular. Wanda, with memories of 'Mignon' and others who had, of late years, nearly come to perform this rôle, resolved to take the plunge with Sandor.

But a practical difficulty arose. The families of both Gross and

Suhr were so inordinately numerous that privacy in either house was non-existent. Even the mildest flirtations aroused attention inconvenient to a sedentary matron with three young children. It was decided that the 'betrayal' must be postponed until a move was made to Budapest in September.

Here the Sacher-Masochs obtained furnished rooms of a rather cramped and unsatisfactory character, for Leopold, as usual, had spent all the money received for the lectures and was now in straitened circumstances again. Nevertheless, young Sandor, who had recently resumed his studies at the University, was invited to dinner. Leopold sent the children to bed early and spent hours decking his wife out for the 'sacrifice.' She received the callow guest in ermine and white satin. Leopold, in evening dress, insisted upon waiting at table.

The law student could not but be elated at the prospect of Frau von Sacher-Masoch's forthcoming capitulation to his long, if diffident, siege of her virtue. But he was seriously incommoded by the obsequious solemnity of her husband. He still stood in considerable awe of the distinguished Austrian visitor and could not reconcile himself to the part of insolent seducer which he was supposed to play.

After dinner Leopold ostentatiously withdrew to the kitchen. Sandor respectfully enquired of Wanda the reason for his curious behaviour. She found herself obliged, not for the first time, to try to get into this young man's rather obtuse head the nature and effects of her husband's sexual eccentricities. She spoke with some asperity. Sandor, who was nearly as frightened of this haughty beauty as he was of her 'brilliant' husband, began to feel that the situation was getting beyond him. He understood and enjoyed coquetry, normal inhibitions and sheer lasciviousness. But he certainly did not understand or enjoy what was in question here. It semed to him as baffling as the Hungarian property laws.

Wanda was reduced, after a final indication, in the plainest terms, of what his general attitude should be, to simply telling him to obey her orders.

She began, both so as to prove to Sandor that he stood in no danger from conjugal resentments and also to reassure herself on this score, by ringing for Leopold and commanding him to bring 'the paper,' i.e. the 'treaty,' authorizing her to do as she pleased with regard to 'lovers.' She had not seen it for some months and feared he might have destroyed or lost it.

But Leopold produced the document at once. He read it aloud, with great solemnity, in a sonorous tone, then handed it, on his knees, to Sandor for inspection. Wanda dismissed her husband brusquely, after this ceremony, locked up the 'treaty' and proceeded, as previously instructed by her spouse, to rig out the embarrassed undergraduate as a 'Turk,' in a fez bought for the occasion and Leopold's best fur overcoat. She then planted him in an armchair, sat on his knee and called in her harshest voice for the author, who, she knew, had been standing to attention in the kitchen ever since his dismissal.

On Leopold's entrance she informed him, from her position on Sandor's lap, that she was about to 'betray' him and that henceforward he would have to obey her 'Turkish' lover. Sandor, prompted vigorously by his prospective mistress, called, rather nervously, for wine. It was brought with deliberate delay and clumsiness. Wanda reached for a whip, which had been prepared in readiness for this thoroughly rehearsed scene, and gave the 'servant' a few energetic cuts with it. Leopold fled in terror, shut the kitchen door and glued his eye to the keyhole, which gave him a restricted view of the room beyond.

After some theatrical laughter and a brief carouse, during which the parties behaved as though in a cheap brothel, the act of adultery for which Leopold had been waiting, through disappointment after disappointment, for ten long years, duly took place.

Almost immediately afterwards Wanda herself flung open the door, whip in hand. Leopold was flagellated, obliged to kiss her hands and feet and to help Sandor to put himself to rights for the street. That young gentleman, who could not bear to look his disgracefully accommodating host in the face, fumbled, as ordered by

Wanda in a fierce whisper, for his cigarettes. He hurriedly tipped his host with one of these, representing an even greater humiliation than the passage of a coin, and fled.

The guilty wife, with a sigh of relief, enquired grimly of her legitimate partner whether he was now satisfied.

He threw himself at her feet in a perfectly genuine ecstasy.

"You were wonderful, tremendous! Oh, I shall never forget this! Oh, how I fear you and love you — I am horribly, excruciatingly jealous — it was terrible — terrible —— "

He went on like this for a long time, writhing in a hysterical agony of delight. She had never seen him reach such a point of orgiastic rapture and was quite fascinated at the sight.

When he at last grew calmer, she tried to explain her own point of view and also Sandor's. She was sure that the boy was thoroughly ashamed of himself and terrified of Leopold's 'vengeance.' But her husband, prancing about the room in a frenzy of triumph and excitement, laughed this idea to scorn. He fell at her feet again. The long physical estrangement between the couple ended, that night, in an orgy of primitive passion which almost compensated Wanda for all the years of bitter disillusionment, anxiety and disgust which had again and again brought her to the verge of despair since her grand design to marry a rich and famous man had culminated in the church of Saint Sang in 1873.

But this mood did not last. She found that Leopold expected the intrigue with Sandor to be a permanent feature of their lives together. Gradually, the perpetual artificial stimulation of her senses dulled her original feelings of ignominy and self-contempt. Her nature was coarse enough to find, for a time, a real pleasure in regular commonplace debauchery. Sandor himself grew jealous of her cynical promiscuity.

Its effect upon Leopold was, to begin with, agreeable. But he was too sensitive to feminine charms not to become aware, as time went on, of his once resplendent wife's steady physical and mental degeneration. He felt, at times, that he really could not stand her much longer. But habit remained decisive. There was no definite psychological or material break during the ensuing months. But misunderstandings and quarrels grew more and more frequent. There could be no doubt, as the year 1881 drew to a close, that the matrimonial experiment upon which both parties had founded such high hopes was at last coming to an end.

CHAPTER SEVEN

Hulda Meister

A SERIO-COMIC episode occurred this year which illustrates both Leopold's characteristic nervous irritability in matters which had nothing to do with sex, the peculiar social conditions of the time and place and the fact that Wanda, for all the coarsening of her temper at this period, still retained a typically bourgeois sense of duty to the husband she really, by now, detested.

He had been writing for a Viennese paper, perhaps in imitation of Turgenev, with whom he had some literary affinities, a series of light, satirical sketches of well-known personalities. In one instance he went too far. The disguise under which a powerful publisher, Froeben by name, appeared in these word-caricatures, had been too thin. Froeben prosecuted the author for slander and won his case. A sentence of eight days' imprisonment was decreed by the Austrian Courts and could not be commuted.

Leopold was safe for the time being in Budapest, where this variety of Austrian law had no validity. But he made a great fuss about the affair and no secret of his fright at the idea of becoming a convict, if only for a week. This kind of humiliation, since it had nothing to do with women, did not appeal to him. He made strenuous efforts to get the sentence quashed, but without success.

In his despair he turned to the woman whom he had once believed capable of doing anything she liked with a man.

"You must go to the Emperor, Wanda."

"I? Why, what on earth can I do?"

"Everything. He will listen to a beautiful woman, though he will not listen to a man. Braun, my father's friend, who is Chief of the Privy Council, will get you the audience. You have only to appear in your furs and your white satin and use your eyes. Talk vaguely about the dishonour to your husband, the Chevalier von Sacher-Masoch. These kings and emperors only care about women and rank. You might even be able to seduce him. Think of that!"

His dark eyes glittered feverishly. She smiled cynically.

"You are hopeless, Leopold. Well, I don't mind trying. I've never seen an emperor in my life before so far as I can remember, certainly not in private."

Francis Joseph, however, though extremely courteous, as usual, was not encouraging.

"I am a constitutional monarch, Frau von Sacher-Masoch. I cannot interfere with the administration of the laws of my country. In any case, I can assure you that neither I nor any man of sense in Austria considers it a disgrace for an eminent intellectual like the Chevalier to be imprisoned for a few days for speaking his mind. Writers of any creative originality are always in hot water, and a very good thing, too, for civilization. It is their business to keep us old fogies from stagnating. I can do nothing for your husband, most gracious lady. But you can tell him from me that I shall always regard him as my loyal and patriotic subject, however often he gets into prison."

On receipt of Wanda's report Leopold first raved, then wept, then wired in all directions for money to enable him to leave Austria-Hungary altogether. For while Wanda was at Court he had ascertained from the Hungarian police that an extradition order from Vienna would have to be complied with.

A friendly Jew sent him the necessary travelling expenses. The Sacher-Masochs took refuge in Henbach, a German village just over the frontier, where, for the second time, they lived in an old mill. It was during this period that the 'Anatole' mystery was finally cleared up by Dr. Grandauer. Leopold was now notified that the prison sentence had been reduced to four days only. But he remained obstinately in exile, taking a fearful joy, sometimes, in walking ten steps over the frontier into Austria. He told Wanda that he would never return to that ungrateful country after the way its rulers had treated him.

In September 1881 he heard through friends that a Jewish publisher in Leipzig, one Leon Baumgärtner, would like to see him with a view to starting a special periodical. Leopold instantly transferred himself to the German city, found Baumgärtner young, handsome, cultured and apparently extremely wealthy and very soon came to terms with him.

The projected review was to be of the highest possible intellectual standard — it was even to be called *On The Heights*. It would be internationally minded, pacifist, philo-semitic and francophile. It was to be afraid of nothing and would teach the Germans a much-needed lesson in cosmopolitan good manners, aesthetics, practical philosophy and social reform.

Leopold, in the highest spirits, summoned Wanda to join him at once and meet this altogether exceptional 'Greek,' who put even Sefer Pasha in the shade. She arrived quite ready, in her present mood, to prove as complacent as anybody could wish, particularly now that their livelihood and the future of their children seemed to depend upon it.

But trouble began almost at once. Baumgärtner proved to be so highly serious and respectable an intellectual that Wanda could make nothing of him. Her methods, it is true, had become rather vulgar since the days of Alexander Gross. They seemed to shock the sensitive young publisher, who gave her clearly to understand that he was not interested in adultery.

Leopold lost his temper. He staged a furious scene with his wife in which he told her, for the first time, a few home truths about her tactlessness and primitive mentality. He warned her that unless she went to work with more discretion and realized that she was dealing with a man of refined sensibility and education, not a coarse adventurer like herself, he would leave her to stew in her own juice with Mitschi and Linerl, while he removed himself, with Sacha, beyond her baneful and degrading influence.

Wanda, in a real panic, for there had been a scene something like this a few months before, when he had torn up the 'papers,' promptly went into hysterics. She told him, on recovering, that she had never loved him and was now determined to give him as good as he gave her. She threatened him physically, perhaps with a confused idea that this time-honoured expedient might bring him, as so often before, to heel. He rushed out of the house, calling for the police. She flung herself onto a couch and burst into a violent tempest of sobs.

In the end she gave in. Relieved at her new docility but with his mind now made up to get rid of her with as little fuss as possible, Leopold sounded Baumgärtner, in a general way, about his views on marriage. But this rather unusual Jew, it turned out, was a confirmed bachelor. He smilingly informed the anxious author that his intellectual exertions left him no energy to pay proper attention to a wife.

Leopold saw that the case was hopeless. For once, he had met his match in obstinacy. His miraculous powers of persuasion had no effect upon a man who was his intellectual equal, perhaps his superior in sophistication, though inferior in sheer verbal facility and felicity.

Baumgärtner now began to be rather difficult of access. He told Leopold, at last, that he felt he had been mistaken in his judgment that the time was ripe for educating Germany. For the time being, he believed that he could serve the cause of cosmopolitan civilization better in Vienna. He imparted this information with the greatest possible delicacy and courtesy. But his decision remained unalterable. *On The Heights* must temporarily cease publication. It was not a business proposition.

The disappointed editor vented his spleen, as was becoming habitual with him now, upon Wanda. She kept her temper this time. For she had reached a point of desperation, by now, when she felt that nothing could save her and the children but a cool head. She talked of ways and means, of 'starting again.' It was Leopold's turn to burst into tears.

In the very nick of time, a letter arrived from Nuremberg which revived Leopold's remarkably resilient spirits. Always susceptible to flattery, he read with delight the smooth phrases of a certain Monsieur Armand, then just completing, in the Bavarian city of Albrecht Dürer, an exhaustive study of that very painter. M. Armand went on to say that he had read with deep appreciation a copy of *On The Heights* and heard with inexpressible despair of its imminent dissolution. He had, however, a ray of hope to offer the distinguished editor. He had been talking to a publisher named Morgenstern, who seemed willing to back a somewhat similar venture. Could M. Armand give himself the barely imaginable pleasure of meeting the Chevalier von Sacher-Masoch in the near future?

The reply was a foregone conclusion. M. Armand duly arrived in Leipzig in January 1882 and made an excellent impression on both parties. He was a rather heavily built, soft-spoken, youngish man, very well dressed and groomed in the French style, but of unmistakably Jewish extraction. Wanda took to him at once and he, apparently, to her. Leopold found him knowledgeable and sensible, with a wonderful air of quiet confidence where money was in question. He was one of those men who wave such difficulties aside with convincing assurance. Morgenstern, he said, would look after the commercial side. And he himself, Jacques Armand, was by no means a child in these matters and commanded resources which, he hinted with a charmingly deprecatory smile in Wanda's direction, would not be easy to exhaust.

The whole atmosphere in the Leipzig home of the Sacher-Masochs seemed to change almost overnight from bitter brooding to lively activity. Morgenstern, an absolute expert, it seemed, in publishing, with every whit as confident a manner as M. Armand and a somewhat similar personal appearance, soon became a valued intimate of the family circle. Leon Baumgärtner's departure for Vienna, from which city, incidentally, he never returned, passed nearly unnoticed in the general bustle.

The serious but thoroughly discreet love affair between Wanda and M. Jacques Armand, which rapidly reached consummation and permanence, found its natural and gratefully acknowledged place in Leopold's new outlook of the rosiest optimism. Money became plentiful. Distinguished visitors, among them the composer Saint-Saëns

and Juliette Adam, editress of the *Nouvelle Revue Française* and
mistress of France's greatest living statesman, Léon Gambetta, came
to call.

A far less brilliant personage, but one destined to play a decisive
part in the remainder of Leopold's life, now also made her appearance. He had engaged for the new periodical, on the strength of an
exceptionally impressive list of qualifications, a lady named Hulda
Meister as his chief translator. She was by birth a West Prussian and
now just twenty-six years old. She had spent all her short adult life as
a governess in various parts of Germany, Switzerland, Italy, Ru-
mania and even Central and South America, specializing in wealthy
cosmopolitan families. She disposed of a long series of uniformly
flattering testimonials to her industry, sobriety, intelligence, patience,
linguistic erudition and affectionate nature. Leopold was to find all
this evidence perfectly well founded in Hulda's typically German
character. She was a perfect monument of conscientiousness and
shrewd sense, utterly honest and as courageous as becomes a young
woman whose plain looks were not likely to involve her in any very
severe tests.

Her friends called her, she told him ingenuously, 'the little bee'
and she tried her best to live up to the nickname. Leopold was
gracious and appreciative. But it never occurred to him, just then,
that there might be anything in Hulda but a useful member of his
staff. He was busy at the time, not only with the new paper, but also
with Jenny Marr, a young Jewess of enormous size, whom he was
training to take Wanda's place. This affair, however, broke down
after a few weeks, owing to the incongruous sentimentalities of the
giantess. It was not until the middle of March, when Wanda was
absent in Berlin with Armand and Morgenstern, that Hulda Meister
first attracted his serious attention.

It had been arranged that she, as the Sacher-Masochs' most
responsible woman friend, should look after the children and run
the household while Wanda remained away. On the first evening of
Fräulein Meister's residence in the house she and Leopold had a long
talk together.

It was impossible for him to converse for more than half an hour with a young or even middle-aged woman of any sensibility without introducing her to his views on the ideal sexual relationship. The looks and temperament of any such listener might be the very opposite of stately and domineering. Leopold would always find, once he was fairly launched into his exposition, some significant feature, in her appearance, comments or gestures, of an encouraging nature.

Hulda Meister was, in fact, something more than a typically friendly and bustling little business woman, thoroughly practical and efficient. Her travels and the logically enquiring mind which had made her such a good linguist had led her to an intelligent sympathy with psychological traits alien from her own, particularly if they were to be found in an agreeably indulgent employer distinguished in his own line of business and apparently well on the way to still further distinction in it.

She underwent the spell of Leopold's rhetoric with a trained relish for its literary qualities and without surprise at its barely concealed basic content. She was not swept off her feet by a blind infatuation for the brilliant personality of the lecturer. But she would not have been a warm-hearted and broad-minded young German governess without much sexual experience of her own if she had not felt some compassion for his erotic woes and a real admiration for the gifts and the charm which were being stifled by them.

She assured Leopold, of her own accord, that he did not 'frighten' her.

His eyes burned.

"Will you help me, Fräulein Hulda?"

"Well — "

The furs and the whip were produced. Hulda carried through her part of the business with all the earnest docility she showed in her everyday work. Leopold was delighted with her. Twenty years before he would have deeply regretted the fact that she was, quite definitely, not of the 'imperial' type. Now he was simply grateful for her natural adroitness, sincerity and energy. She became, that same evening, the most satisfactory mistress he had known since he first encountered Wanda herself.

That strong-minded lady, on her return from Berlin, was of course at once informed by Zenzi, her maid, that Leopold and his translator had been regularly sleeping together during her absence. Wanda had been, for some time, according a similar privilege to Monsieur Armand. It may have been for this reason that Leopold had taken so little trouble to conceal his new erotic orientation from Zenzi. He can hardly have been prepared, in any case, for the extravagant violence of Wanda's behaviour on her discovery of his latest intrigue.

She dragged Zenzi into the presence of the guilty couple, made her repeat her story and interrupted immediately, with raucous abuse, Leopold's too casual admission of the irregularity. He was stupefied when, with her heavy face distorted and empurpled by passion, she seized the ever-present whip and flung herself, in a storm of reckless fury, not upon himself, but upon the trembling 'little bee,' who had been given to understand by her lover that his wife would be wholly indifferent to their proceedings, since she had a well-established 'friend' of her own.

Wanda had cut Fräulein Meister hard over the face, twice, with the heavy whip, and brought it down again and again on her cowering shoulders, before Leopold and the maid managed to intervene. It was no part of his sexual plan to allow assaults, however splendidly terrific, upon helpless girls in his presence. He could not help admiring, in a detached way, his wife's Valkyric rage. But he concluded, within a second or two, that it resembled a washerwoman's rather than an empress's. He hated her at that moment. Yet even so Zenzi, who had been used to this sort of thing at home, played the chief part in securing the termagant.

Meanwhile, Hulda had fainted. Leopold hastened to revive her to some extent and managed to escort her from the house, while Wanda, in hysterics, struggled with the sturdy Zenzi. The former's frenzy on this occasion can only be put down to a sudden fit of irrational jealousy, exacerbated by her recognition of the new mistress's superiority to herself in every respect except the purely physical. Husband and wife had long been estranged. The association with Armand was an open secret. But Wanda was too crudely vindictive by nature, too resentful of the failure of her anxiously and cunningly premeditated and at first triumphantly realized marriage, to give her 'degenerate' partner the satisfaction of a cosy intrigue with a more congenial companion.

Next day, the 22nd of March, 1882, Leopold received the following characteristic letter from the victim of his wife's ferocity.

"Honoured Sir,

After what happened to me in your house today you will readily understand that I feel obliged to resign my post in the office. I will finish what I have still to prepare for the May number and then return to my home or else go to Berlin. I shall be glad if you will be so good as to have the remuneration due to me remitted to my future address.

At Berlin I shall take the necessary steps to obtain legal redress for the assault committed upon me."

The Chevalier instantly rushed to Fräulein Meister's Leipzig lodgings, threw himself at her feet, declared his eternal love for her and offered her marriage at the first opportunity that could be contrived. He explained to her that until the paper was fairly launched it was absolutely necessary for him to remain on good terms with Armand, who, so far as he could gather, had no present intention of taking on Wanda and her children as a permanent liability. Leopold added, however, that this was the object he himself wished to achieve, provided he could keep his favourite Sacha with him, and he was working steadily and tactfully to this end. Matters so delicate could not be rushed. But Hulda must understand that the goal ever present to his mind was a peaceful and happy life with the only woman he had ever met in his whole life who thoroughly understood him and whom he could thoroughly love and respect.

She saw at once that he was sincere, promised to be patient and to resume her duties with the paper. At the same time she urged him, in her practical way, to consult his lawyers as to the best manner in which the 'impossible' Wanda could be removed from their path to respectable domesticity. Leopold agreed to bend all his energies and ingenuity to this end, so far as the Roman Catholic Church, to which both he and Wanda belonged, would permit him to do so.

This uneasy position lasted until New Year's Day, 1883, the twenty-fifth anniversary of the publication of *Rebellion in Ghent,* the first printed work of Leopold von Sacher-Masoch. A formal celebration of this event was staged by Armand and Morgenstern in the author's house at Leipzig. Correspondence poured in. An album of international autographs was presented to Leopold containing the names of Zola, Dumas, Saint-Saëns, Ibsen, Bjornson, Bret Harte, Pasteur, Daudet, Gounod and the Duc de Broglie, to mention only figures who are still world-famous. A special telegram came from Victor Hugo. Juliette Adam sent to the Chevalier von Sacher-Masoch the ribbon of the French Légion d'Honneur. Public ceremonies took place in Lemberg and Prague as well as in Leipzig. However badly Leopold's private life was going, there was no doubt of his public eminence. Armand and Morgenstern privately congratulated each other as well as their *protégé,* who was especially popular, they noted with serious attention, among the Jewish communities of Europe.

Leopold's forty-seventh birthday occurred on the 27th of that month. On the 29th he informed both Wanda and Armand of his decision to leave his wife, taking Sacha with him, and to live openly with Hulda Meister. This step seems to have been influenced not only by the fact that the latter lady had recently received a legacy but also by Leopold's feeling, after the recent demonstrations of his solid literary reputation abroad, that he need no longer nurse Armand. Wanda of course stormed. Armand argued. But the Chevalier departed the same day, with his son, to Fräulein Meister's apartments.

This move merely regularized a situation which had existed for nearly a year. But it had the effect, upon Wanda, of hardening her whole attitude towards her husband into a determination to make him suffer in any way she could for the humiliation of being deserted in favour of Hulda. She was accordingly determined, come what might, to remain his official wife and thus to disgrace him and his 'paramour' in their turn. In this intention Wanda was supported by her lover. Jacques Armand now confessed to her that his real name was Jacob Rosenthal, that he had been born a Hungarian Jew and had lived on his wits ever since he could remember, mostly in France. He assured her that he loved her devotedly and was prepared to throw in his lot with hers, but that divorce would only weaken both their prospects, which depended so very largely upon their several connections with the Chevalier. He added that he would take the same care of the children as if they had been his own.

About this time, however, Linerl, who was now twelve years old and showing a strong resemblance, mentally, to her mother, the vivacious and casual Mademoiselle Clairemont, disappeared. She simply walked out of the house one day and did not return. It was evident that she, like Armand-Rosenthal, intended henceforth to live on her wits. Leopold had always rather neglected the child and Wanda, though she seems to have acted as conscientiously, in the matter of bringing up another woman's daughter, as could be expected, hardly regretted this early relief of her responsibilities. The search for the deplorably precocious Linerl did not succeed and was soon given up.

Hulda Meister, just then, was not, apparently, prepared to imitate her predecessor in this respect. For when Sacha, shortly afterwards, fell ill again, he was returned by Leopold to Wanda for attention. But the father soon realized that he could not bear to be parted long from his favourite. He descended upon his wife, who had retired with her two boys to a country cottage near Leipzig, and, while she was in her bath, persuaded little Sacha to accompany him back to the city.

On The Heights was now showing the signs of financial instability which always affect purely cultural periodicals of a high standard sooner or later. Neither Leopold's nor Hulda's devotion to the literary side could save it, nor could all Rosenthal's and Morgenstern's business ability improve the circulation. The paper had to cease publication. Both Leopold and his mistress and Rosenthal and his had now to fend for themselves. Wanda, for her part, retired to Neuville in Switzerland, oddly enough the birthplace of the formidable Kathrin Strebinger, and her lover soon followed her.

In 1884 Hulda bore the Chevalier a daughter, whom they named Olga. Then Sacha's recurrent ill-health culminated in a dangerous attack of typhoid fever. Leopold, in a panic, wired to Wanda, with whom he had, characteristically, never ceased to correspond, and she dashed from her Swiss refuge to the bedside in Leipzig. But she had scarcely arrived before Rosenthal telegraphed urgently for her return. He feared, perhaps, that a reconciliation would follow this meeting of the boy's parents. As the child seemed to be recovering, Wanda complied with the telegram. But the illness, in her absence, ended fatally, plunging the father, for many weeks, into a state of stupefied despair.

When he came to himself, it was in a mood of bitter hostility to all the world that had treated him so ill. He instituted divorce proceedings in grim earnest, riding rough-shod over the lawyers' protests. He wrote, at last, a coldly vindictive letter to his wife which effectually removed any lingering hopes she may still have cherished of their ever coming to live together again.

"You reproach me with my 'fancies,'" he told her loftily, in his sternest style. "I would never have entertained them if you had not, for your own selfish purposes, aroused and encouraged them.

A few weeks after our marriage you were already telling me that you did not love me, that you could never love anyone again after your betrayal by the painter" — a lover of Wanda's in her pre-Leopold period — "that you were unhappy, that happiness had come too late for you. Shortly afterwards you refused me conjugal rights.

If you had loved me I would have wished for nothing more. But your indifference, your ingratitude and your cruelty were the true origin of those 'fancies' of mine, with which no one can reproach me, since they harmed only myself. You understood remarkably clearly that your husband, whose heart could find no hospitality in your own, could only be bound to your side by the devilish fetters of sensuality. This is the real truth."

The Chevalier certainly rather flatters himself here. His obsessions were far too deeply based, as his whole life shows to its very end, ever to have been removed, far less 'originated' by any individual woman. The truth of the matter is somewhat more elaborate than he states here. He cultivated Wanda and married her in the hope that he would be able to turn her into an ideal 'sultana.' Many men of genius have made similar mistakes in their choice of partners. Leopold's was particularly tragic in the thoroughness of its illusion, the utter blindness to the woman's fundamental nature, one calculated, more than any other conceivable, to strike him fatally in his most vulnerable and exquisite part, his artistic sensibility. There can only be mutual detestation, never any kind of compromise, between a coarse and shoddy materialism and the profound intuitions of a genuine, almost automatic, aesthete. Both parties were precluded, by all that was deepest in them, from doing each other anything but harm.

The long association, doomed from the start, was now essentially over. Wanda and Leopold were to meet again, even to live under the same roof. But they were to do so only for a brief and final period, not indeed as strangers, but more as business acquaintances, casually thrown together and as casually parted. The dream of creating a wild and poignant poetry from the crabbed prose of common brutality had failed again, as it always must fail, even when the dreamer seems born to achieve the impossible.

Leopold and Hulda now decided to leave Leipzig, which had so many bitter memories for both of them. They migrated west, to Lindheim, a picturesque little village in the heart of Hesse, with narrow, crooked streets of two-storied houses and a mysterious old ruin in the neighbourhood, the *Hexenturm,* said to be still haunted by the souls of the witches burnt alive there in medieval times. The couple from Leipzig took a small house close to this sinister relic and settled down to the uneventful calm of a rustic retirement.

The divorce hung fire. Wanda remained obstinate, threatened scandalous revelations if her husband persisted in charging her with adultery. Rosenthal continued to encourage her to maintain this attitude, for his own towards her had already changed. He now perceived, as Leopold had always known, that the distinguished author's wife was the last person on earth to be of assistance to an ambitious journalist. Leopold had not cared twopence about this aspect of his late spouse. He was already well known when he married her. But Jacques Ste. Cère, as Rosenthal now called himself, still had his way to make and proposed to make it in Paris, where he had influential friends. They would not care much for Wanda, he felt. He required a mistress of a far different type, someone, for instance, like Juliette Adam.

In Switzerland he had written a topical skit on the new Imperial Germany. The piece had been well received in a Paris which had still not forgotten 1871. He now moved to the French capital, taking Wanda and Mitschi with him, for he was far too discreet to break with her openly at this stage. He was, however, determined to replant her on Leopold at the earliest opportunity, since no one else, in his opinion, would be so likely to accept her.

With this end in view he got Wanda to write a friendly letter to the author, telling him that Jacques Ste. Cère had already obtained a conspicuous post on the *Figaro* and was prepared to launch him in Paris, where a far more hospitable public awaited him than he could ever find in Germany.

Leopold, as the astute Jacques had foreseen, could not resist this temptation. Like all cosmopolitan writers of that day, he was convinced that residence in Paris would set a seal upon his reputation, which was now declining, for one reason and another, elsewhere. Hulda, who saw the danger, protested, but in vain. On the 14th of December, 1886, the Chevalier arrived, alone, in the French capital.

Wanda and her lover met him at the station and were struck by the change in his appearance. He was carelessly dressed, and looked very thin in the face, with the corners of the big mouth sunk in, the hair grey at the temples, the moustache straggling and unkempt. His manners, too, they decided, had grown very 'Slavonic.' He said he had no money.

Rosenthal found him quarters, cleaned him up, bought him clothes and introduced him to Henri Rochefort, Kathrin Strebinger's first lover, who had now returned to Paris under a political amnesty. Leopold was also presented, by the affable Jacques, to the novelist Paul Hervieu, the poet Catulle Mendès, the actor Mounet-Sully and even to the popular war minister, the man of the moment, General Boulanger.

The Chevalier now began to recover a good deal of his old charm and to enjoy himself. He was genial to Wanda, talked business with her lover, and actually proposed marriage to a strange young woman, daughter of the painter Schlesinger, a girl who received her visitors in short knickers of black velvet, riding-boots and a red silk sash. For the sake of this vision he cut an engagement to take Wanda to dinner with the Daudets, the last appointment he was ever to have with her.

For early in the new year two events occurred which changed the whole situation. Hulda Meister, tired of waiting for her lover, who had promised to return to Lindheim 'very soon,' appeared in Paris and almost instantly gave birth to another daughter, who was named Marfa. Shortly afterwards Leopold was informed that the divorce had at last been pronounced. He at once left France, with Hulda and his new daughter, for Heligoland, then English territory and an easy place to get married in. After celebration of this long postponed ceremony the couple went back to their village in Hesse and resumed the tranquil existence which had so briefly, yet excitingly, been interrupted by the Paris episode.

That spring Jacques Ste. Cère told Wanda that it had become necessary for him to leave Europe at once. His attitude to her had long been equivocal, now became distraught and indifferent. The lovers parted with promises which deceived neither of them. Wanda returned with Mitschi to Switzerland and settled in Lausanne. A few weeks later she heard that Rosenthal-Ste. Cère was still living in Paris, still functioned as one of the *Figaro* editors and had induced the wife of Bismarck's Press representative in the French capital to leave her husband and devote her energies and fortune to the promotion of those of her enterprising new companion.

The divorced wife and abandoned mistress refused to acknowledge herself beaten. She spent the rest of her life writing not only the pot-boiling novelettes which Leopold had taught her to compose but also her memoirs, directed to 'putting the Chevalier in his place' as a wretched liar and gasbag, a repulsive sensualist and a poor-spirited creature generally, who was well suited to his sly little, old-fashioned, unattractive 'bee' of a Hulda Meister.

One must not be too hard on Wanda, who was no worse a character, to begin with, than innumerable other young women who rely on their physique to carry them to heights where they ultimately find that they cannot breathe and where they remain, finally, completely bewildered and therefore snappish and soured. It is perfectly true that so far as she was capable of love, she loved Leopold, and no other, all her life. Her misfortune was that she was constitutionally incapable of understanding who it was that she was loving.

CHAPTER EIGHT

The Mantling Flame

THE isolated little community of Lindheim was inhabited mainly by stolid peasants. A few sharper-witted Jews ran the shops and organized trade. The name of Sacher-Masoch meant little or nothing to these people. As usual, they began by resenting and despising the 'interlopers' who had come to live in the little house near the *Hexenturm*. If any of the villagers had ever been admitted to Leopold's study on the first floor they would probably have left the building crossing themselves or muttering prayers from the Talmud.

The room was by no means luxuriously furnished. But a conspicuous feature of it was the number of pictures, either purchased by the occupant himself or presented to him by the artists who had painted them. The overwhelming majority of the canvases regaled the spectator with drawings or paintings of ladies of imposing build and sternly set features, clad in furs which, although sumptuous and voluminous, were so arranged as to expose a good deal of the naked and robustly developed flesh beneath them. Some of these figures held whips and scourges of types varying from those used on horses and dogs to the implements employed in ecclesiastical and penal establishments of an earlier day. One of them had very obviously been inspired by *The Pelisse* of Rubens.

Apart from this peculiarity, the new residents lived very simply. They were even chronically hard up. Leopold's receipts from his professional work were now relatively slender and in any case went largely to pay old debts. Hulda also made a little money with her translations and occasionally obtained small legacies. But she now had little time for any but household duties and those connected with her children. The latter were in the following year reinforced by a son, Ramón.

Leopold had published in 1874, as one of the tales making up the second Part, *Property,* of *The Legacy of Cain,* the story of an ideal rural community, which he had called *Paradise on the Dniester.* He now felt it might be possible to incarnate this idyll, to some extent at least, in Lindheim. He laid himself out to charm the dour inhabitants. But they took little interest in his enthusiasms until he threw himself, with great energy, into the project for a local water supply which had hung fire for many years. By eloquent representations in exalted quarters he managed, at last, to get this amenity installed. Thereafter, the Lindheimers regarded him with much respect and were constantly at his house to ask his advice about practical administrative matters.

Gradually and tactfully he came to use his new prestige in the interests of promoting hitherto unheard of social and cultural institutions in the village. Before long Lindheim had an Educational Club, a library, a concert hall and even a theatre. Fairy tales and comediettas were produced in this improvised building and once even Goethe's *Geschwister.* But most of the pieces were written or rehashed by Leopold himself in a style to which not the strictest moralist in residence could object. Hulda, with her practical sense and tireless industry, was a great help to him on the organizational side. She understood the peasants. He understood the Jews. Between them, the husband and wife extinguished, more than once, the flames of mutual hostility always liable to break out in the uneasy alliance of Gentile and Hebrew which characterized the village.

The Hessians and Rhinelanders, in common with most Germans, as contrasted with Austrians and Frenchmen, had largely ignored the Chevalier's previous works, if they had not, indeed, thundered against them as immoral. But now they began to hear of him as a writer of a much milder type, not the eloquent analyst and revealer of the darker passions of humanity, but the author of pastorals and innocently humorous fantasies for children of all ages. It was true that he still wrote a certain amount in the old vein. Titles from these years include *The Soul Snatcher* (in the feminine), *The Bloody Wedding at Kiev,* and *The Snake in Paradise.* But these tales were mostly sold abroad. In Germany the lighter, more sentimental sketches began now to be appreciated, as well as the Tolstoyan social pathos of *The Sated and the Hungry* and *The Poor and the Rich.*

Invitations occasionally arrived from neighbouring towns. Would the Chevalier lecture or give a series of readings from his works in Paderborn, in Arnsberg or in Wildungen? Later the great cities of Frankfurt and Mannheim offered him employment. He visited France again, and north Germany. His interests beyond Lindheim grew steadily and he had to invent a card index system to keep track of his correspondence.

But Hulda remained static and he found it necessary for both his bodily and his mental health to return to her regularly. She was so calm, so sober, so omniscient and so reasonable! He delighted in comparing her with Wanda, for the one 'torture' he allowed himself at this period was an occasional exchange of views, incredible as it may seem, with that lonely and virulently embittered exile. His own communications were deliberately composed in a style of somewhat sanctimonious rebuke, in order to elicit a scarifying retort which would overwhelm him with confusion, guilt and dread.

> "How comes it," he enquired of her on one of these occasions, "that my present marriage is in every respect a blameless union, in which my 'fancies' play no part? It is because I now have a wife who truly loves me and peace and concord reign in my house."

Wanda replied to this baiting with a boiling stream of invective and menace. She would show him up for what he was if it killed her, she would hound him to his grave, she would make the whole world sicken at his name, etc., etc. After a fit of exquisitely enraptured anguish he replied self-righteously:

> "Let the fight begin! I have nothing to lose by it, you everything. I have long since ceased to make any claims on the world

or on literary fame. I have nothing to fear where I find my only happiness. My wife knows me as quite a different person from the monster you try to represent me as. My children will come to know me through their mother, who loves and respects me."

So the game went on. He tired of it, sometimes, for months, but could not help returning to it at intervals. Wanda still fascinated him by her sullen animosity and he enjoyed his easy verbal triumphs over her vulgar abuse. Meanwhile, he felt that he was retiring further and further into the shell of Hulda's cool protection, from which he issued only to play the part of an industrious and sober-minded literary hack.

The Legacy of Cain remained an ambitious but barely identifiable torso. Part I, *Love,* and Part II, *Property,* had been published in 1870 and 1874 respectively. Isolated tales, really belonging to subsequent Parts, had been issued separately, since the latter year, at various times and places. *The Black Cabinet* and *The Ilau,* from the section entitled *The State,* dealt with the institution of a secret police and with the effect upon science of political absolutism. *The Old Castellan,* from *Work,* described the conquest of suffering by industry and self-denial. *The Mother of God,* from *Death,* described life among the woman-worshipping Doukhobor fanatics. The heroine, designated 'God's Mother' by her co-religionists and bearing a distinct resemblance to the blonde Lesbian, 'Nora,' from Graz, uses her unlimited power with appalling results, crucifying her lover, in the end, with every circumstance of dramatically sombre horror.

The ideas, however, which Sacher-Masoch noted as forming the basis of this gigantic life-work, never took detailed and complete shape on paper. He had begun, in 1869, with an indictment of the ruin of social hopes perpetrated, generation after generation, by those whom power corrupts, 'great princes, great generals and great diplomats.' These people, he held, as the Marquis de Sade had held before him, deserved the gallows or the prison far more richly than most common murderers, thieves, forgers or swindlers.

In *The State* he had intended to prove that the only remedy for the eternal deceptions of even 'constitutional' governments would be a 'United States of Europe,' with the same legal code valid in all parts of the continent. The principle of militarism, disguised by governments as 'self-defence,' was to be attacked from every angle, including the patriotic. *Work* was to lay bare the ignoble roots of the contemporary economic system, to show how it sapped the normal delight of the average man in his mental and physical energy and encouraged his opposite tendency to idleness, greed and the cruel exploitation of the economically weak. It was to point to the cure of such abuses by an organization which would preclude both economic servitude and the parasite.

Finally, a vision of true Christianity would close the sequence, proposing altruism as its basic motive, involving the disappearance of personal ambition and selfishness, of all desire for exclusive possession in the fields of sex and property, of all insular patriotism and aggression upon others.

Whatever one may think of the naïvety of such idealism, coincident in a surprising number of particulars with the utopian notions of the Marquis, but leaving room, as he did not, for specifically Christian feeling, there is no denying the generosity or the moral fervour of the Chevalier's vision. Nor can the general truth of its intellectual diagnosis, its logic, be set aside as wholly irrelevant. It is perfectly certain that primitive dog-in-the-manger greed, with its inevitable accompaniment, in a developed society, of hypocrisy, is as rife and powerful among men, in every field of human activity, from the sexual to the economic, as ever it was in the simpler days of *pithecanthropus*. It is equally unquestionable that every outstanding philosophic mind in history, from Plato to Tolstoy, has believed, at one time or another, that it may be feasible, by one means or another, to correct this fatal shortcoming of the animal masters of the world. Leopold was here in good company and, at his best, showed himself not unworthy of it.

His philo-semitism, in which he was almost alone among prominent writers of the period, derived in part from the preoccupation with politics, economics and morals that had led him to design *The Legacy of Cain*. He had been born in Galicia, where Jews of every type were extremely numerous. He was attracted by their conspicuous mysticism and the strangeness of the forms it took in Western society, both the romanticism and the materialism of which differed so fundamentally from the oriental varieties. But it was mainly the Jew as the typical underdog of central Europe that Leopold felt to be an essential starting point for his projects of political, economic and moral reform.

He once wrote in a newspaper article:

"I know I have made many enemies, especially in Germany, where I am abused as a franco- and judeo-phile. But that doesn't worry me. I got to know the Jews where they are poorest, in Galicia. I saw them providing services to society in the most industrious manner and yet persecuted by their Slav masters simply and solely because they were Jews. I was profoundly touched by the constancy of this helpless people to the manners and morals of their forefathers. When I came, later on, to achieve some position and influence in the world, I used both, to the best of my ability, in the interests of the weak. It was never the rich and powerful who interested me. I have always thought it my duty to take the side of the poverty-stricken and oppressed. When I am confronted by a victim of misfortune I do not first ask: Are you Jewish or Aryan?"

Such were the Chevalier's most edifying characteristics, in his prime, both as a writer and as a man. Something must be allowed for the discretion required in approaching a public so often hostile or contemptuous. Much of his work, especially as the peculiarities of his purely sexual behaviour, which he never took much trouble to conceal, became better known, bears a slightly smug and self-righteous air. He was somewhat unheroically concerned to defend and justify himself. He always preferred, on principle, persuasion to aggression. He was no Nietzsche. He stands much lower, therefore, intellectually and morally, than the stormier prophets. His character was undoubtedly flawed, rendered disproportionately apologetic, by his sexual obsessions. And yet they were responsible for much of his originality in abstract thought and literary impact. The idea of the terrible power of Aphrodite originated in ancient Greece. But it was Sacher-Masoch who gave it the logical, the symbolic, the ultimately physical twist, so prolific of poetry, by which the insidiously intoxicating goddess became as towering a demon as any Attila or Genghis Khan.

The subordination of the male to this destructive female deity, more familiar to oriental than to European mythologies, and therefore more comprehensible to the Slav than to the Teutonic or the Latin mind, suggested, it is highly probable, to Leopold the subjection of Jew to Gentile, of the mass of mankind to a few powerful individuals, of decency and reason, love and generosity, to tyranny, lust and selfishness. This analogy may well have been the spur that drove him to the heights he reached, not perhaps sensational, but still eminences of some consequence, as an artist and a thinker.

But the purely physical side of Leopold's erotic complex was only slumbering during these first years at Lindheim. In his lighter moods he was glad of Hulda's sobriety, common sense and practical loyalty, pleased with the three children she had given him, with the respect of his neighbours, both humble rustics, hard-working traders and the administrative and cultural leaders of society in provincial towns. Yet there were times when he was overwhelmed by memories of Wanda, of Anna von Kottowitz, of Fanny, of many another mistress who had once symbolized for him a sexual ideal which the estimable 'little bee,' however seriously she took her conjugal duties, could never even approach. They had all failed him in the end. Their images came and went, while he lay sleepless beside Hulda, wandered in the Hessian woods or paced the streets of Frankfurt or Mannheim, so different from those of Paris or Vienna, even from those of Lemberg, in their stolid conventionality. And behind the images of these momentarily incarnate 'sultanas' crouched the prototypes of them all, the Isis or the Astarte, the Kali of the Hindus, Amazons and Valkyries, historical figures like Elizabeth Bathory, the 'hyena of the Puszta,' or Lucretia Borgia. These abstractions haunted him as they had haunted the young Swinburne twenty years before. Leopold was now well into his fifties. But the lonely, restless man, irretrievably frustrated now, as he saw fewer and fewer people who seemed capable of understanding him, still returned again and again, especially when he was away from home, on his long, solitary journeys in distant parts of Germany, to the building of the old fantasies.

On one of these occasions, in the summer of 1891, he was returning to Lindheim through the little Hessian village of Stockhausen when one of the three horses of the *troika* he had hired foundered. It was found impossible to proceed further that night. The Chevalier, who was in the habit of taking with him on these prolonged expeditions, to beguile the tedium of the way, not books, but kittens, had one of these alluring little animals on his shoulder as he wandered off to the village inn in search of accommodation.

He was interested to find, not only that this isolated hostelry was under purely female management and that the innkeepers were, as usual in this part of Germany, Jewish, but that the youngest of the three women who received him, daughter of one of the two older hostesses, was a pretty and intelligent-looking girl of sixteen. He was still more delighted to be told that they knew perfectly well who he was, the girl having seen his photograph in a magazine. The final culmination of his pleasure came when the precocious young lady informed him that she was actually the authoress of a story called *Balm in Gilead,* which he now remembered having noticed, among many other such callow effusions, in his mail at Lindheim recently.

He was quite unable to recall any details of the contents of this novelette, but hastened, of course, to compliment the youthful composer of it on her 'literary talent' and, as usual, to add that he was ready to help her if she proposed to adopt a professional career as a writer.

The three ladies were delighted with their distinguished guest, his affable manners, and his lovely little kitten. Confidences were exchanged which did not include, on Leopold's part, the existence of

Hulda and her three children. His whole family, just then, happened to be on a visit to Warsaw. He gathered that the girl, whose name was Miriam, was due to return to school in Berlin the following morning. He at once offered to escort her at least part of the way, as far as Frankfurt, where she proposed to catch the Berlin express. His own house at Lindheim, he informed her, stood on the Frankfurt road, so that he would be able to offer her hospitality, in the care of his aged housekeeper, on the journey.

This proposal by the famous author was enthusiastically agreed to by all concerned. Next morning Leopold, the kitten and Miriam drove off together in the rehabilitated *troika* through the forest to Lindheim. The Chevalier, as they bowled along through this leafy paradise of sun and shadow, talked of the 'intellectual freedom' of Paris, where people could do just as they pleased so long as their reasons for doing so satisfied their friends. He was embarking upon a description of the arrogant and dictatorial ladies to be found there when one of the horses dropped a shoe, fortunately only a mile or so from the house by the *Hexenturm*.

"Let us walk, Miriam," he proposed. "I will carry your luggage."

She laughed.

"Oh, no, *Herr Doktor!* That's absurd. I'm far stronger than you are!"

"Are you really?" He was smiling delightfully, if somewhat ferally.

"Of course!"

She swung the heavy bag, with youthful pride, to the ground. He watched her intently. The smile faded. But he merely continued, in a more serious tone:

"You know, Miriam, it would give me great pleasure to carry that bag for you. And all the more if it should prove to be beyond my strength. To suffer, you know, for those whom we — find attractive and charming — can be a most exquisite rapture. You wouldn't deprive me of that, would you?"

Miriam, unlike the driver of the *troika,* who was staring at his oddly assorted 'fares' with stupefaction, found this dialogue most amusing and exciting. She deliberately prolonged it, but in the end yielded to her prospective host's eloquence. Leopold carried the bag with the devoted expression he had so frequently assumed, when he was in Italy with Fanny, as 'Gregor.' Miriam, half politely solicitous, half giggling, was memorizing the episode as hard as she could for recitation in Berlin. The girls would never believe their eyes, she told herself triumphantly, if they could see her now, with the great Leopold von Sacher-Masoch trudging at her heels like a footman.

They were received at the house, as Leopold had told her, by his housekeeper, a gaunt old Galician, with a submissive expression but a Roman profile, who was wearing, the girl noticed to her astonishment, a set of heavy furs, though it was an extremely hot afternoon. The matriarch had seen the two travellers coming some distance off. If she felt any surprise at the youth and innocence of the Chevalier's companion, her impassive countenance showed nothing but a conventional welcome. Miriam, as she bustled enthusiastically into the author's sanctum, heard him assure his dependent that the guest would be staying 'for one night only.'

In the study there were more furs. They seemed to be lying about everywhere. Leopold insisted upon her trying them on and adopting 'queenly' attitudes, a form of charade to which Miriam applied herself with girlish zest. Afterwards, as twilight fell and the moon rose, they went for a walk in the park. Leopold extended his literary powers to the full as he drew attention to the sinister bulk of the *Hexenturm* in this theatrical setting and told his companion all the dreadful legends of its haunted past. Miriam had quite enough romanticism in her to appreciate, with a delicious shudder, these old stories.

They returned to the house for dinner, at which the taciturn but courteous old housekeeper, herself resembling a fairy-tale witch playing a preliminary part of subtle flattery before revealing herself in her true colours, joined them.

Miriam did most of the talking. For Leopold, too, had now fallen very silent.

The dining-room had something of the character of an ancient armoury. Old-fashioned weapons and some odd-looking implements, which he told her gravely were instruments of torture, hung upon the walls. In one corner a set of fetters, much more modern in appearance, were suspended.

The girl enquired casually, as they sat over coffee, whether these chains could still be effectively used. Her host turned very pale.

"You shall see," he answered quietly and rose to his feet, with a significant glance at the Galician, who also got up. The old woman, with the greatest tranquillity, detached the fetters from their iron frame, fastened them upon her master and then clamped them again to the wall in such a way that Leopold now stood, securely chained, with his back to the room, facing the corner.

The girl giggled delightedly. But the facetious comment died on her lips as the tall 'witch' approached her with a heavy dog-whip, which she seemed to have picked up in the same corner, in her hand. The Galician's expression, however, remained impassively obsequious. She spoke in a low, serious tone to the young guest.

"The Chevalier is not feeling well. He wishes you to whip him with this."

She presented the handle of the dog-whip to Miriam. The girl stared, smiling incredulously.

"To whip him? What, hard, do you mean? What good will that do him?"

"As hard as you like, *Fräulein*. Those are his doctor's orders. I can't tell you any more. I am afraid I am very ignorant of medical matters. But I know my master. He will be very ill if you don't help him in this way."

"Well, how extraordinary —— "

Miriam laughed a little as she held out her hand for the whip. Like many girls of her race and age, she was rather exceptionally courageous and self-confident. Moreover, the strangeness of the scene appealed to her literary sense. The walk with the bag, the furs, even the *Hexenturm,* were nothing to this. How the girls at school would be thrilled! She couldn't even imagine what they would say to it all.

As she walked towards the prisoner the housekeeper, a step behind her, whispered:

"Just suppose you are a priest exorcising a devil. You know what I mean. That's all."

Miriam swung up the dog-whip, her youthful features glowing with excitement. In the end, after a rather slow start, she acquitted herself quite well, from the victim's point of view, if not brilliantly. The young authoress's tender years and ingenuous appearance made up to some extent for her lack of inches, *avoirdupois* and 'queenliness.' Leopold managed to whimper and writhe with some sincerity.

When she grew tired, the housekeeper, after a glance first at the executant's flushed but still humorous expression and then at her master's prostrate and quivering form, touched the girl on the shoulder.

"That will do now, *Fräulein*. Come with me. I will do the rest."

Miriam shrugged her shoulders and, after a final survey of the now motionless and silent Chevalier, followed the Galician.

The night passed without further incident, so far as the guest was concerned. In the morning Leopold appeared to have regained his normal charm and equanimity. He made no reference whatever to his post-prandial thrashing. The girl felt that it would be tactful for her, too, to ignore it. They spent the morning talking of literary matters. In the afternoon he drove with her to Frankfurt, saw her into the train for Berlin and behaved in every respect as she supposed distinguished old men of letters always do behave to promising young authors.

Miriam never saw Leopold again. She was destined to become, eventually, under the name of Myriam Perrault-Harry, quite a well-known writer of books of travel and mysticism, from a rather emphatically Jewish point of view, but with no particularly tendentious sexual orientation. The strange experience at Lindheim left no decisive mark upon her character.

For Leopold, too, it had been a mere incident, without much significance, in the long procession, now growing more and more shadowy and sinister, as age and loneliness began to tell upon his vitality, of his erotic fantasies. He kept up a fairly normal façade to such of his fellow-beings, trivial enough creatures in general, as he had to face in the ordinary way of business. But when he was alone, and now more and more even when he was alone with Hulda, he found it increasingly difficult to distinguish reality from dreams. The flame of his mind flickered kaleidoscopically as its hues changed along the spectrum of his moods, now childishly clear and tender, now sentimentally roseate, now richly dark with meditative speculation and melancholy yet lovely visions, now shot with mad, fiery gleams of agony and horror as his obsession leaped suddenly from the dark to strangle him in an orgy of lust and panic.

Hulda was constitutionally incapable of being seriously frightened. But she grew uneasy, as these last moods multiplied under her very eyes. She was no psychologist. She took little interest, really, in her husband's abnormal remarks and behaviour. She was only concerned to prevent them, if she could, from affecting his physical health. But a year or two after the affair with Miriam her eyes were opened to the real physical danger in which she herself and her children stood from the incalculable brain-storms of this ordinarily gentle and considerate artist.

One afternoon, when the children were out, he called her from his study in an agonized, barely recognizable tone. She entered the room without haste, but caught her breath at the sight of her husband's fixed, staring eyes, the blood on his face and hands.

"Leopold! What are you doing? What is the matter?"

He sobbed.

"I have killed him! Look, look! I have killed him!"

She saw that his favourite grey Angora kitten lay on his knees, motionless. He was breathing heavily, as though he had been running. He told her, in gasping, half-incoherent sentences, that he had had a sudden, irresistible impulse to strangle the animal, as he sat caressing it. The creature, in its death-struggles, had scratched his face and hands badly.

"Ah, to kill what one loves, Hulda! What appalling rapture! It is like killing oneself. Ah, Hulda! To crush, tear, suffocate and destroy another's handiwork, to set the seal of death, of annihilation where another, where God Himself, has enthroned life! That is indeed to take a vengeance that no one can misunderstand —— "

He grimaced at her, his jaw fallen, teeth showing above the big underlip.

She compressed her own lips instinctively, regarding him warily. "Are you going mad, Leopold?"

"Mad?" He sprang to his feet, shaking his fist at her. "Don't you dare to call me mad! Don't you mention that word to me, or I'll kill you —— "

He was trembling from head to foot, his great eyes blazing. The carcass of the kitten had fallen to the carpet. He kicked it out of his way as he advanced upon her. Hulda threw up her chin angrily, darted out of the room and locked the door upon him.

By the evening, after a long fit of weeping, he was calmer, begged her pardon and crept about the house in a silent misery of remorse. But in the dead of night he awoke with a shriek, seizing her in his arms with shocking violence.

"I am being eaten alive! I am being eaten alive! It's the cats — the cats — they are after me —— "

He screamed and fought for some minutes before she could master him. These nightmares now became unpleasantly frequent. The 'stimulants,' too, were required to be of an altogether grimmer, more drastic character. The whips had to be of steel hooks or nails. They were called for several times a day. Denial of them merely resulted in terrifying attacks of homicidal mania. Other resources demanded, not now for purely sexual purposes but simply to prevent dangerous 'scenes,' were boiling poultices for application to the patient's bare flesh, red-hot needles for piercing his arms and legs, razors and salt for incisions on back and chest.

Hulda would not have been Hulda if she had not kept her head. But by March 1895, after consultation with a specialist, she decided to add a couple of robust male nurses to her domestic staff. Leopold was by now beyond noticing such changes in the background of his existence. The 'attendants' were luckily within call on an occasion

when he caught his wife by the throat after treating her to a dis-
quisition on the pleasures of murdering persons to whom one was
deeply, irrevocably, even metaphysically, attached.

These guardians in all probability saved her life that day. She felt
obliged to report the whole affair in detail to the specialist, who took
a serious view of it. He insisted upon Leopold's immediate removal
to a lunatic asylum. He reminded Hulda of her duty to her children.
He advised her, in the strongest possible language, to save her husband from a disgraceful arrest for her own assassination. The matter of the necessary certificate of insanity and subsequent tactful
detention could be arranged, he assured her, without the least
publicity. But he could hold out no hope, now, of the patient's
recovery.

Hulda had been tried to the limit of her endurance during the last
few years. For some months, already, Leopold had ceased altogether
to be, for her, the man she had loved and married. She considered
him mentally dead. The doctor now added his scientific corrobora-
tion of this opinion. In the literary world the reputation of Leopold
von Sacher-Masoch had been declining for many years, though he
still wrote and published. No one would be surprised if he fell suddenly silent. Hulda, for her own part, was characteristically confident
of her own personal capacity to face the future and bring up her
children alone.

As a result of all these conclusions, on the 9th of March, 1895, the
living body of the man who had once been the Chevalier Leopold
von Sacher-Masoch, an author comparable with the greatest of contemporary Europeans and certainly a good deal more attractive, as a
human being, than most of them, was escorted to a discreet place of
detention for the insane at Mannheim. A report of his death from
natural causes was given to the Press. Flattering obituaries were
published. Wanda, from Switzerland, read them and began to agi-
tate for recognition as the only true and legitimate widow of the
dead man. In 1901 the Freiherr C. F. von Schlichtegroll published a
study of 'Sacher-Masoch and Masochism' which, since it contained
slighting references to Wanda, as well as a number of errors of fact,

decided that lady to issue a counterblast in the form of her 'Confessions,' which appeared, eventually, in 1906.

By that date Leopold had been dead, not for ten years, as she, in common with almost everyone who had known him supposed, but for one. His life actually ended in the asylum at Mannheim in the year 1905.

Epilogue

~~~~~~

As the nineteenth century closed, a distinct intensification began of the cults of 'sadism' and 'masochism.' Such preoccupations, in that secure generation and in view of the intellectual stature of the eponymous heroes, were largely theoretical, in other words, literary or philosophic in character. The age, like that of the Renaissance, prided itself upon its sophistication, its emancipation from 'vulgar' or 'bourgeois' prejudice. The relatively wealthy and leisured strata of society, numerous, and often, especially in Europe, comparatively erudite, since the pursuit of learning was not then interrupted by repeated social cataclysms, controlled the climate of opinion.

The secular aristocratic tradition had been revived as the revolutionary thunders of 1848 died away on the temporal horizon. In that last golden afternoon of the old order the typical intellectual aesthete, bored with the even tenor of his exquisite highway among the impressive monuments of a civilization that seemed, then, to be immortal, wandered very readily into strange, sometimes grim byways, through which he strolled, like Oscar Wilde, with the air of a disguised prince, a dilettante determined never to be surprised at anything, though hoping, perhaps rather forlornly, to achieve a new sensation.

Upon this equivocal paradise of experimental epicureanism there burst the momentous impact of the first German War, followed almost immediately by the epoch-making discoveries, in psychology, of Sigmund Freud. Both these phenomena were taken very seriously upon the continent where they had originated. They transformed

society there. With the release of international violence and under
the irresistible, uncompromising light of pure science, thrown so
suddenly upon the most remote recesses of the human heart, the
more or less fastidious amateur and private sado-masochist went
down under a horde of crude, more or less public and professional
practitioners of his art, the perpetrators of war-time 'atrocities' and
those who quoted the Viennese psychologist as they broke the conventions which had ruled European sexual relations for nearly two
thousand years.

The cynical, pseudo-scientific gaiety of the nineteen-twenties resembled in some respects the Paris into which the marquis de Sade
had been born. But the former's motive force was despair, not arrogant self-confidence. Freud and the war, between them, coupled
with the decay, suddenly accelerated, of religious tabus which had
been going on ever since the time of Voltaire, seemed to have rendered an orderly society, favourable to reflection and the growth of
wealth and refinement, impossible for ever.

The words 'sadism' and 'masochism' passed from the usage of a
cultured few to that of the police-court, the newspaper and the street-
corner. These expressions were now indiscriminately applied to every
kind of cruelty on the one hand and every kind of self-denial on the
other. The psychologists worked hard to impose their special remedy
of 'sublimation.' But the average citizen found this type of control as
far beyond him as the schoolmaster does who prefers to suppress his
rowdy pupils rather than canalize their turbulent energies into more
creative directions. The phobias and obsessions resulting from the
individual's forcible repressions of his sado-masochism, which both
Sade and Masoch, still unread by all but a few scholars, had affirmed
to be perfectly natural and indeed inevitable in the majority of us,
became as common as the actual crimes proceeding from the psycho-
sis of a conviction that restraint, besides being a nuisance, was positively bad for one.

How far this unsatisfactory state of mind in the ordinary inhabitants of Europe may have been responsible for the social upheavals
of the ensuing decade, culminating in the second German War, is a

question beyond the scope of a work concerned only to present a few data for the assessment of the general significance of the Marquis and the Chevalier. It is, however, at least possible that if more people in the nineteen-thirties had known more about these geographers of the human soil and had been less affected by the gross vulgarization of Freudian concepts, they would not have fallen such easy victims to the disingenuous political theories which are now dragging the world into a third holocaust.

One of the principal causes of the sinister conditions under which we live today is undoubtedly the ludicrous self-righteousness of those who apply solely to their enemies what they are pleased to conceive as 'vices,' while reserving the equally illusory 'virtues' to themselves. Humanity is basically the same everywhere. One of its chief bases is algolagnia, sado-masochism, however disguised. The bold affirmation and the equally bold illustration of this simple fact in the writings and in the lives of Sade and Masoch together comprise their out-standing contribution to the character of a truly civilized world. The fact can only be unpalatable to those whose sublimations of this foundation of general human nature have for one reason or another gone so far as to be mistaken by such moralists for equally fundamental psychological constituents and, on occasion, illogically enough, for their own exclusive private property.

Appendix

The numbers of titles of published works by these two authors amount in the case of the Marquis to 16 and in that of the Chevalier to 90. The great majority of these volumes, as of the few translations that exist, are in present circumstances very difficult to obtain.

The outstanding productions are named and briefly described in my text. Readers desirous of further study are referred to the works mentioned in the Bibliography, a number of which, in the case of de Sade, give substantial extracts from his writings. G. Apollinaire's book (1912) contains a bibliographical essay which identifies all the Marquis's major works. As regards Sacher-Masoch, a bibliography in the *Deutsche-Österreichische Literaturgeschichte* (*Handbuch zur Geschichte der deutschen Literatur in Österreich-Ungarn*) by J. W. Nagl and J. Zeidler, Ed. E. Castle, Vienna, 1926, Vol. III, pp. 955 sqq., lists everything written by the Chevalier which is still worth reading today. A check list may be found in the *Deutsches Literatur-Lexikon* by W. Kosch, Vol. II (Halle, 1930, M. Niemener).

In the circumstances noted above it has not been thought necessary to repeat in the present work a bibliography of all the books known to have been written by these two authors and subsequently published.

Select Bibliography

(Exclusive of general works on psychology and of works by the Marquis and the Chevalier themselves)

Brunet, P. G., *Le Marquis de Sade,* 1866.
Duehren, E., *Der Marquis de Sade und seine Zeit,* 1901.
Schlichtegroll, C. F. von, *Sacher-Masoch und der Masochismus,* 1901.
Alméras, H. d', *Le Marquis de Sade,* 1906.
Sacher-Masoch, A. von, *Meine Lebensbeichte,* 1906.
Sacher-Masoch, A. von, *Masochismus,* 1908.
Apollinaire, G., *L'Oeuvre du Marquis de Sade,* 1912.
Summers, A. M., *The Marquis de Sade,* 1920.
Dawes, C. R., *The Marquis de Sade,* 1927.
De Shane, B., *De Sade,* 1929.
Sarfati, S., *Essai Médico-psychologique sur le Marquis de Sade,* 1930.
Flake, O., *Der Marquis de Sade,* 1930.
Stern, L., *Sacher-Masoch,* 1933.
Gorer, G., *The Revolutionary Ideas of the Marquis de Sade,* 1934.
Amiaux, M., *La Vie Effrénée du Marquis de Sade,* 1936.
Amiaux, M., *Le Chevalier de Sacher-Masoch,* 1938.
Desbordes, J., *Le Vrai Visage du Marquis de Sade,* 1939.
Nadeau, M., *Oeuvres du Marquis de Sade,* 1947.
Klossowski, P., *Sade Mon Prochain,* 1947.
Lély, G., *Morceaux Choisis, etc.,* 1948.

Index

‸‸

DATE DUE